Palgrave Games in C

C000053492

Series Editors
Neil Randall
The Games Institute
University of Waterloo
Waterloo, ON, Canada

Steve Wilcox
Game Design and Development
Wilfrid Laurier University
Brantford, ON, Canada

Games are pervasive in contemporary life, intersecting with leisure, work, health, culture, history, technology, politics, industry, and beyond. These contexts span topics, cross disciplines, and bridge professions.

Palgrave Games in Context situates games and play within such interdisciplinary and interprofessional contexts, resulting in accessible, applicable, and practical scholarship for students, researchers, game designers, and industry professionals. What does it mean to study, critique, and create games in context? This series eschews conventional classifications—such as academic discipline or game genre—and instead looks to practical, real-world situations to shape analysis and ground discussion. A single text might bring together professionals working in the field, critics, scholars, researchers, and designers. The result is a broad range of voices from a variety of disciplinary and professional backgrounds contributing to an accessible, practical series on the various and varied roles of games and play.

More information about this series at
http://www.palgrave.com/gp/series/16027

Todd Harper • Meghan Blythe Adams
Nicholas Taylor
Editors

Queerness in Play

Gerald Voorhees
Managing Editor

palgrave
macmillan

Editors
Todd Harper
Division of Science, Information Arts
and Technologies
University of Baltimore
Baltimore, MD, USA

Meghan Blythe Adams
Department of English and Writing Studies
University of Western Ontario
London, ON, Canada

Nicholas Taylor
Department of Communication
North Carolina State University
Raleigh, NC, USA

Palgrave Games in Context
ISBN 978-3-319-90541-9   ISBN 978-3-319-90542-6   (eBook)
https://doi.org/10.1007/978-3-319-90542-6

Library of Congress Control Number: 2018957198

Cover design by Fatima Jamadar

This Palgrave Macmillan imprint is published by the registered company Springer Nature Switzerland AG
The registered company address is: Gewerbestrasse 11, 6330 Cham, Switzerland

Acknowledgments

We are greatly indebted to the many reviewers who generously donated their time and expertise evaluating manuscripts for this volume. The editors would like to thank Bridget Blodgett, Chris Kampe, Erika Behrmann, Alexandra Orlando, and Elise Vist for their service, without which this work would not have been possible.

Considerable thanks are also due to the editorial teams for the companion volumes to our own: Gerald Voorhees, Kishonna L. Gray, and Emma Vossen. Situated as it is in the liminal space of queerness, our work both stands on its own but is deeply enmeshed in the scholarship on gender in games these other volumes are engaged with. The knowledge and insight our fellow editors shared with us during this process has been invaluable.

Contents

Notes on Contributors

Meghan Blythe Adams is a PhD candidate at the University of Western Ontario, Canada. Her research interests include representations of androgyny in media, as well as death and difficulty in games. Her work has appeared in *Loading, Kinephanos*, and *First Person Scholar*. She tweets at @mblytheadams.

Maresa Bertolo is a researcher in the Department of Design at Polytechnic University of Milan, Italy, where she deals with game studies, with attention to games as a vehicle for communication, learning, and social dialogue.

Evelyn Deshane has appeared in *Plenitude Magazine, Briarpatch Magazine*, and *Bitch Magazine*. Evelyn (pronounced Eve-a-lyn) received an MA from Trent University, Canada, and is completing a PhD at the University of Waterloo, Canada. Her most recent project #Trans is an edited collection about transgender and nonbinary identity online. Find more info on http://evedeshane.wordpress.com or follow @evelyndeshane.

Sarah Evans is a PhD candidate at North Carolina State University, USA, in the Communication, Rhetoric, and Digital Media program. She is an editorial board member for the international, student-run *Press Start Journal*. Her research has appeared in *QED: A Journal in GLBTQ Worldmaking* and *Hyperrhiz: New Media Cultures*.

Mark Filipowich is a curator at Critical Distance, a video game criticism database. He is pursuing his PhD in Communications at Concordia University, USA.

Clara Gargano graduated in BFA Graphic Design at Brera Academy, Italy, and is finishing her MSc in Communication Design at Polytechnic University of Milan, Italy. She got closer to the LGBT community during her five-month exchange program at the University of Michigan, USA, in 2015. Since then she has been focusing her thesis research on LGBT and gender studies. Her investigation led her to center the inquiry of her studies on the relationship between parents and their kids, in a non-heteronormative situation, with the promise of a ludic outcome, due to the acknowledged persuasive power of these means.

Randall Hammond is a third-year student in the Communication, Rhetoric and Digital Media program at North Carolina State University, USA. His work focuses on advocacy for underrepresented populations in video game communities, as well as novel approaches to gameplay study.

Todd Harper is Assistant Professor in the Division of Science, Information Arts and Technologies at the University of Baltimore, USA. His research centers on games as culture and communication.

Elyse Janish is a doctoral candidate in the Department of Communication at the University of Colorado Boulder, USA. She received her Master's degree in Communication and Rhetorical Studies from Syracuse University, USA. Her research interests include digital culture, intersectional feminisms, queer theory, and identity in online spaces, especially video games.

Yowei Kang is an assistant professor in the Department of Film and Creative Media, Kainan University, Taoyuan, Taiwan. His research focuses on digital games, game rhetoric and technology, and new media.

Evan W. Lauteria is a PhD candidate in Sociology at the University of California, Davis, USA, where he works in the UC-Davis ModLab. He is the co-editor of *Rated M for Mature: Sex and Sexuality in Video Games* (2015), and his work appears in *Reconstruction and Analog Game Studies*. His dissertation explores the history of the Japanese video games industry during the "console wars" in the 1980s and 1990s.

Chris Lawrence is a PhD candidate studying at the University of Waterloo, Canada's Games Institute. His research examines the relationship between narrative and mythology in digital games. He serves as the commentary editor for the middle-state games scholarship publication *First Person Scholar*.

Ilaria Mariani (PhD in Design, Polytechnic University of Milan, Italy) designs, investigates, and lectures in games and interactive narratives as systems for communication and social innovation. Her research—theoretical and practical—mainly addresses the meaningful experiences games for social change create to activate reflection and social impact. She focuses on (interactive) ludic artefacts that challenge players to explore civic, social, political, moral, or ethical issues, encouraging reflection and/or alteration of entrenched attitudes. To comprehend the impact on players and assess these games effectiveness in transferring meanings, she combines qualitative and quantitative research and employs interdisciplinary mixed methods. As an author of scientific essays and articles, journal contribution, and as co-author of *Game Design* (2014), she presents her work and research at national and international conferences.

R. Travis Morton is a PhD candidate in English Literature at the University of Waterloo, USA. His research areas include game studies, linguistics, political theory, American literature, horror fiction, and folklore studies. He completed his MA at Trent University, Canada, where he wrote his thesis on narrative structures in video games on Bethesda Studios' *Fallout 3*. His dissertation involves independent survival horror games, with a focus on *Slender: The Awakening* and the proliferation of online folklore.

Tanja Sihvonen is Professor of Communication Studies at the University of Vaasa, Finland. Her research interests span the areas of digital media and games, participatory culture, and virtual work. In her book *Players Unleashed! Modding The Sims and the Culture of Gaming* (2011), she focused on the cultural appropriation of computer games. At the moment, she is studying the algorithmic power of social media.

Daniel Sipocz is a former sports reporter turned academic, teaching journalism courses at Berry College, USA. His research focuses on the intersection of representation of women and minorities in popular culture. He has been publishing works about sexuality in the *100 Greatest Characters* edited volume (2017) and race in sports in *The Routledge Companion to Media and Race* (2016) and *The ESPN Effect: Examining the Worldwide Leader in Sports* (2015).

Carol A. Stabile researches the history of gender, race, and class in media institutions. Her books include *Feminism and the Technological Fix* and *White Victims, Black Villains: Gender, Race, and Crime News in US Culture*. Her articles have appeared in *Camera Obscura*, *Cultural Studies*, and *South Atlantic Quarterly*. She is Managing Editor of the Fembot Collective, co-editor of *Ada: A Journal of Gender, New Media, and Technology*, and edits the *Feminist Media Studies* book series for University of Illinois Press. Her forthcoming book, *The Broadcast 41: Women and the Broadcast Blacklist*, tells the story of a group of women who were driven from US media industries during the Cold War. She is chair of the Women's Studies Department at the University of Maryland, College Park, USA.

Jaakko Stenros (PhD) is a game and play researcher at the Game Research Lab at the University of Tampere, Finland. He has published five books and over fifty articles and reports and has taught game studies and internet studies for almost a decade. He is working on the aesthetics of social play, but his research interests include norm-defying play, role-playing games, pervasive games, and playfulness. Stenros has also collaborated with artists and designers to create ludic experiences.

Laura Strait is a doctoral candidate in Media Studies at the University of Oregon, USA. She received her BA in Cultural Studies at Columbia College Chicago. Her research interests include technology and gaming, social movements in the digital age, and race and gender issues on social media. Her dissertation research looks at the historiography of the women's liberation movement and its complicated relationship to conservative and pro-life feminisms.

Nicholas Taylor is Assistant Professor of Digital Media in the Department of Communication at North Carolina State University, USA. He is also the associate director of their Communication, Rhetoric and Digital Media (CRDM) PhD program. His work applies critical, feminist, and socio-technical perspectives to experimental and mixed-methods research with digital gaming communities.

Nathan Thompson is a PhD candidate in Sociology at the University of New Brunswick, Canada. His research focuses on audience participation in the production of video games and video game content.

Kenneth C. C. Yang is an assistant professor in the Department of Communication at the University of Texas at El Paso, USA. His research and teaching interests are advertising, new media and advertising, international advertising, and consumer psychology and advertising.

List of Figures

List of Tables

1

Queer Game Studies: Young But Not New

Todd Harper, Nicholas Taylor, and Meghan Blythe Adams

"Queer." Depending on one's point of view, it's a word with a variety of readings and interpretations, many of them emotionally or socially charged. To some, it's a painful reminder of slurs and hatred; for others, it's a symbol of reclamation and pride. For academics, "queer" evokes images of deconstruction and liminality, a point of view that questions existing structures and binaries and a diverse range of theoretical work that has, at its core, a critique of how heteronormative power structures serve to limit and compress our understanding of the world.

The study of games from a queer perspective is an enterprise that is already well underway in the scholarly community. Much like game studies itself, queer theory is open, multidisciplinary, and is a space where "hyphenations became common and hybrid theories borrowing from a variety of views promised rich opportunities for analysis" (Raymond 2003, 99). Work specifically exploring or examining gender in games is as old as the discipline of game studies itself, with the work found in Cassell and Jenkins' *From Barbie*

T. Harper (✉)
University of Baltimore, Baltimore, MD, USA

N. Taylor
North Carolina State University, Raleigh, NC, USA

M. B. Adams
Western University, London, ON, Canada

© The Author(s) 2018
T. Harper et al. (eds.), *Queerness in Play*, Palgrave Games in Context,
https://doi.org/10.1007/978-3-319-90542-6_1

1

to *Mortal Kombat* (2000) being perhaps the most well-known example. However, even research and writing that doesn't specifically focus on gender or sexuality is often still informed by the philosophical underpinnings of feminist and queer scholarship. In the past few years, however, the amount of work being done that explicitly takes a queer perspective, or addresses queerness directly, has become exponentially greater.

Scholars studying the intersection of queerness and games owe much to the work of Adrienne Shaw, one of the foremost scholars working on the subject. Shaw's *Gaming at the Edge: Sexuality and Gender at the Margins of Gamer Culture* (2014) is without question a key text for any scholar interested in video games and queerness (or marginalization of any kind). However, by the same token, they owe as much to queer designers and scholars who thread queer ideas and concepts into their designs at every level. Works such as Mattie Brice's *Mainichi* (2012) and Robert Yang's recent *The Tearoom* (2017) represent ways that queer lives and queer politics become part of the critical conversation through game design. In her work for this volume, Sarah Evans deftly and thoroughly presents considerable work done in queer game studies over the past decade.

Rather than imply that queer game studies are new or uncharted territory, however, it might be better simply to say that the idea of it as a *discipline* is young. While the work itself has been ongoing for some time, it's experiencing a period of unprecedented—and, given the politics of global life in 2017, entirely needed—growth. In their introduction to their volume *Queer Game Studies*, Ruberg and Shaw (2017) discuss multiple influences on this sudden surge. One factor is the rise of queer game developers making challenging and expressive queer games, often in conversation with queer games critics and scholars. Another is the unfortunate spike in abuse and harassment in games culture of recent years, which puts the need for scholarship that examines both the identity politics and the power dynamics of games in sharp relief indeed.

Whatever the reasons, however, this "veritable wave" (Ruberg and Shaw 2017, ix) of queer games work, both design and scholarship, is the reality. It is in the spirit of that growth that we offer this volume and the perspectives therein: work that continues in the tradition of queer game studies. The work in this volume explores a considerable range, from explorations of how gender is queered in representations of video game characters, to the queering of characters in fan-modding practice, to the use of game design to help non-queer players understand the experience of being closeted and coming out.

As a companion to the other volumes in this series, it is our hope that the scholarship presented in this book will offer a glimpse of the *possibilities* of the work that can be done in this field. If we are to view queer game studies as "young," then it is essential that—as with any growing thing—we focus on its potential, on what it can offer us, rather than on defining it into a small box. Just as the other volumes in this series explore the range of masculinities and femininities at work in games, this book too hopes to present a slice of those possibilities as well.

Queerness, Games, and Possibility Space

One may wonder, then, how we define "queer" for the purposes of this volume and how that definition impacted the way the book came together. Certainly, the editors had a working definition of queerness in mind; we considered queerness as a topic area broadly. As part of a three-volume series examining gender in games, we were naturally focused on work that centered gender and sexuality and their intersection with games, particularly in ways that didn't necessarily fit cleanly into binary notions of either.

In the introduction to her 1996 book *Queer Theory: An Introduction*, Annamarie Jagose is quick to mention that queer theory as a then-nascent discipline was characterized by how difficult it is to pin down exactly what falls under its umbrella. "It is not simply that queer has yet to solidify and take on a more consistent profile," Jagose writes, "but rather that its definitional indeterminacy, its elasticity, is one of its constituent characteristics" (1). Jagose does not necessarily claim that queer theory is vague or amorphous; rather, her argument is that because queer theory as a perspective relies so heavily on the destabilization and critique of norms and what's "natural," attempts to limit or codify it are quite probably antithetical to the very nature of the work.

It is clear that queer theory is connected to gender and to sexuality, particularly since much of its disciplinary origin—in the work of scholars like Eve Kosofsky Sedgwick and Judith Butler—comes from feminist and gay/lesbian studies. But even that relationship is complicated by an understanding of queerness as something that destabilizes or questions normative assumptions. David Halperin draws a distinction between gay identity and queer identity, which:

> …does not name some natural kind or refer to some determinate object; it acquires its meaning from its oppositional relation to the norm. Queer is by definition *whatever* is at odds with the normal, the legitimate, the dominant. *There is nothing in particular to which it necessarily refers.* It is an identity without an essence. (1995, 62)

Thus queer theory certainly encompasses the study of gender and sexuality, but it is not *limited* to those things. Rather than presenting an alternative name for the study of LGBTQ identity, queer theory instead is defined by its relationship—an often adversarial one—to existing power structures.

Lest this description paint queer theory as wholly "negative" in affect, however, it is important to point at the work of theorists and writers like José Esteban Muñoz, who very clearly position queerness and queer theory as a realm of possibility, something rife with potential. In their attempt to question and problematize long-held norms, queer theorists work toward a new and better future: "[q]ueerness is that thing that lets us feel that this world is not enough, that indeed something is missing" (Muñoz 2009, 1). The idea of queerness as a "horizon" of potential toward which we continually strive, the pursuit of which fuels our critique of the here and now, is a powerful one.

There is a game design concept called "possibility space," the loosely defined idea that within the play of a game, there is a bounded freedom, a space in which there are certain potential actions that can be taken. Katie Salen and Eric Zimmerman, in their foundational design text *Rules of Play*, refer to this space of possibility thusly:

> But game designers do not directly design play. They only design the structure and contexts in which play takes place, indirectly shaping the actions of the players. We call the space of future action implied by a game design the *space of possibility*. It is the space of all possible actions that might take place in a game, the space of all possible meanings which can emerge from a game design. …The space of possibility is the field of play where your players will explore and cavort, compete and cooperate, as they travel through the experience of playing your game. (Salen and Zimmerman 2004, 67)

If this description of how games work sounds as if it has resonance with Muñoz's description of queer futurity in *Cruising Utopia*, that's unsurprising. Queerness as playful or explorative is a common theme in queer theory; in essence, queer theory describes a "space of possibility" for our concepts of gender, sexuality, identity, and power. As scholars who employ that theory, we "explore and cavort, compete, and cooperate" through our work in a playful way. Queer theory and games are a natural fit because, at the core, they work inside two highly complementary philosophical frames. The study of games, therefore, should similarly be approached with those frames in mind.

In a similar sense, Nikki Sullivan's framing—drawing on numerous foundational queer theory scholars—of queerness and queer theory as something that is "done" rather than something one "is" meshes well with visions of games as things that players *do* as well. Sullivan argues that "it may be more productive to think of queer as a verb (a set of actions), rather than as a noun" (2003, 50). This idea of what we might consider an identity category, a way of being, as instead being a set of actions is not limited to sexuality, either; a core tenet of Judith Butler's conception of gender is the argument that it is a "stylized repetition of acts" (Butler 1990, 179), a thing that individuals both do and have done to them on a regular basis.

Returning to Salen and Zimmerman's description of the possibility space, we see again the strong potential link between queer theory as a practice and games as a medium. As players, we engage a pre-configured, bounded set of potential actions through which meaning is built and values are shared and explored.[1] Gender and queerness, too, are similarly bounded; speaking of Butler's notion of performativity, Jagose suggests they are "constrained—not simply in the sense of being structured by limitations but because ... constraint is the prerequisite of performativity" (1996, 87). In both queerness and in games, the idea of boundless freedom is a mirage, but also for both, there is meaning in exploring the possibilities that occur *within* the boundaries, especially when that exploration allows us to see the ways in which those boundaries can be tested, expanded, or reconfigured.

Much like the identity politics to which much early queer theory was a reaction and movement away from (Turner 2000, Sullivan 2003), games (particularly digital ones) also find themselves mired in a modern debate about their nature and their scope. Nowhere is this more visible than in arguments about the "walking simulator," an often-pejorative term leveled at first-person narrative games where the gameplay focus is on exploration and story rather than combat. The deployment of "walking simulator" is a specific, targeted rhetoric about a broader ontological stance: these are not "games." They are something else, some other category, a category that—for some—does not merit the prestige that comes with being a "game."

It will likely come as no surprise that many of the games accused of this lack of game-ness are both titles that deal with marginalization of some kind, or which are connected with the post-Gamergate sneer of choice, "social justice warriors" (Lemarchand 2015; Kain 2016). The very nature of the accusation is exclusionary, its end goal about the staking of territory more than the advancement of the medium.

Of what use to us—as scholars, players, critics, or designers—is a rhetorical approach so rooted in the preservation of a status quo, one which locks down possibilities and inhibits growth? How can we not view games as fertile ground for exploring and embodying queerness? More importantly, how can we in good conscience limit ourselves and the potential that both queerness and games provide by becoming lost in ontological prescriptivism about their nature or their scope?

To that end, and in the spirit of the queer theorists discussed above, in this volume we are similarly disinterested in a definition of queerness, or queerness in games, that polices or excludes. Rather than sit in judgment, engaged in the endless mastication of "is this queer? are these games?" we choose instead to see the queerness in the act of analysis, study, and interpretation itself.

The Queerness in Games

In her piece "Finding the Queerness in Games," designer and scholar Colleen Macklin considers the various avenues by which queerness can be found in games, the number of which is quite vast:

> We can find traces of queerness—or at least its potential—in the characters and worlds of games. We can find it in the actions of the game, in the people who make them, how they are made, in how we play, in who plays, and how we talk about games. We can find the queerness in many aspects of games, not just these ones we have just explored. (2017, 255)

Much as we have done above, Macklin cites Muñoz's idea of queer futurity and queer utopia to position the queerness of games firmly in their potentiality: their capacity for interesting failure, for unexpected pleasure, for exploration and discovery. For Macklin, it's not that there is queerness in games; rather, games *are* queerness: "Instead of the question 'Where is the queerness in games?' we can ask 'Where is the queerness?' and answer 'In games'!" (256).

The spirit of queerness, of queer theory, and—if Macklin is to be believed—games themselves is both in questioning what we think we know (or have always felt we knew) and exploring the possibilities of what we don't. The work presented in this book is, in our view, a worthy contribution in both regards.

Ruberg and Shaw refer to the writing in *Queer Game Studies*—which includes the Macklin piece quoted above—as a "snapshot … capturing a transitional historical moment" (2017, xix); rather than being definitional, they provide a look into the possibility (and peril) of the moment. Informed by that snapshot, and other work in similar vein, this volume aims to continue that process: to explore and memorialize each moment, each progressive step, toward that messy but exciting queer futurity.

Book Structure

This volume is organized into four parts that examine the methodological and theoretical foundations for the collected works, the representations of gender in games, the ways gender is constructed in and through the cultural and material apparatuses that constitute game cultures, and the emerging opportunities for future research intervention to make games and gaming cultures more hospitable for a plurality of identities—particularly, but by no means limited to, sexual and gender identities.

Our short but vital opening part, "Queer Foundations," provides a review of the terrain of queer game studies (as of 2016); while research in this area has grown rapidly since this chapter was first written, Sarah Evans offers a robust framework for approaching the key themes and sites of production, contestation, and growth for this dynamic field. In a similar vein, Evan Lauteria provides a productive theoretical orientation to research on queerness and gaming, asking how queer studies inflects and alters traditional game studies approaches to knowledge production.

The second and largest part, "Representing Queerness," consists of works that attend to the ways games portray non-normative characters, game mechanics, and relationships. Certainly, Adrienne Shaw's research explored the (often limited) significance of these portrayals to queer-identified players' enjoyment of, and appreciation for, digital games (2014). A decade earlier, Helen Kennedy suggested that the representational elements of Lara Croft can only take us so far in unpacking her cultural significance, as a playable character that operates as much as a vehicle for queer(ing) pleasure as for the heteronormative male gaze (Kennedy 2002). Despite questions over the importance of representational elements to digital play, however, avatars and their (stated and/or reimagined) gender and sexual identities remain foundational to considerations over whether, and in what ways, digital games and their attendant cultures are welcoming of queer subjectivities. As other scholars have stated, repeatedly and more eloquently (Doty 1993), representation in media is a vital site of political struggle, through which the experiences and perspectives of marginalized identities might find greater purchase. The chapters assembled in this part build on and extend the vital work of applying queer theory via literature and film studies to analyses of playable characters, game mechanics, and relationships between characters.

The third part, "Un-gendering assemblages," engages queer (queering?) relationships between digital game players and texts and practices beyond gameplay. This part proceeds from two complementary insights: the first, stemming from recent studies of player communities and their paratextual practices acknowledges that digital gaming supports a range of technologically mediated activities aside from play, including modding, hacking, critiquing, cosplaying, and so on. The second, stemming from STS-driven accounts of media and identity (Slack & Wise, others) holds that our identities are constituted through our engagements with (and via) multiple technological devices, practices, and systems. Combining these two theoretical starting points, the chapters in this part explore the ways queer identities and queer practices are made possible through reconfiguration of certain elements of gaming's conventionally hetero-normative sociotechnical assemblages, including mods, fan fiction, and rule-books. We see these chapters building on and extending scholarship that explores how we might think of (and enact) queer relationships and forms of queer expression, not just in relation to gaming characters but to the underly-ing "algorithmic ecologies" of games (Phillips 2014), game mods (Lauteria 2012), and authoring platforms (Harvey 2014).

The final part, "No Fear of a Queer Planet: Gaming and Social Futures," explores the challenges facing queer-identified players as they negotiate gaming communities and industries that are often virulently homo- and transphobic. This work understands that digital gaming is not only a site of identity forma-tion and hobbyism; for many, digital play provides pathways to professional fulfillment and financial stability, particularly with the rise of new media industries such as live streaming and e-sports that transform play into eco-nomic production. As a site of political struggle, gaming is increasingly about inclusive and equitable labor practices as it is about representation and self-expression. Chapters in this volume draw productively from social scientific research on queer communities—including gaming guilds (Sundén 2012) and online forums (Condis 2015; Pulos 2013)—and on research into whether and how contexts of play can be made safe(r) for queer folk (Stabile 2014).

Queer Foundations

Sarah Evans' "Queer(ing) Game Studies: Reviewing Research on Digital Play and Non-normativity" helps anchor the rest of the work in this volume. Evans' essay is a thorough review of existing research on queerness and non-normativity in digital games aimed at not only identifying key insights but also contextualizing which disciplines and publishing venues have most prominently produced them. Evans' chapter provides a contextualizing meta-analysis of queer game studies that our editors hope will help readers frame the rest of the volume's selections.

The other chapter in this part provides a second contextualizing analysis, one that looks specifically at the intersection of queer game studies and ludology. Evan Lauteria's essay "Envisioning Queer Game Studies: Ludology and the Study of Queer Game Content" examines the possibilities and limitations of ludology as an approach to queer game content. Additionally, Lauteria asks how queer game studies might inform the ludological approach.

Representing Queerness

Opening our next part, Kenneth C.C. Yang and Yowei Kang's essay "The Representation (or the Lack of It) of Same-Sex Relationships in Digital Games" specifically addresses the exclusion of queer game content, taking a step away from the ludological approach analyzed by Lauteria. Using textual criticism of the exclusion of same-sex relationships from the 2013 game *Tomodachi Life* as a case study, the authors explore discourses surrounding same-sex relationships in games. Ultimately, Yang and Kang identify key factors in the proliferation of queer relationships in games.

In contrast to Yang and Kang's analysis of queer absence, Daniel Sipocz's "Affliction or Affection" examines queer presence in the franchise *The Last of Us*. Sipocz examines the depiction of key queer characters in the franchise, including Ellie, Riley, and Bill. Using textual and paratextual analysis, Sipocz draws on the work of Adrienne Rich, Mia Consalvo, and Jane Pinckard in order to problematize developer Naughty Dog's representation of queer characters.

Next, Chris Lawrence's "What if Zelda Wasn't a Girl? Problematizing *Ocarina of Time*'s Great Gender Debate" begins this part's transition from chapters focused primarily on sexuality as a marker of queerness to chapters focusing on gender coding. The author examines fan debates regarding the role of gender in Zelda's transformation into her male alter-ego Sheik. Using theories of gender performance and gender normativity, Lawrence traces the evolution of Sheik in the *Legend of Zelda* franchise.

Following Lawrence's essay is "Maidens and Muscleheads, White Mages and Wimps, From the Light Warriors to *Lightning Returns*" by Mark Filipowich. Returning to the vein of textual criticism seen in earlier selections, this chapter traces the evolution of gender coding in the *Final Fantasy* series. Building on an examination of the cultural and inter-cultural contexts of the series' depiction of gender, Filipowich explores the differing treatment of feminized and masculinized characters.

Part II next selection analyzes not gender coding but rather key tropes surrounding transgender identity in media. Evelyn Deshane and R. Travis Morton build on the work of Brianna Wu and Ellen McGrody asserting *Metroid* heroine Samus Aran is a trans woman in "The Big Reveal: Exploring (Trans)femininity in *Metroid*." Deshane and Morton read this assertion in the context of dramatic reveals of transgender identity in cinema, drawing on player affect and the work of Bob Rehak on avatar identification to center potential player reactions to Samus' identity.

Withdrawing from Deshane and Morton's close look at *Metroid* back to the broader scope of reading gender variance across genres, "Bye, Bye, Birdo: Heroic Androgyny and Villainous Gender Variance in Video Games" by Meghan Blythe Adams examines the distinctions made in games between heroic, masculine-leaning androgyny and villainous gender variance. Using textual criticism, Adams closes Part I with a comparison of depictions of androgyny and gender variance in key game franchises including *The Legend of Zelda*, *NiGHTS*, and *Super Mario*.

Un-gendering Assemblages

Tanja Sihvonen and Jaakko Stenros begin Part III focus on queering game play by examining possibility spaces and affordances for queer play in multiplayer role-playing games in "Cues for Queer Play: Carving a Possibility Space for LGBTQ Role-Play." Sihvonen and Stenros emphasize going beyond textual analysis to examine player interventions in and negotiations with "urtexts" to create spaces of queer possibility.

Similarly, Nathan Thompson's "'Sexified' Male Characters: Video Game Erotic Modding for Pleasure and Power" looks at structural opportunities for queer play by analyzing erotic modding in *Skyrim*. Using interviews and thematic analysis of blog content and responses, Thompson reads the transformative potential and pitfalls of fan efforts to sexualize male characters.

Maresa Bertolo, Ilaria Mariani, and Clara Gargano close Part III with an analysis of the queer affordances of a game of their own design, using qualitative data and player ethnographies to determine the impact of their game in "Let's Come Out: On Gender and Sexuality, Encouraging Dialogue and Acceptance." Looking at the effect of gameplay on players' understanding of LGBTQ stereotypes in a specifically Italian context, Bertolo, Mariani, and Gargano assert the usefulness of the "magic circle" as a space in which players can question discrimination.

No Fear of a Queer Planet: Gaming and Social Futures

Our opening selection for Part IV, Nick Taylor and Randall Hammond's "Outside the Lanes: Supporting a Non-normative *League of Legends* Community" presents an ethnographic study of a *League of Legends* club based at North Carolina State University. Taylor and Hammond document the club members' efforts to be inclusive in the context of the stereotypically skill- and gender-based exclusivity of e-sports culture.

Following Taylor and Hammond, Elyse Janish's "The Abject Scapegoat: Boundary Erosion and Maintenance in *League of Legends*," is similarly focused not only on e-sports culture but the contemporary context of *League of Legends*. Janish examines abjectification as a tool to reinforce the cissexist, heteronormative, masculine privilege of e-sports culture. Using the experiences of professional player Remilia as a case study, Janish asserts that abjection is a key element of transphobia and offers potential recourse to the prevalence of transphobia in e-sports.

Carol A. Stabile and Laura Strait's essay "Out on Proudmoore: Climate Issues on an MMO" closes Part IV visions of queer futures. The chapter offers both an examination of the history of the *World of Warcraft* server Proudmoore and the strategies and transformative practices that can make an online space more inclusive. Stabile and Strait explicitly aim to balance their critique with a call to action, noting transformative change efforts in spaces like the *League of Legends* community.

Note

1. See Mary Flanagan and Helen Nissenbaum's *Values at Play in Digital Games* for an excellent examination of how values are coded into games through their design on every level.

Bibliography

Butler, Judith. 1990. *Gender Trouble*. New York: Routledge.
Condis, Megan. 2015. No Homosexuals in Star Wars? BioWare, 'Gamer' Identity, and the Politics of Privilege in a Convergence Culture. *Convergence: The International Journal of Research into New Media Technologies* 21 (2): 198–212. https://doi.org/10.1177/135485651452720.

Doty, Alexander. 1993. *Making Things Perfectly Queer: Interpreting Mass Culture*. Minneapolis: University of Minnesota Press.

Halperin, David. 1995. *Saint Foucault: Toward a Gay Hagiography*. New York: Oxford University Press.

Harvey, Alison. 2014. Twine's Revolution: Democratization, Depoliticization and the Queering of Game Design. *GAME Journal: The Italian Journal of Game Studies* 1 (3): 95–107. http://www.gamejournal.it/wpcontent/uploads/2014/04/GAME_3_Subcultures_Journal.pdf.

Jagose, Annamarie. 1996. *Queer Theory: An Introduction*. New York: New York University Press.

Kain, Erik. 2016. On Walking Simulators, Game Journalism and the Culture Wars. *Forbes*, October 5. https://www.forbes.com/sites/erikkain/2016/10/05/on-walking-simulators-game-journalism-and-the-culture-wars.

Kennedy, Helen W. 2002. Lara Croft: Feminist Icon or Cyberbimbo? On the Limits of Textual Analysis. *Game Studies: The International Journal of Computer Game Research*. http://www.gamestudies.org/0202/kennedy/.

Lauteria, Evan W. 2012. Ga(y)mer Theory: Queer Modding as Resistance. *Reconstruction: Studies in Contemporary Culture* 12 (2): 1–34. http://reconstruction.eserver.org/Issues/122/Lauteria_Evan.shtml.

Lemarchand, Richard. 2015. *Infinite Play*. Presentation at the Game Developer's Conference, San Francisco, CA, March 4–6, 2015.

Macklin, Colleen. 2017. Finding the Queerness in Games. In *Queer Game Studies*, ed. Adrienne Shaw and Bonnie Ruberg, 249–257. Minneapolis: University of Minnesota Press.

Muñoz, José Esteban. 2009. *Cruising Utopia: the Then and There of Queer Futurity*. New York: New York University Press.

Phillips, Amanda. 2014. (Queer) Algorithmic Ecology: The Great Opening Up of Nature to all Mobs. In *Understanding Minecraft: Essays on Play, Community, and Possibilities*, ed. N. Garrelts, 106–120. Jefferson, NC: McFarland.

Pulos, Alexis. 2013. Confronting Heteronormativity in Online Games: A Critical Discourse Analysis of LGBTQ Sexuality in World of Warcraft. *Games and Culture* 8 (2): 77–97. https://doi.org/10.1177/1555412013478688.

Raymond, Diane. 2003. Popular Culture and Queer Representation: A Critical Perspective. In *Gender, Race, and Class in Media: A Text-Reader*, ed. Gail Dines and Jean M. Humez, 98–110. Thousand Oaks: Sage.

Ruberg, Bonnie, and Adrienne Shaw. 2017. *Queer Game Studies*. Minneapolis: University of Minnesota Press.

Salen, Katie, and Eric Zimmerman. 2004. *Rules of Play: Game Design Fundamentals*. Boston: MIT Press.

Stabile, Carol. 2014. 'I Will Own You': Accountability in Massively Multiplayer Online Games. *Television & New Media* 15 (1): 43–57. https://doi.org/10.1177/1527476413488457.

Sullivan, Nikki. 2003. *A Critical Introduction to Queer Theory.* New York: New York University Press.

Sundén, Jenny. 2012. Desires at Play: On Closeness and Epistemological Uncertainty. *Games and Culture* 7 (2): 164–184. https://doi.org/10.1177/1555412012451124.

Turner, W. 2000. *A Geneaology of Queer Theory.* Philadelphia: Temple University Press.

Part I

Queer Foundations

2

Queer(ing) Game Studies: Reviewing Research on Digital Play and Non-normativity

Sarah Evans

Recently, efforts by LGBTQ game players, designers, and activists have been instrumental in broadening public understandings of gaming's gender and sexual diversity (though not necessarily its inclusivity). The popularity of Scarlett, a highly ranked transgender *Starcraft 2 Pro* gamer, the conversations initiated by the games journalism of Samantha Allen, Katherine Cross, and Mattie Brice (among others), and Anna Anthropy's successes in creating and promoting queer games collectively contribute to a growing understanding of the experiences and perspectives of communities that have, throughout digital gaming's history, gone largely ignored. Despite this increased visibility, academically accredited research in the area of queerness and digital play remains underdeveloped.

By way of systematic literature review, this chapter considers how game studies scholarship has (and has not) approached queer players, communities, and perspectives. My goal is to map a vital terrain of scholarship, in order to outline opportunities for research related to queer and non-normative digital games, players, and play practices. I aim to ascertain not only *what* insights scholarship has produced with regard to LGBTQ games, gamers, and gaming but to critically consider *where* and *how* as well: which disciplines, methodological traditions, and publishing venues are most active in this area. My analysis deliberately focuses on peer-reviewed journals, monographs, and

S. Evans (✉)
North Carolina State University, Raleigh, NC, USA

© The Author(s) 2018
T. Harper et al. (eds.), *Queerness in Play*, Palgrave Games in Context,
https://doi.org/10.1007/978-3-319-90542-6_2

17

book chapters, excluding academic blogs and conference presentations; my method here is purposeful, to ascertain to what extent research on queer gaming is appearing in those venues that conventionally have most "currency" in terms of academic career advancement, so as to advocate for efforts to recognize and legitimate other vibrant—though less institutionally accredited—forms of intellectual work in this subject area.

This chapter begins with an operational (if imperfect) definition of "queer gaming," as it relates to game studies scholarship. I then describe my approach to compiling and reviewing literature in this area, including research on queer gamers and gaming communities, as well as the application of queer theories and perspectives to analyses of games. Engaging with this growing field, I consider what methodologies are employed, where such scholarship is being published and what issues prevail. I end with a consideration of where and how game scholars and their communities can build on existing work in this area, in order to both contextualize and advance the efforts of LGBTQ players, critics, designers, allies, and activists.

Definitions

In keeping with contemporary queer theory (Ahmed 2006; Butler 1990; Cohen 1997; Halberstam 2005; Sedgwick 2009), the notion of "queerness" I operate with pertains to non-heteronormative sexual identities, as well as to non-normative positions to and within institutions that work to police sexuality. As Jenny Sundén and Malin Sveningsson (2012, 157) state: "queer is often used as shorthand for multiple ways of positioning and orienting oneself as non-straight, and simultaneously as a way of rendering problematic every fixed definition." Following this, if "straight" is positioned as the norm (as it applies to sexuality or otherwise), a queer orientation turns away from it. Working on this more expansive notion of queerness, this review includes research with LGBTQ players and communities, as well as research that intentionally disrupts heteronormative approaches to game design, play, and analysis. For this reason, I adopt the term "queer gaming" to indicate the inclusion of research exploring non-normative game-related practices, as well as studies of LGBTQ gamers.

Approach

The systematic literature review began with a keyword search through academic research databases, including North Carolina State University's Summons, JSTOR, Sagepub, and EBSCOhost using search terms like queer + gam*, lgbt + gam*, glbtq + gam*, lesbian + gam*, gay + gam*, trans* + gam*.[1] I employed the same search terms (queer, LGBT, etc.) paired with "video game" to determine if new results were revealed. These searches were then repeated within Google and Google Scholar, drawing from the first 10 pages of sources for each. I conducted keyword searches using these same criteria in the contents of specific gaming and media studies journals such as *Ada, Games and Culture, The Journal of Virtual Worlds Research, The Journal of Gaming and Virtual Worlds, Eludamos,* and *Convergence.*

After accessing the relatively limited number of peer-reviewed articles (10) from the keyword search, I mined their references and observed publication announcements on social media and academic LISTSERVs, taking note of sources that referenced or alluded to queer theories and LGBTQ issues, identities, and communities. These searches took place primarily between March and August 2015, and the list was supplemented throughout the publication process. In total I found 44 publications that fit my criteria across primarily gaming and media journals as shown in Table 2.1. The "other" category was comprised of journals in the fields of communication, cultural studies, LGBTQ studies, studies on the origins of names and naming, and geography. Notably, less than half of the relevant journal articles were published in gaming journals.

To determine the ranking of any individual publication venue I used several methods, including searching the journals' names in services such as the SCImago Journal & Country Rank, Google keyword searching the journals' names with terms such as "rank" or "ranking," and drawing from professional experience from being immersed in the field (e.g. knowing that university presses are often viewed as most rigorous and which journals are highly respected). Additionally, some journals such as *Convergence, Games and Culture,* and *New Media and Society* advertise their ranking and impact factor on their landing page.

Where This Work Appears

Figure 2.1 details the connections between the collected literature across three distributions: publication venue, method, and discipline. The height of the node (the black or gray bar behind each text item) indicates the frequency of

Table 2.1 Overview of queer gaming research by publication venue

Articles published in peer-reviewed gaming journals	11
Articles published in peer-reviewed media journals	10
Articles published in other peer-reviewed journals	12
Books published by scholarly presses	3
Book chapters published by scholarly presses	8

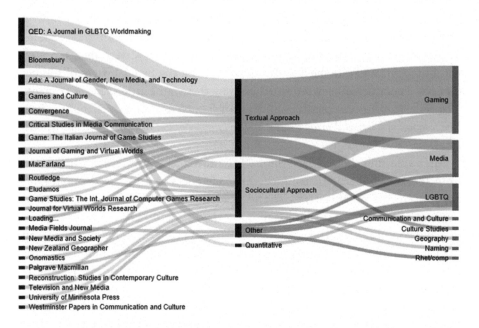

Fig. 2.1 Publication venue, method, and discipline of collected literature

occurrences. The first distribution, publication venue, consists of the specific names of the journals or publishers where relevant literature appeared.[2]

Though methodological genres can be indistinct, the middle distribution represents the methodological background from which the sources drew their modes of inquiry. Publications demonstrated a diversity of research methodologies, including literacy studies, qualitative research, textual analysis, theory, criticism, and critical discourse analysis. The findings indicate the majority of studies (23) used textual approaches, applying methods like close reading, rhetorical criticism, and textual analysis to games, tools, fan magazines, and so on. Sixteen of the studies took sociocultural approaches that focused on players and communities.[3] One study was quantitative and four classified as "Other." Here, "Other" designates a mixed or personal experience-driven (e.g. interview) method. The third distribution represents the disciplinary backgrounds wherein this work is situated, previously discussed in more detail with Fig. 2.1. Taken with Table 2.1, this visualization provides insight into where and through what methods and disciplines work in queer gaming has been published.

Methodologically, it is noteworthy that there has been very little quantitative research to date that considers the experiences and perspectives of LGBTQ gamers. Indeed, where it has done so, quantitative research on online role-playing games frames queer players in terms of "gender deviance" (Williams et al. 2009). As de Castell et al. (2014) contend, such findings reproduce the very same discourses around gender binarism that queer theory itself has long problematized. Despite the advantages of concurrent, parallel analyses of gender and sexuality (Eklund 2011), binary constructions of these characteristics fail to accurately describe what is going on for players and in games.

Engaging the "Gaymers": Sociocultural Approaches

Using sociocultural approaches allows scholars to understand how LGBTQ players and communities experience (and produce) contemporary games culture. Deploying methods such as autoethnography, participant observation, interviews, discourse analysis, and content analysis, scholars have explored how and why sexuality matters in gaming; various forms of rebellion against norms, beliefs, and challenges concerning representation; and discrimination. Adrienne Shaw and Jenny Sundén are two of the more prolific scholars working in this area, and their research serves as both a foundation and touchstone.

In one of the earliest published monographs about queerness and gaming, Sundén and Sveningsson (2012, 2) compare ethnographies of "'straight' and 'queer' guilds in *World of Warcraft*" to highlight differences between "player cultures and expectations [as enacted through] ways of moving, sensing, and making sense of particular norms and contexts of play." Beyond the broad categories of gender and sexuality, Sundén and Sveningsson elaborate on their findings in terms of coming out, passion and desire, flirting, queerness, and research methodology. This work derives from Sundén's previous studies analyzing queerness in games as a form of transgression.

Sundén (2009) defines transgression as any of the ways non-normative players might disturb social imaginaries of the "ideal" player implied by a game (typically white, hetero, cisgender man). Transgressive players are those whose actions and sometimes just existence in game spaces defy the normative disciplining forces inherent to gaming culture, such as players who are openly gay. Janne Bromseth and Sundén (2010, 2012) argue women's presence in games work to queer game spaces simply by existing within the masculinely coded video games culture that binds technology to masculinity and designates the default player as male.

This concern with intersections between players' identities and games' representations of gender and sexuality is at the core of Shaw's research. In early work, she dispels the myth of homophobic exclusion (alone) being the primary factor contributing to the overall lack of representation of LGBTQ sexualities and experiences in games (2009). Shaw "parse[s] the connected but distinct issues of identity, identification, and media representation" (2014, loc 233) of marginalized players. Elaborating on themes of her previous work (Shaw 2012a, b, 2013), Shaw (2014) focuses on the ways disenfranchised players across gender, sexuality, and race view their own positions in a hobby and lifestyle culture designed for, and dominated by, people who are not them. Using mostly qualitative interviews, Shaw (2012a, 2014) finds that, despite minimal representation of LGBTQ identities in games and gaming culture, players who might identify as lesbian, gay, bisexual, transgender, or queer demonstrate ambivalence toward "more" representations of their sexual identity, focusing instead on "the search for a queer sensibility and a safe space from the gay-bashing of other gamer communities" (2012a, 81). Shaw's intersectional research is instrumental in mapping out the ways in which LGBTQ players respond to and negotiate the heteronormativity of games.

Research by James B. Kelley (2013), Alexis Pulos (2013), and Megan Condis (2015) focus on heteronormative discourses circulating on gaming forums. Kelley compares discussions of armor and the male body in *Age of Conan* between GayGamer.net forums and the *Age of Conan* official forums. Resistance to the game's heteronormativity through appraisals of the scantily clad male characters was lauded in the gaygamer.net forums but charged with hostility in the game's official forums. In studying *World of Warcraft* forums, Pulos (2013) uses discourse analysis to decipher how LGBTQ community concerns are constructed by both players and Blizzard Entertainment, the game's publisher. Pulos argues that Blizzard's preoccupation with moving discussions of gender and sexuality away from gameplay and into an "authorized" forum space condoned the homophobia exhibited by the broader *WoW* community. Condis' (2015) study of the *Star Wars: The Old Republic* forums revealed similar sentiments via a series of threads where participants argued the inclusion of optional homosexual relationships unnecessarily politicized the game. It is through such documentation of the rampant homophobia in some video gaming communities that mainstream games culture's intolerance of queerness becomes starkly evident. As Kelley (2013), Pulos (2013), and Condis (2015) demonstrate, analyses of player discourses reveal the ways these gaming communities (often in unofficial collaboration with publishers) perpetuate a cultural domain that is hostile to queer subjectivities.

This attitude is not bound to forums, as Lisa Nakamura (2012) contends; in games journalism and other settings in games culture, those with hegemonic identities (straight white men) are understood as inherently being interested in and skilled at games (having gaming capital), while people whose identities deviate from that norm face skepticism at levels concomitant with their degree of perceived deviation. Under this framework, queer women of color face the most discrimination in games culture, while straight white men receive inherent credibility.

This intolerance and hostility toward "outsiders" manifests in-game too, even in game spaces like *Second Life* that give players agency to choose their play style. Robert Alan Brookey and Kristopher L. Cannon (2009) argue that despite the openness of *Second Life*'s character creation and player world, players often enact existing gender and sexuality norms; LGBTQ players are discriminated against and women often positioned as sexual objects. In contrast, Jonathan Cabiria's (2008) qualitative study of gay and lesbian *Second Life* players found that in-game experiences positively benefitted their out-of-game lives through the freedom it gave them to express their sexuality. Players reported increases in their sense of belonging, connection to others, and self-esteem.

Jonathan Alexander et al. (2007) also see productive uses in those online gaming experiences and discourses authored by and for LGBTQ players. Through an exploratory, mixed-methods study including analyses of gay gamer message boards, Alexander et al. (2007, 172) contend that "the communication, interpretation, and reading of sexual orientations, identities, and knowledges about sexuality" collectively shape players' understanding of what sexuality is and means both inside and outside game contexts. These practices likely extend to the ways LGBTQ players employ language to communicate with others online while avoiding discrimination.

Kelley's (2012) work with the gaygamer.net forums revealed insights into how LGBTQ players self-identify themselves (or not) through avatar and guild naming practices that utilize strategic language choices that both conceals and reveals their sexuality. Such measures are viewed as necessary considering Carol Stabile's (2014) study that found players enact gender category accountability measures when faced with the gender ambiguity player-avatar combinations can pose. To discover a player's "true" gender, players may consult up to "four layers of communication" (Schmieder 2009, 12) which include the visual appearance of the avatar, in-game written chat, communication from the player on guild forums (in MMORPGs), and voice chats.

These norm-enforcing practices complicate the transgressive possibility of gender bending (or sex swapping, Jenson et al. 2015) in games. Cherie Todd's (2012) qualitative study of female gamers aged 30+ suggests that gender bending in online games is largely a normative practice. Other studies also suggest that the practice is commonplace (Yee 2005), especially for male players (Jenson et al. 2015). However, if play becomes sexual—such as often occurs in *WoW*'s Goldshire (dubbed "Pornshire" by fans because of the frequent erotic role-play that occurs there)—the normative boundaries of gender and sexual orientation can be queered as players "experiment with their own sexual and gender embodiment and desires" (Thompson 2014, 10). Sex swapping in these circumstances can challenge heteronormativity as some players reported not to care who was behind the avatar as long as the avatar's gender corresponded with their preference.

As evidenced here, gaming scholarship has begun to productively explore the ways LGBTQ players navigate the entrenched heteronormativity of mainstream games culture, documenting their efforts to endorse more inclusive spaces and practices—often, as in Sundén, Svengisson, and Stabile's work, via exploiting the ambiguity and queer potentiality of avatar-mediated online game spaces. I now turn to scholarship that focuses on game content and tools, rather than players and communities.

Queer Playthroughs: Textually Driven Approaches

Textual approaches to queer game studies, most commonly employing queer theory and techniques of "queer reading" (Doty 2000), allow researchers to explore the potential for non-normative pleasures and perspectives associated with ostensibly "straight" commercial games.

Romancing the Avatar

Helen Kennedy's (2002) textual analysis of *Tomb Raider* offers one of the earliest of such readings. Kennedy's account considers that Lara may not simply (or only) be a sexualized object for the heterosexual male gaze but may in fact enable both male and female players to explore queer desire. However, Kennedy recognizes these potentials pose little challenge to an overwhelmingly heteronormative and masculinized gaming culture. The character of this masculinized culture is laid bare in Arne Schröder's (2008) analysis of the single-player *Gothic* series as its content reinforces normative gender and sexuality roles through stereotypical depictions of subservient women and parodic depictions of gay men. Examining two other single-player games, Mia Consalvo (2003a) compares *The Sims* to *Final Fantasy IX* to examine the ways queer desire might be cultivated and expressed. Consalvo (2003a) describes the ways the implied heteronormativity of *Final Fantasy IX* may be undermined when women or gay men play as a hetero male protagonist. According to Consalvo, the male playable character does not conform to the stereotypically hypermasculine game protagonist mold, offering players an opportunity to read (and play) him as queer. However, the burden of finding or making inclusive game spaces is shifted to players.

In another study, Consalvo (2003b) conducts a queer reading of *The Sims*; she describes the ways in which the game's character customization and open play style enable players to experience non-normative romantic relationships. By allowing players this agency, *The Sims* leaves room for resistance against heteronormative notions of romance. However, yet again, it is the (imagined) player who brings diversity to the game. Further, Stephen Greer (2013, 5) argues that the queer possibilities available to players via in-game relationships in the *Fable* and *Dragon Age* series are "primarily constructed and validated on the same terms as playing straight." Decentering these norm-enforcing practices may only be possible when players are prescribed to play as a character with a queer orientation. Meghan Blythe Adams (2015) also discusses the ways compulsory heterosexuality is enforced in games and highlights how even progressive games like those of the *Mass Effect* series could benefit from more radical challenges to normative sex and gender hierarchies.

Jordan Youngblood (2013) offers a textual analysis of *Persona 4*, a game in which the protagonists directly negotiate sexual identity. Players work through the story as "a young punk named Kanji terrified that he might be gay, and his relationship with a young cross-dressing female detective named Naoto." By experiencing the tension between resistance and attraction toward the cross-dressed Naoto, players grapple with these opposing embodiments and desires via a machine/player co-construction that defies traditional understandings of a gendered body.

Evan Lauteria and Matthew Wysocki's edited collection *Rated M for Mature: Sex and Sexuality in Video Games* (2015) offers four chapters that focus on queerness. Lauteria's (2015) chapter uses case studies of *Final Fight* and *Chrono Trigger* characters to discuss the controversies and subversions surrounding representations of queer-identified characters in these translated-from-Japanese Super Nintendo games. Summer Glassie (2015) also analyzes representations of sexuality in her chapter about the single-gendered asari race in the *Mass Effect* series. Here she describes the pros and cons of representing a non-normative sexuality and gender in a sci-fi game, ultimately concluding that the inclusion of this race reflects positively on the video game industry since it offers opportunities to play with gender and sexuality. Youngblood (2015) treats queerness as a spatial feature of the puzzle game *Catherine* to provide a queer reading of the compulsory heteronormativity inherent to the game's plot. Last, Bridget Kies (2015) analyzes *Gay Fighter Supreme*, a fighting game that stars LGBTQ characters in nonsexual contexts. Kies argues this game resists heteronormativity by presenting queer characters that are represented not by their sexual behaviors but by queerness as an identity.

Taking the Black Box Out of the Closet: Queer Approaches to Mechanics and Tools

While the humanistic works examined thus far offer queer readings of commercial games to point to the potentials (or lack thereof) for transgressive representations and interactions, scholars have also sought to apply the work of queer theorists to analyses of game mechanics, practices, and devices. This strand of research is vital in exploring, and disrupting, connections between heterosexuality, conventionally masculinized technologies for play and design, and the broader political economies within which games circulate.

Lauteria and Harvey each respectively look to retool games away from normativity through design. Lauteria (2012) looks at game mods produced by LGBTQ gamers, in response to many developers' superficial treatment of sexual diversity in games. He notes how modders can effectively create "meaningful political alternatives to ... commercialized and normative manifestations of LGBT content" (27). By analyzing the ways modders shift gameplay toward queer alternatives in mods of *Mass Effect*, *Dragon Age: Origins*, *The Sims II*, and *Fallout New Vegas*, Lauteria argues that these constitute acts of playful resistance opposing gaming's compulsory heteronormativity. Alison Harvey (2014) similarly engages with radical retooling, as it applies to the free, text-based game platform Twine and its user community. Harvey suggests games produced using Twine contradict "the dominant norms and values of mainstream game design" (99). The tool's accessibility allows those who fall outside of the normal conception of the (white, male, straight) game designer to communicate their perspectives and experiences through creating games with Twine.

Applying concepts from queer theory to obscure gaming communities, Rob Gallagher (2014) guides readers through gradations of esoteric fandom that might go unrecognized if analyzed through other modes of analysis. Gallagher illustrates the ways subscribers to the 1990s publication *Sega Saturn Magazine* lionized and appropriated Japanese games unintended for them, revealing the idiosynchronous, self-guided, and self-gratifying queerness the (Western) Sega Saturn console fandom exemplified. By framing the latter console fandom as identifiable with "camp" (a cultural and aesthetic style marked by "contradictoriness, perversity, and excess" (39)), and contrasting it with the ways contemporary fandoms have been "kitsched" (deindividualized by cynical, targeted marketing dictated by quantitative analyses), Gallagher draws attention to one way queer theory can productively inform perspectives on gaming cultures.

Queer theory has also been applied to game mechanics. Amanda Phillips (2014) draws from Jack Halberstam's (2005) work to argue *Minecraft* employs a queer algorithmic ecology. Phillips (115) argues that no "primary life orientation" is privileged for gameplay, and therefore players are free to inhabit the space in any way they choose. Even the game's temporality is queer in that "time marked by reproductive life stands still" (116). Similarly, Shira Chess (2016) uses queer theory to establish that video games employ a queer narrative structure that withholds the climax (or rejects it altogether), delaying players' gratification and therefore making the process of playing—not the final boss battle—the pleasure. Indeed, these readings would not be possible without the use of queer theory as it offers nuance to well-tread topics and opportunity for topics that might otherwise go unexamined.

Bending the Rules: Alternative Models of Academic Inquiry

This hybridizing of game studies and queer theory is not achieved via methods alone. Game studies have been further enriched by queer perspectives when alternative publishing models were used. An example of this occurs in *QED: A Journal in LBGTQ Worldmaking*, a journal that welcomes the voices of scholars, activists, and artists alike. Their special issue on queerness and games includes two commentaries by queer game designers (Conn 2015; Sens 2015) and an interview by Carly Kocurek (2015) with queer tabletop game designer Michael De Anda paired with five more traditionally academic articles. Topics covered in the academic articles include the ambivalent nature of queer potentialities in *World of Warcraft* and *FrontierVille* (Chang 2015), solo players (Shaw 2015), the masochistic pleasure of playing games (Ruberg 2015), and online activism in the face of GamerGate (Evans and Janish 2015). This issue also includes the only example of quantitative methods applied to this subject, taking the form of a survey analyzing players' in-game romance preferences (McDonald 2015). Academic publishing models that include works from scholars, activists, and practitioners offer a bridge between scholarly publication and other work on queerness and games that occurs outside the academic pipeline.

Publication venues that offer content that is viable and accessible to, and encourages discussion between, a diversity of audiences are invaluable to both queer game studies researchers and LGBTQ gaming communities. Excellent work on the topic has appeared in midway academic publications like FirstPersonScholar.com and *In Media Res*, at conventions like GaymerX and QGCon, on personal blogs and journalistic publications like Gamasutra.com, and countless curated exhibitions, such as those from Babycastles that bring both scholars and non-scholars together. Special journal issues such as the aforementioned example from *QED* and Shaw and Ruberg's forthcoming (at time of publication) edited collection, *Queer Game Studies: Gender, Sexuality, and a Queer Approach to Game Studies*, offer diverse perspectives from voices inside and outside of academia that have the potential to reach multiple audiences. More collaborations between scholars and community members will enrich queer game studies and gaming culture. Importantly, if this model is taken up, nonacademics who contribute to academic publications should be compensated for their time and effort. The importance of forging and bolstering supportive, ethical bonds with members of LGBTQ communities in gaming culture should be implicit as we move forward.

Challenges and Opportunities

There continues to be rich opportunity for research that disrupts and challenges the compulsory, and often toxic, heteronormativity that saturates gaming culture. From a theoretical perspective, queer approaches to gaming are instrumental in problematizing the sex-based binaries that inundate both commercial games and much games research. Documenting the experiences, practices, and perspectives of queer players and designers is central to the project of unsettling the long-standing gender inequities that pervade mainstream gaming industries and cultures. These approaches also open opportunities for more nuanced understandings of the complex, messy, and often unpredictable intersections between games and players' embodied subjectivities. I also think it important to reiterate Harvey's (2014, 104) call for more research focused on designers "making games outside of the dominant, professional, and industrial context." Efforts of queer game designers—across the aforementioned contexts as well as in commercial game development studios—deserve more scholarly attention and, accordingly, support.

A greater variety of case studies might keep pace with, and support, not only the burgeoning awareness of sexual and gender diversity across multiple gaming contexts but foreground opportunities where queer theory might enhance understandings of commonplace or overlooked gaming practices and discourses. In addition to exploring the experiences of LGBTQ gamers and designers operating in different contexts, games researchers might also follow contemporary feminist and queer activism in drawing greater attention to (and support for) the challenges faced by transgender individuals and communities involved in digital play. To borrow from the Feminists in Games network, and traditions of feminist interventionist research more generally, research that both creates and documents safe spaces for LGBTQ-identified youth and adults to cultivate game design skills might bring change to the overwhelming heterocentrism of the games industry or minimally greater awareness.

A stronger presence of scholarship in recognized journals and high-profile conferences will undoubtedly do good for the disciplines, authors, and communities who care about issues surrounding queerness and games. Open-access journals such as *Ada* excel at welcoming academically rigorous research on queerness in games. However, academic systems also need to acknowledge alternative modes of knowledge production.

By way of conclusion, it is important to reiterate a point I made at the outset: scholarly work on/in queer gaming *is* happening. Vibrant discussions around sexuality and digital gaming are taking place. And yet, each of the academic works I discuss in this chapter identifies a dearth of visible, notable research in the area. This suggests not so much a lack of activity on the part of scholars—but rather a lack of support from the conventional gatekeepers to academia. I therefore encourage the gatekeepers—editors, conference organizers, editorial boards, tenure and hiring committees, dissertation committees, and journal reviewers—to make a more concerted effort to encourage and support work that not only documents queer gaming communities and contexts but that also, significantly, queers conventional theoretical and methodological traditions. To make this work matter—to ensure that its impact can be measured not only in terms of journal rankings but in the lives of LGBTQ game enthusiasts—requires a rigorous and multifaceted set of strategies related to the production and communication of queer gaming knowledge.

Notes

1. Here, a wildcard character indicates a search term that will return results that are not exact matches, therefore broadening the scope of the search. For example, the search gam* will return results with terms such as game, games, gaming, gamer, and so on.

2. *QED* published a special issue on queerness and gaming, and Bloomsbury published a book in which several chapters contained research on the topic. This is not insignificant in terms of total numbers, but further clarification is prudent to prevent misrepresentation of the data in Fig. 2.1. For further detail, refer to the references list.

3. Based on the results of this systematic review, a categorization between sociocultural and textually based approaches offers the most productive means of mapping existing research related to queer gaming; the former reports on empirical studies of LGBTQ-identified game players, groups, and communities, while the latter applies queer theories and frameworks to analyses of games, gaming practices, tools, and games-related texts.

Bibliography

Adams, Meghan Blythe. 2015. Renegade Sex: Compulsory Sexuality and Charmed Magic Circles in the Mass Effect Series. *Loading … The Journal of the Canadian Game Studies Association* 9 (14): 40–54.

Ahmed, Sara. 2006. Orientations: Toward a Queer Phenomenology. *GLQ: A Journal of Lesbian and Gay Studies* 12 (4): 543–574. https://doi.org/10.1215/10642684-2006-002.

Alexander, Jonathan, Mack McCoy, and Carlos Velez. 2007. 'A Real Effect on the Gameplay': Computer Gaming, Sexuality, and Literacy. In *Gaming Lives in the Twenty-First Century: Literate Connections*, ed. Gail Hawisher and Cynthia L. Selfe, 167–190. New York: Palgrave Macmillan.

Bromseth, Janne, and Jenny Sundén. 2010. Queering Internet Studies: Intersections of Gender and Sexuality. In *The Handbook of Internet Studies*, ed. Robert Burnett, Mia Consalvo, and Charles Ess, 270–300. Sussex: Wiley-Blackwell.

Brookey, Robert Alan, and Kristopher L. Cannon. 2009. Sex Lives in *Second Life*. *Critical Studies in Media Communication* 26 (2): 145–164. https://doi.org/10.1080/15295030902860260.

Butler, Judith. 1990. *Gender Trouble: Feminism and the Subversion of Identity*. New York: Routledge.

Cabiria, Jonathan. 2008. Virtual World and Real World Permeability: Transference of Positive Benefits for Marginalized Gay and Lesbian Populations. *Journal of Virtual Worlds Research* 1 (1): 1–13.

Chang, Edmond Y. 2015. Love is in the Air: Queer (Im)Possibility and Straightwashing in Frontierville and *World of Warcraft*. *QED: A Journal in GLBTQ Worldmaking* 2 (2): 6–31.

Chess, Shira. 2016. The Queer Case of Video Games: Orgasms, Heteronormativity, and Video Game Narrative. *Critical Studies in Media Communication* 33 (1): 84–94. https://doi.org/10.1080/15295036.2015.1129066.

Cohen, Cathy J. 1997. Punks, Bulldaggers, and Welfare Queens: The Radical Potential of Queer Politics? *GLQ: A Journal of Lesbian and Gay Studies* 3 (4): 437–465. https://doi.org/10.1215/10642684-3-4-437.

Condis, Megan. 2015. No Homosexuals in *Star Wars*? BioWare, 'Gamer' Identity, and the Politics of Privilege in a Convergence Culture. *Convergence: The International Journal of Research into New Media Technologies* 21 (2): 198–212. https://doi.org/10.1177/135485651452720.

Conn, Matt. 2015. Gaming's Untapped Queer Potential as Art. *QED: A Journal in GLBTQ Worldmaking* 2 (2): 1–5.

Consalvo, Mia. 2003a. Hot Dates and Fairy-Tale Romances: Studying Sexuality in Video Games. In *The Video Game Theory Reader*, ed. Mark J.P. Wolf and Bernard Perron, 171–194. New York: Routledge.

———. 2003b. It's a Queer World After All: Studying *The Sims* and Sexuality. *GLAAD Center for the Study of Media & Society*. http://archive.glaad.org/documents/csms/The_Sims.pdf.

de Castell, Suzanne, Jennifer Jenson, Nick Taylor, and Kurt Thumiert. 2014. Re-Thinking Foundations: Theoretical and Methodological Challenges (and Opportunities) in Virtual Worlds Research. *Journal of Gaming and Virtual Worlds* 6 (1): 3–20. https://doi.org/10.1386/jgvw.6.1.3_1.

Doty, Alexander. 2000. *Flaming Classics: Queering the Film Cannon*. New York: Routledge.

Eklund, Lina. 2011. Doing Gender in Cyberspace: The Performance of Gender by Female *World of Warcraft* Players. *Convergence: The International Journal of Research into New Media Technologies* 17 (3): 323–342. https://doi.org/10.1177/1354856511406472.

Evans, Sarah, and Elyse Janish. 2015. #INeedDiverseGames: How the Queer Backlash to GamerGate Enables Nonbinary Coalition. *QED: A Journal in GLBTQ Worldmaking* 2 (2): 125–150.

Gallagher, Rob. 2014. From Camp to Kitsch: A Queer Eye on Console Fandom. *GAME Journal: The Italian Journal of Game Studies* 1 (3): 39–50. http://www.gamejournal.it/wp-content/uploads/2014/04/GAME_3_Subcultures_Journal.pdf.

Glassie, Summer. 2015. 'Embraced Eternity' Lately? Mislabeling and Subversion of Sexuality Labels Through the Asari in the *Mass Effect* Trilogy. In *Rated M for Mature: Sex and Sexuality in Video Games*, ed. Matthew Wysocki and Evan Lauteria, 161–174. New York: Bloomsbury.

Greer, Stephen. 2013. Playing Queer: Affordances for Sexuality in Fable and Dragon Age. *Journal of Gaming and Virtual Worlds* 5 (1): 3–21.

Halberstam, Judith. 2005. *In a Queer Time and Place: Transgender Bodies, Subcultural Lives*. New York: New York University Press.

Harvey, Alison. 2014. Twine's Revolution: Democratization, Depoliticization and the Queering of Game Design. *GAME Journal: The Italian Journal of Game Studies* 1 (3): 95–107. http://www.gamejournal.it/wpcontent/uploads/2014/04/GAME_3_Subcultures_Journal.pdf.

Jenson, Jennifer, Nick Taylor, Suzanne de Castell, and Barry Dilouya. 2015. Playing with Our Selves: Multiplicity and Identity in Online Games. *Feminist Media Studies* 15 (5): 860–879. https://doi.org/10.1080/14680777.2015.1006652.

Kelley, James B. 2012. Gay Naming in Online Gaming. *Names: A Journal of Onomastics* 60 (4): 193–200.

———. 2013. The Virtual Male Body as Site of Conflicting Desires in Age of Conan: Hyborian Adventures. In *Conan Meets the Academy: Multidisciplinary Essays on the Enduring Barbarian*, ed. Jonas Prida, 144–173. Jefferson, NC: McFarland Press.

Kennedy, Helen W. 2002. Lara Croft: Feminist Icon or Cyberbimbo? On the Limits of Textual Analysis. *Game Studies: The International Journal of Computer Game Research*. http://www.gamestudies.org/0202/kennedy/.

Kies, Bridget. 2015. 'Death by Scissors': *Gay Fighter Supreme* and the Sexuality That Isn't Sexual. In *Rated M for Mature: Sex and Sexuality in Video Games*, ed. Matthew Wysocki and Evan Lauteria, 210–224. New York: Bloomsbury.

Kocurek, Carly A. 2015. Tabled for Discussion: A Conversation with Game Designer Michael De Anda. *QED: A Journal in GLBTQ Worldmaking* 2 (2): 151–172.

Lauteria, Evan W. 2012. Ga(y)mer Theory: Queer Modding as Resistance. *Reconstruction: Studies in Contemporary Culture* 12 (2): 1–34. http://reconstruction.eserver.org/Issues/122/Lauteria_Evan.shtml.

———. 2015. Assuring Quality: Early-1990s Nintendo Censorship and the Regulation of Queer Sexuality and Gender. In *Rated M for Mature: Sex and Sexuality in Video Games*, ed. Matthew Wysocki and Evan Lauteria, 42–59. New York: Bloomsbury.

McDonald, Heidi. 2015. Romance in Games: What Is It, How Is It, and How Developers Can Improve It. *QED: A Journal in GLBTQ Worldmaking* 2 (2): 32–63.

Nakamura, Lisa. 2012. Queer Female of Color: The Highest Difficulty Setting There Is? Gaming Rhetoric as Gender Capital. *Ada: A Journal of Gender, New Media, and Technology* 1 (1). https://doi.org/10.7264/N37P8W9V.

Phillips, Amanda. 2014. (Queer) Algorithmic Ecology: The Great Opening up of Nature to all Mobs. In *Understanding Minecraft: Essays on Play, Community, and Possibilities*, ed. Nate Garrelts, 106–120. Jefferson, NC: MacFarland.

Pulos, Alexis. 2013. Confronting Heteronormativity in Online Games: A Critical Discourse Analysis of LGBTQ Sexuality in *World of Warcraft*. *Games and Culture* 8 (2): 77–97. https://doi.org/10.1177/1555412013478688.

Ruberg, Bonnie. 2015. No Fun: The Queer Potential of Video Games That Annoy, Anger, Disappoint, Sadden, and Hurt. *QED: A Journal in GLBTQ Worldmaking* 2 (2): 108–124.

Schmieder, Christian. 2009. World of Maskcraft vs. World of Queercraft? Communication, Sex and Gender in the Online Role-Playing Game *World of Warcraft*. *Journal of Gaming and Virtual Worlds* 1 (1): 5–21.

Schröder, Arne. 2008. 'We Don't Want It Changed, Do We?' Gender and Sexuality in Role-Playing Games. *Eludamos: Journal for Computer Game Culture* 2 (2): 241–256.

Sedgwick, Eve Kosofsky. 2009. *Epistemologies of the Closet*. Berkeley, CA: University of California Press.

Sens, Jeffrey. 2015. Queer Worldmaking Games: A Portland Indie Experiment. *QED: A Journal in GLBTQ Worldmaking* 2 (2): 98–107.

Shaw, Adrienne. 2009. Putting the Gay in Games. *Games and Culture* 4 (3): 228–253. https://doi.org/10.1177/1555412009339729.

———. 2012a. Talking to Gaymers: Questioning Identity, Community and Media Representation. *Westminster Papers in Communication & Culture* 9 (1): 67–88.

———. 2012b. Do You Identify as a Gamer? Gender, Race, Sexuality, and Gamer Identity. *Games and Culture* 14 (1): 28–44. https://doi.org/10.1177/1461444811410394.

———. 2013. On Not Becoming Gamers: Moving Beyond the Constructed Audience. *Ada: A Journal of Gender, New Media, and Technology* (2). https://doi.org/10.7264/N33N21B3.

———. 2014. *Gaming at the Edge: Sexuality and Gender at the Margins of Gamer Culture.* Minneapolis, MN: University of Minnesota Press.

———. 2015. Circles, Charmed and Magic: Queering Game Studies. *QED: A Journal in GLBTQ Worldmaking* 2 (2): 64–97.

Stabile, Carol. 2014. 'I Will Own You': Accountability in Massively Multiplayer Online Games. *Television & New Media* 15 (1): 43–57. https://doi.org/10.1177/1527476413488457.

Sundén, Jenny. 2009. *Play as Transgression: An Ethnographic Approach to Queer Game Cultures.* Proceedings of DiGRA 2009: Breaking New Ground: Innovation in Games, Play, Practice and Theory, West London, UK.

———. 2012. Desires at Play: On Closeness and Epistemological Uncertainty. *Games and Culture* 7 (2): 164–184. https://doi.org/10.1177/1555412012451124.

Sundén, Jenny, and Malin Sveningsson. 2012. *Gender and Sexuality in Online Game Cultures: Passionate Play.* New York: Routledge.

Thompson, Nathan James A. 2014. Queer/ing Game Space: Sexual Play in the *World of Warcraft. Media Fields Journal* 8: 1–12.

Todd, Cherie. 2012. 'Troubling' Gender in Virtual Gaming Spaces. *New Zealand Geographer* 68: 101–110. https://doi.org/10.1111/j.1745-7939.2012.01227.x.

Williams, Dimitri, Mia Consalvo, Scott Caplan, and Nick Yee. 2009. Looking for Gender: Gender Roles and Behaviors Among Online Gamers. *Journal of Communication* 59 (4): 700–725. https://doi.org/10.1111/j.1460-2466.2009.01453.x.

Wysocki, Matthew, and Evan Lauteria. 2015. *Rated M for Mature: Sex and Sexuality in Video Games.* New York: Bloomsbury.

Yee, Nick. 2005. *WoW Gender Bending. The Daedalus Project: The Psychology of MMORPGs.* http://www.nickyee.com/eqt/genderbend.html.

Youngblood, Jordan. 2013. 'C'mon! Make me a man!': *Persona 4*, Digital Bodies, and Queer Potentiality. *Ada: A Journal of Gender, New Media, and Technology* (2). https://doi.org/10.7264/N3QC01D2.

———. 2015. Climbing the Heterosexual Maze: *Catherine* and Queering Spatiality in Gaming. In *Rated M for Mature: Sex and Sexuality in Video Games,* ed. Matthew Wysocki and Evan Lauteria, 240–252. New York: Bloomsbury. https://doi.org/10.7264/N3QC01D2.

3

Envisioning Queer Game Studies: Ludology and the Study of Queer Game Content

Evan W. Lauteria

In his infamous introduction to "The Gaming Situation," Markku Eskelinen (2001) boldly and brashly stated "if I throw a ball at you I don't expect you to drop it and wait until it starts telling stories." In doing so, Eskelinen both summarized the academic goal of ludology—its investment in identifying the particular modes of meaning-making found in games and play—and its short-sightedness, an unabashed dismissal of representative features of games. Ludology gave game studies a powerful set of analytic tools for understanding games broadly and video games in particular, highlighting their ergodic features (Aarseth 1997), their configurational properties (Eskelinen 2001), and their ordering of meaning through future-oriented simulations (Frasca 2003b). Indeed, ludology helped clarify the form of the game, identifying its ontological properties and core-defining structures (Juul 2003). Simultaneously, however, ludological approaches were fraught with numerous "conceptual blind spots" (Jenkins 2004, 670), namely, around representation and the interplay between narrative, mechanics, experience, and play, which ultimately limited scholarship working within and through those frames.

This chapter seeks to explore and unpack the affordances and limitations of ludological concepts and approaches in addressing queer game content. Ludology's attempt to isolate and identify features of the gamic form and its

The author wishes to express a special thanks and gratitude to his research assistant, Ben Snow Sipes, who collected a majority of the quantitative data for this study.

E. W. Lauteria (✉)
University of California, Davis, CA, USA

© The Author(s) 2018
T. Harper et al. (eds.), *Queerness in Play*, Palgrave Games in Context,
https://doi.org/10.1007/978-3-319-90542-6_3

distinct approach meaning-making both afforded scholars new language for analysis and constrained scholarship within its purview to a certain set of analytical precepts. Both these affordances and limitations, however, can inform and be informed by queer studies. I open this chapter by exploring the limitations of ludology's early scholarship by adopting a queer reading of early ludological work and suggest one major point of oversight—the messy construction of the player-subject position—has been a primary focal point in much of queer game scholarship since the early days of ludology. I suggest that many queer game studies complicate and expand ludology's frame of analysis through its commitment to understanding simulated relations—relations between player and avatar (Shaw 2012, 2015; Consalvo 2003; Phillips 2017), between player-character and non-player characters (Belmonte 2011; Glassie 2015; Lauteria 2012), between non-player characters (Youngblood 2013), and between player and medium (Alexander 2007; Cabiria 2008; Condis 2015; Pozo 2015). That is, many queer game studies explore how games hail and interpellate players and construct diegetic and mechanical sexual and gendered realities through the discursive and material relationships between player and avatar, between user and apparatuses, both material and mediated, and between in-game characters and discourse. The study of relations is central to queer games analysis.

I then attempt to merge ludology's commitment to the ergodic, configurational, and simulative elements of games with past queer game studies' focus on relations by exploring a sample of 17 transgender characters in 91 commercial mainstream games from 1987 to 2015. I opt for a content analysis approach over a close reading approach to show how relational game analysis can be deployed as an epistemological and analytical frame beyond a single method, such as close reading, much as we understand ludology as a theoretical and methodological frame rather than a distinct method. Through this study, I show how simulated relations to and between characters in games with transgender characters help us to understand how transgender identities circulate in gamic spaces, how these relations have changed over time, and how the representational and simulative facets of queer game content across the entire sample are intimately tied together through the very relations identified by queer games scholarship.

Queering Ludology and the Study of Play Relations

In the late 1990s, following a consumer boom around video games with the release of the Sony PlayStation in 1994 and Nintendo 64 in 1996, scholars from multiple disciplines began expressing an intellectually invigorated interest in video games, beyond studies of media effects prior. Scholars like Espen Aarseth (1997), among others—both ludologists and not—began to develop a language for understanding cybertext and cyberspace from a humanistic, formal perspective. Aarseth argued that cybertexts, including video games, are "ergodic," from "the Greek words *ergon* and *hodos*, meaning work and path." By this, he suggests that "nontrivial effort is required to allow the reader to traverse the text" (1997, 1), that video games and cybertexts as a whole operate differently than the media of the past because of their mechanistic, formalistic qualities. Traversing cybertexts invariably requires some sort of meaningful input—choices, strategies, selections—to become legible.

This orientation to video games' formal qualities birthed an academic movement in game studies known as "ludology." Ludology, from the Latin *ludus* for "game," emerged as a scholarly approach and a polemic oriented to dismissing pre-existing schools of thought, such as new literary criticism, narrative theory, or performance studies, in the service of creating a unique set of concepts, methods, and theories for the analysis of games. European ludological scholars such as Jesper Juul (2003, 2005), Markku Eskelinen (2001), Miguel Sicart (2003), and Gonzalo Frasca (2003a, b) drew heavily from a constructed "classical canon" of game studies: *Homo Ludens* (1955) by cultural historian Johan Huizinga; *Man, Play, and Games* (1961) by sociologist Roger Caillois; and *The Grasshopper: Games, Life and Utopia* (1978) by philosopher Bernard Suits. Suits in particular invested much, both through the Platonic dialogues of *The Grasshopper* and elsewhere (1967, 1969), in developing a salient notion of just what a game is. He offers a simplistic definition: "playing a game is the voluntary attempt to overcome unnecessary obstacles" (1978, 55). More complexly, however, he asserts:

To play a game is to attempt to achieve a specific state of affairs [prelusory goal], using only means permitted by rules [lusory means], where the rules prohibit use of more efficient in favour of less efficient means [constitutive rules], and where the rules are accepted just because they make possible such activity [lusory attitude]. (Suits 1978, 54–55)

While Suits suggests that his simplistic definition is merely a "more porta-ble version" of the longer, the expanded definition offers a greater focus on these so-called unnecessary obstacles, all of which are organized around for-mal rulesets and their functions. This preoccupation with the gamic form, its binding rules, shaped and informed ludological analysis on the whole (see Frasca 2003b; Juul 2003), despite the classical canon of Huizinga, Caillois, and Suits that overwhelmingly emphasized the importance of meaningful play rather than the formal and functional qualities of a game.

Returning to Markku Eskelinen's (2001) flippant description of ball throw-ing, an exemplar of ludology's formalist approach, ludology seemingly fore-closed the possibility of symbolic and representational meaning operating at the level of simulation, or, at best, rendered it distantly secondary. Games are configurational media, as he suggests, but ludology's polemic repudiation of narrative approaches to games—again, "if I throw a ball at you I don't expect you to drop it and wait until it starts telling stories"—overlooked the locus of representational meaning in games. Processes of play in games are not asu-bjectively configurational; games simultaneously hail and interpellate player subjects by inviting participation in configurational practices. That is, to be a "player" is to hold a subject position in the gaming experience, bound up in symbolic and representational processes. Indeed, the word "player" alone is a signifier.

By Louis Althusser's (1971) account, ideological state apparatuses like schools, police, and corporations "hail"—that is, summon, call, request—individual actors and in doing so interpellate actors as subjects within a given ideological order. "Student," "criminal," and "consumer" are imbued with dis-cursive and ideological power which constructs a subject position with appro-priate behaviors, thoughts, and role sets. With respect to gender, Judith Butler (1990) articulated how gendered moments such as the declaration of "it's a boy/girl" produce the subjectivity of the identified boy/girl through this very hailing and interpellation process. To be a viable subject in the world requires this sort of institutional and discursive naming and performative ascription. What it means to navigate any social space, then, is to be hailed and interpel-lated as a specific subject within the confines of an ideological state, as under state-sanctioned capitalism, or discursive relations, such as binarily con-structed gender.

This same process is centrally important to games as media and interactive systems. James Paul Gee argues that "games recruit identities and encourage identity work and reflection on identities" (2007, 51). Identity through game play operates at three levels—virtual, real, and projective—through which, unlike traditional non-ergodic texts, players are active and the relationship between player and character is reflexive (58). That is, game-encouraged identification is not absolute or all-encompassing but rather a complex relationship between the simulative features of a game's rules and mechanics, the pre-existing and extra-gamic identities and frames of the player, and the mediation and interaction between the two. Indeed, the act of ball throwing produces symbolic relations between participants—pitchers and catchers—and symbolic characterization of additional rulesets simultaneously hierarchizes those symbolic roles—winners, who comes out "on top," even culturally imbued concepts as "the bigger man." Even in these anecdotal examples, issues of identity, power, gender, and status are central to the meaning-making around a simple game of ball throwing, divorced of the ball's capacity to "tell stories."

But those roles must be actively adopted and negotiated by players. Simulation and configuration produce symbolic meanings through relational ties between subjects, objects, and procedures, and those meanings are enacted through material behaviors of players themselves. I offer the ball-throwing example both for its (im)potency as Eskelinen's primary counterpoint to narrative and representational meaning and for its immediate potential for queer interpretation. The symbolic meanings of pitchers and catchers take on additional meaning through queer lenses, referring to explicit sexual positions, particularly between men who have sex with men. The production of new identities through win-states illustrates the pervasive power of competitive masculinity and discomfort with homosociality, complicated further by queer sensibilities regarding gender identity and performance. Queer interventions in general take place at the level of relations: between actors, between bodies, and between discourses.

Queer game scholarship has, at least since Helen Kennedy's (2002) exploration of transgender identification through Lara Croft and Mia Consalvo's (2003) first attempt to explore the role of sexuality in games using *The Sims* and *Final Fantasy IX*, regularly questioned relations in some form. By Kennedy's account, the relation between a (male) player and avatar, a "complex relationship between *subject* and *object*," produces "a kind of queer embodiment, the merger of the flesh of the (male) player with Lara's elaborated feminine body of pure information." To Kennedy, the hailing of the male player into the world of *Tomb Raider* yields a transgender or drag embodiment of Lara, while simultaneously and messily facilitating Lara's objectification. Consalvo, in her analysis of player-avatar relations in *Final Fantasy IX*, explores the plausibility of applying Eve Sedgwick's (1985) erotic triangle to heterosexual pursuit in games. She concludes that, unlike the competitive rivalry of homosociality in literary texts, games endeavor to collapse the difference between player and avatar, ultimately unifying subjects in a symbiotic relationship of shared interests and goals, both a relationship to the female sex object and "the (normative) validation of masculinity—heterosexuality—that is conferred through this relationship" (2003, 179). Like Kennedy, Consalvo inquires about the relationship between subject and object, directly asking "what if the player is a heterosexual female, or a gay male? Viewing the game (or playing the game) from these subject positions demonstrates how norms can be made visible and problematized" (179). Here, Consalvo identified the notion of the "implied player" years before Espen Aarseth (2007) used the term and in doing so through queer theory better articulated the role of player positionality and the central function of normative hailing and interpellation in games embedded in heterosexism and cultures of compulsory heterosexuality. That is, in identifying the messiness of subject-object, player-avatar relationships, Kennedy and Consalvo highlight the importance of gamic role signifiers, how games hail and interpellate player subjects, at least in part through the symbolic management of gendered and sexual desire divorced of game's formal rulesets.

Queer games studies since have further unpacked issues of relations in the analysis of games in myriad ways. In regard to mediated desire, scholars have illustrated that games produce and facilitate desire through play, often replicating or emblemizing contemporary logics and discourses of sex, sexuality, and gendered relations (Kryzwinska 2015; Navarro-Remesal and García-Catalán 2015). They do so through hailing and interpellating player subjects into the diegesis of a game's world and into the ludic mechanics of a game's system. In doing so, seemingly inclusive mechanics like same-sex romance options in games produce limited and confined sorts of subjectivities. Juan F. Belmonte (2011) argues that the navigation of same-sex romance options in *Dragon Age* yields "rhizomatic" identity production for players, though the mechanics simultaneously limit and confine as they permit such identity production. The romances and proclamations of identities of non-player and allied characters, too, lend itself to the mediation of desire by producing sexual and gendered others (Glassie 2015; Youngblood 2013) and sexual and gendered spaces (Chang 2015; Schmieder 2009; Sherlock 2013; Thompson 2014; Youngblood 2015). And games' material bases of input and interaction (Phillips 2017; Pozo 2015) and production of certain affective ties (Lauteria 2016; Ruberg 2015) similarly hail and interpellate players by constructing relations between the player-body, machine, and imagined worlds.

In turn, queer game studies have responded to the aforementioned intellectual blind spot of ludology, its polemic dismissal of representational meaning that is centrally important to processes of play. But simultaneously, they have expanded the capacity for ludological concepts and frames—a focus on the form, how simulation and configuration produce meaning, the functional role of ergodicity in game play—to properly address queer content. That is, by expounding upon the initial inquiry of subject-object relations and the hailing-interpellation processes of play, queer game scholars have illustrated the importance of unifying textual, symbolic, formal, and sociocultural dimensions of games for effective analysis.

Queer Relations: An Analysis of Transgender Game Content

In the following pages, I further illustrate how explicit attention to relations within games provides fruitful analytical outcomes for queer games analysis. I drew from a sample of 17 transgender characters appearing in mainstream video games between 1987 and 2015. This sample was formed by combining lists of video games with transgender characters from transgamersociologist. wordpress. com[1] and Out.com[2] (see Table 3.1), both of which exclude transgender content that relies solely on player/protagonist choice (as in the *Fable* or *Saints Row* series) or on cross-dressing as a mechanic in the absence of otherwise transgender-identified or gender non-conforming characters (as in *Final Fantasy VII*). These lists were designed to catalogue transgender representation in games, though the lists

Table 3.1 Trans* characters by first game appearance

Character	First appearance	First game
Birdo (Catherine)	1987 (JP)	*Yume Kōjō: Doki Doki Panic*
Poison	1989 (Arcades)	*Final Fight*
Faris	1992 (JP)	*Final Fantasy V*
Flea (Mayoné)	1994 (JP)	*Chrono Trigger*
Sheik	1998 (JP)	*Legend of Zelda: Ocarina of Time*
Quina Quen	2000 (JP)	*Final Fantasy IX*
Bridget	2002 (JP)	*Guilty Gear X2*
Vivian	2004 (JP)	*Paper Mario: The Thousand Year Door*
Guillo	2006 (JP)	*Baten Kaitos Origins*
Leo	2007 (JP)	*Tekken 6*
Naoto Shirogane	2008 (JP)	*Persona 4*
Kainé	2010 (JP)	*NieR Gestalt & NieR RepliCant*
Erica Anderson	2011 (JP)	*Catherine*
Serendipity	2011 (NA)	*Dragon Age II*
Gwyndolin	2011 (JP)	*Dark Souls*
Beauty Brigitte	2013 (JP)	*Pokémon: X/Y*
Cremisius Aclassi (Krem)	2014 (NA)	*Dragon Age: Inquisition*

were compiled with different underlying cultural frames—academic vs. popular, insider vs. outsider experience, and so on. In this regard, combining the lists overall provided a more thorough, though still incomplete, picture of transgender representation in mainstream games. The combined list avoided only including "positive" representations or regulating trans*[3] identity to only include a subset of transgender experiences and behaviors (e.g., sex change or binary gender identification).

On the other hand, however, this list is also a curated sample rather than a full census of all transgender representation. From these lists, I identified 91 different games where these characters appear and a total of 97 appearances, accounting for moments where more than one transgender character was included in a single game. I drew data for this project from information in formal release documents, Wikipedia entries, and fan-curated wikis and "shrines." In the interest of privileging relational features of these characters and their related games for analysis, the quantitative and categorical dataset codified primarily "demographic" information for the characters and their games—sites of production and dissemination, game genre, character "role" (e.g., playable vs. non-playable), and so on. Particular attention was given to how game genre, race, nationality, and species, and status as a protagonist, antagonist, or neutral character served to construct certain kinds of possible relations and discourses for players. That is, non-human, regionally foreign, and enemy transgender characters were understood to hail and interpellate players regarding gender in a manner different than human and player or allied non-player characters, clarified further below.

Table 3.1 is the complete list of trans* characters included in the sample. The column "First appearance" lists the year of their first appearance in a game release, followed by the first region of release in parentheses ("JP" for Japan; "NA" for North America). For Poison, *Final Fight* was released in arcades as a simultaneous "global" or multiregional release. Gwyndolin in *Dark Souls* experienced a similar "global" release, though the Japanese version was released a week prior to the North American and European versions. Games' first regions of release generally reflect the nationality of games' development companies; all games released in Japan first were designed and developed by Japanese companies such as Nintendo and Square, while the two North American releases were designed by Canadian company BioWare. Poison and *Final Fight* were designed by Japanese company Capcom, and non-arcade releases of her game were released in Japan prior to shipment abroad.

The inclusion of transgender video game characters seems to be a largely Japanese affair, with only one non-Japanese company—BioWare—creating and releasing games with unique transgender characters. On one hand, this is a product of cultural differences around the expression and representation of queer genders and sexualities in the Japanese context. Birdo and Poison, for instance, reflect a then-growing popularity of the *new-half* (male-to-female transgender sex workers) as a spectacle on television and in print in Japan during "the *new-half* boom" (McLelland 2004). Serendipity's appearance in *Dragon Age II* too reflects the Anglophone North American cultural popularity of the drag queen; as anecdotal evidence, *Dragon Age II* was released midway through the third season of the still-popular competitive drag queen television show *RuPaul's Drag Race*.

On the other hand, inclusion of transgender characters might simultaneously be an issue of site of production and of genre conventions within games. Figure 3.1 illustrates the distribution of games with transgender characters by genre. As Mark Wolf (2001) suggests, genre for representational media refers to their iconography, the primarily visual and symbolic conventions that build up the construct of a given genre, such as a romantic comedy or a western, but gamic genres are premised on a different set of criteria. "While the ideas of iconography and theme may be appropriate tools for analyzing Hollywood films" he argues, "another area, interactivity, is an essential part of every game's structure and a more appropriate way of examining and defining video game genres" (2001, 114). In this sense, genre conventions are about configurational relationships, or how the player interacts with the possibility space of the game, and its respective environs, characters, and objects. We can, then, discern important, if partial, information about a game's relational dimensions from its genre classification.

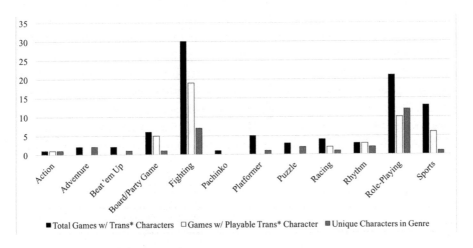

Fig. 3.1 Games and characters by genre

In Fig. 3.1, the first bar in each triplet represents the total number of games with transgender characters in the sample of 97 games. Games containing two characters from the sample were not double-counted, though this only applied to games in the *Super Smash Bros.* series (Birdo, Sheik, and Vivian) and *Final Fantasy Airborne Brigade* and *Final Fantasy Record Keeper* (Faris and Quina). The second column represents the number of games in that genre with playable transgender characters (see below and Table 3.2 for more information on this classification). The third column is the total number of unique characters from the sample in that specific genre, as many characters were featured in more than one game. Genres for each game were taken from both fan wikis and general Wikipedia articles characterizing the games, though slight alterations were made to allow for comparison. "Action-Adventure" was retitled "Adventure" in one case; "Board" and "Party" games were coded together.

"Unique characters" is included as a measure of how many distinct transgender characters appear in a given genre in order to address skewing of the data by repeated and/or cameo appearances. In the case of fighting games, while 30 games include transgender characters, Poison appears in 13 of those games, while Bridget follows closely with 9. Poison greatly skews these data because out of those 13 fighting game appearances, she appears only as a background cameo or in flavor text for other characters in 11. In general, though, fighting games are more prone to retaining and recycling characters in multiple iterations or serial releases than many genres, and so only seven (7) unique fighting game characters actually appear across the total 30 fighting games included in the sample. Fighting games often feature a diverse cast of selectable characters from either across the globe (*Guilty Gear, Tekken,* etc.) or from across franchises (*Super Smash Bros., Street Fighter X Tekken,* etc.). The inclusion of characters like Bridget (*Guilty Gear* series), Leo (*Tekken* series), and Poison (*Street Fighter* franchise) serves to help construct the sense of globality of their respective games' universes. They each represent some form of archetypal or stereotypical person from their region of the world just as their cisgender peers do. For instance, Poison is a rough-and-tough biker chick persona in an American metropolitan street gang, akin to familiar representational tropes seen in characters like Ryu, as a Japanese *karate* martial artist, or Guile, as a member of the US Air Force. But their status as playable within

Table 3.2 Characters by relation to player

	Playable	Enemy	Non-playable	Cameo
Relationship to player/character	47	14	15	21
On North American game cover?	9	2	0	0

those universes also grants a certain degree of privileged relational status, wherein trans-ness is an equally occupiable and livable reality as any other. Poison is a grand example of this, where her moveset in *Ultra Street Fighter IV* comports or at least maps on to the typical *Street Fighter* "*Shōtōkan*" character, the same archetype occupied by the game series' long-time main characters Ryu and Ken.[4] To be interpellated as a player of *Ultra Street Fighter IV* when selecting Poison is to adopt a transgender body that is equally viable and present as any other body within that game world, even with a 13-year delay since her first appearance in *Final Fight* in arcades.

The second most frequent genre in the sample was role-playing games. The inclusion of transgender characters in this genre above others is a predictable result of its genre conventions, which, at least among Japanese role-playing games, are oriented both narratively and mechanically to ensemble drama and teamwork. Out of the 21 role-playing games in the sample, 10 feature playable characters (i.e., a member of your combat team), and there are a total of 12 unique transgender characters among these 21 games. Given the total sample of characters (17), an overwhelming majority (70.59%) appear in role-playing games. Unlike in fighting games, however, transgender inclusion in role-playing games isn't centered on players adopting the pseudo-physicality of a digital trans body. Rather, role-playing games hail and interpellate players into intimate, interactional relationships with transgender characters. Naoto Shirogane's appearance in *Persona 4* is most reflective of this particular genre's conventions, wherein players undergo an extensive recruitment process uncovering Naoto's past and life experiences. To become allied with Naoto means to become familiar with the experience of transgender self-discovery but primarily through a slow unveiling of personal truths dictated by and represented through the player-character's teammates. The player-character, Yu Narukami, is uniformly and unchangeably a cisgender man with only heterosexual romance options through the game's dating mechanics, but the player comes to learn and sympathize with transgender experiences through the intimate narrative and ludic relationship formed with Naoto Shirogane. This strategy of inclusion—education through others—is employed in many RPGs in the sample: Faris, Quina, Guillo, Kainé, Krem, and Vivian all educate the player or player-character on their experiences with gender, identity, and expression through exposition, while their relational proximity to the player-character facilitated through the mechanics of each game produces the possibility to such exposition and disclosure.

The third, fourth, fifth, and sixth most frequent genres in the sample— sports, board/party game platformer, and racing—are all Mario franchise games. Birdo appears in numerous Mario games in these genres—*Mario*

Tennis, Mario Kart, Mario Party, and so on—though her role in each varies. In the cases of these games, Birdo's inclusion is based at least partially on the constant effort of games in the *Mario* franchise to produce and reproduce normative heterosexuality through its character relations. Birdo herself is a pink dinosaur-like creature capable of shooting eggs from her mouth, and she began appearing more regularly as a character in the Mario universe as partnered or paired with Yoshi, another dinosaur character in the series. In one Japanese character profile, Birdo is described as "The one who looks like Yoshi's girlfriend is really his boyfriend!?"[5] Such exclamation is designed to harken back to the spectacle of the *new-half* but simultaneously highlights how inclusion within this specific universe must operate through its internal logics of heteronormativity, such that Birdo's inclusion in the universe is negotiated through Yoshi's perceived male-ness[6] and the functional necessity of heterosexual coupling for the Mario universe's narrative and ludological core. That is, the player-avatar relationship between player and Mario is built around the pursuit of Princess Peach and makes necessary the normalization of heterosexuality and binary gender across the entirety of the series. Birdo and Yoshi's pairing, while facilitating a greater frequency of appearances for Birdo across multiple games, simultaneously serves to normalize heterosexuality and binary gender.

Despite these heteronormative confines, however, Birdo's varied inclusion illustrates how normativity is and can be navigated over time. Indeed, regulated to status as an unspeaking minor boss in *Super Mario Bros. 2*, Birdo, and transgender characters in general, became incorporated into diegetic game worlds as allies and into game mechanics as playable characters more regularly beginning in the early 2000s.

Table 3.2 illustrates the general relational status transgender characters are given to the player. There are 97 total transgender character appearances in this sample in 91 games. In total, 47 (49.00%) of those appearances were as playable characters, either selectable from an ensemble cast, as in fighting, party, or racing games, or as a member of a team, as in role-playing games.

While the percentage of playable inclusion is high, suggesting that transgender characters are represented as main characters with relative frequency, it should be noted that until 2000, over a decade after the first two transgender characters appeared in video games, the only playable transgender character was Faris Scherwiz in *Final Fantasy V*. Faris is, unlike Birdo and Poison before her, not identified as transgender formally within game text or official paratext documentation, included only in transgamer sociologist's list as an honorable mention. In the mid-2000s, however, playability among transgender characters skyrocketed, far overshadowing transgender enemy or non-player characters

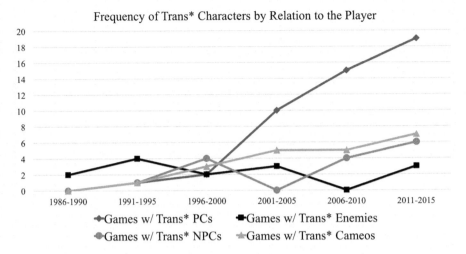

Fig. 3.2 Transgender characters by relation to player

(see Fig. 3.2). Transgender characters also appear more frequently as cameos, as characters in the background of a fighting stage or as trophies for certain accomplishments. The overwhelming majority of these cameo appearances (17 out of 21, or 80.95%) were Poison and Birdo, both appearing as background characters or flavor text for their respective franchises.

The presumption from these data is that transgender inclusion more recently has resulted in hailing and interpellating player processes that render transgender experiences accessible and directly relational to the player. That is, transgender is treated less as "other" over time.

Table 3.3, however, evidences a different sort of "othering" process that remains relatively static across time in the sample. About half (8 of 17, 47.06%) of transgender characters are rendered "other," and thus relationally distant, by being non-human. In some cases, these characters being transgender is a direct result of the gender or sex makeup of that non-human species. Those that are identifiably human (8 of 17, 47.06%) are often rendered ethnically or nationally "other" based on their context of production. Of all the Japanese-created transgender human characters, only Naoto Shirogane is ethnically and nationally Japanese; all other human transgender characters are American or European. In both maneuvers to render transgender as "other," Japanese designers echoed the cultural contexts of the *new-half* boom once again. The media spectacle of the *new-half* in Japan "reinforce[d] the long-standing assumption that transgender performance was something situated in the entertainment world, not in real life" (McLelland 2004, 11). On screen and in print, transgender people were spectacularized and rendered

Table 3.3 Transgender characters by representational features

Character	Representation	Species	Ethnicity/Nationality
Birdo (Catherine)	*New-half*	Birdo	–
Poison	*New-half*	Human	American
Faris	Disguise/butch	Human	Medieval European
Flea (Mayoné)	*Okama*	Mystic	–
Sheik	Disguise	Hylian/Sheikah	–
Quina Quen	Genderless	Qu	–
Bridget	Disguise/femme boy	Human	British
Vivian	*New-half*	Shadow	–
Guillo	Dual gender	Godcraft Puppet	–
Leo	Genderless/butch	Human	German
Naoto Shirogane	Transman/butch	Human	Japanese
Kainé	Intersex	Unknown	–
Erica Anderson	Transwoman	Human	American
Serendipity	Drag queen	Elf	–
Gwyndolin	Trans*	God-like being	–
Beauty Brigitte	Transwoman	Human	French
Cremisius Aclassi (Krem)	Transman	Human	Byzantine-Roman

larger than life; in video games, they were made distinctly "other": non-Japanese or non-human. Popular conceptions of transgender lives, in video games and in Japanese culture broadly, positioned them outside the everyday, and the relations players are invited to participate in with these characters provide a highly mediated and controlled intimacy. These relations remind the player that transgender is—despite possible in-game familiarity—culturally and experientially other.

Conclusion

The above study paints an ambiguous picture of transgender inclusion in games, precisely because the very relations their games facilitate produce and are born out of an anxiety about queerness broadly. The contextual meaning of "transgender" is embedded in each games' relational ties—how players are hailed and interpellated by the game system, how fellow characters construct their peers, and how the game world represents and simulates gendered relationships broadly.

How identity and desire are made manifest and how players are able to express, manage, and pursue identities and desires are intimately tied to the industry-level logics of inclusion, a subject of inquiry tackled most directly by

Adrienne Shaw (2009, 2014) and Todd Harper (2011). Shaw highlights sociocultural and industry discourses and practices that limit and confine the possibility of certain forms of inclusive representation for LGBTQ people. Harper, by contrast, approaches the logics of inclusion as an issue of principled design, articulating the need for what he terms "procedurally and fictively relevant" inclusion of LGBTQ people, themes, identities, and scenarios. Japan's move toward transgender inclusion is a troubled one, fraught with uneasiness about transgender "otherness" and simultaneous spectacularity in the public sphere. North American game designers, on the other hand, have yet to produce a game with a playable transgender character, based on this sample. Both are partial logics of inclusion—Japanese representational otherness and North American simulated and mechanical otherness.

And beyond regional differences, procedures of production, standard business practices, organizational relationships, and corporate cultural frames all inform the creation and dissemination of certain LGBTQ representations and mechanics over others (Lauteria 2015; Ouellette 2013). The emergence of standardized rating systems such as that of the Entertainment Software Rating Board (ESRB), the diversification of console platforms and distribution channels, changing technologies, emergent production standards, and general cultural shifts around LGBTQ people greatly affected the representation of transgender characters in games over time and, in doing so, changed trends in the hailing and interpellation of player subjects in relation to trans-ness generally.

I offer this particular analysis in the attempt to suggest that ludological techniques, frames, and concept still afford powerful methodological toolkits for scholars of queerness in video games, but with messy queer caveats. Unveiling the relational hailing and interpellation processes, particularly around sexuality and gender, in each game aids in the critical goals of queer game studies while reclaiming and reconfiguring an otherwise limited ludological pursuit of "gameness." Textual analyses of games from a queer perspective, then, benefit from understanding hailing and interpellating processes as complex and multileveled—occurring between players, characters, game worlds, and machines and operating at the level of cognition, affect, and identification—and that such processes are intimately tied to discourses of gender and sexuality, both as context of production and as outcome of play. As Marc Ouellette has suggested, "ludic approaches themselves furnish the justification and the methodology for non-ludic approaches to the queering of games and game studies" (2013, 55). And in doing so, I believe queer game studies have aided in the development of a sort of ludology that shies away from pure formalism and apolitical analysis, instead opening avenues for critical work around sex, sexuality, and gender in games.

Notes

1. Garcia, Theresa. 2015. "A Brief History of Transgender Characters in Video Games [Updated]." Accessed online at https://transgamersociologist.wordpress.com/2012/03/26/a-brief-history-of-transgender-characters-in-video-games/.
2. Villagomez, Andrew. 2013. "7 Trans-Friendly Video Game Characters." Accessed online at http://www.out.com/entertainment/popnography/2013/11/03/7-trans-friendly-video-game-characters.
3. The term "trans*" is employed to denote various identity markers and categories under the transgender umbrella, including transgender, transsexual, transman, transwoman, genderqueer, bigender, etc. While some characters openly discuss their identity in their respective games or are granted identities by paratextual documents such as instruction manuals, in many cases the real "identity" of the character is largely unknown, left largely to conjecture based on textual and paratextual evidence. As such, "trans*" is used as a unifying umbrella term for these characters, though their identities or gender categories may vary widely.
4. In the English-language localization of *Street Fighter II*, Capcom referred to the fighting styles of the *Street Fighter* characters Ryu and Ken as "Shotokan" (sic), which has since come to refer to a standard special moveset of a fireball-like projectile (*hadōken*), a rising uppercut (*shōryuken*), and a roundhouse spinning kick (*tatsumaki*). These three moves have become a genre standard, with fans, players, critics, and designers referring to characters with similar movesets, both in the *Street Fighter* franchise and in other games, as "shotoclones." This "*Shōtōkan*" bears little resemblance to the real-world style of karate by the same name developed in Japan in the twentieth century, and thus the current fighting style nomenclature is assumed to be a result of localization error.
5. Original text: 「ヨッシーの彼女に見えて実は彼氏!?」 ("MARIO KART— Double Dash").
6. I write "perceived" here both to note that these are all simulated persons and creatures and to simultaneously draw attention to Yoshi's ability to "pass" as male, and presumably cis, despite producing eggs, a gendered act Birdo attempts to emulate by shooting eggs from her mouth.

Bibliography

Aarseth, Espen. 1997. *Cybertext: Perspectives on Ergodic Literature.* Baltimore, MD: The Johns-Hopkins University Press.
———. 2007. *I Fought the Law: Transgressive Play and the Implied Player.* Situated Play: Proceedings of DiGRA 2007 Conference, Tokyo, Japan.

Alexander, Jonathan. 2007. 'A Real Effect on the Gameplay': Computer Gaming, Sexuality, and Literacy. In *Gaming Lives in the Twenty-First Century*, ed. Cynthia L. Selfe and Gail E. Hawisher, 167–202. New York: Palgrave Macmillan.

Althusser, Louis. 1971. Ideology and Ideological State Apparatuses. In *Lenin and Philosophy and Other Essays*, trans. B. Brewster, 121–176.

Belmonte, Juan F. 2011. *Identity and Choice: Rhizomic and Binary Understandings of the Self in Videogames*. Paper presented at the 2011 Philosophy of Computer Games Conference, Athens, Greece, April 8. http://gameconference2011.files. wordpress.com/2010/10/juan-belmonte-identity-and-choice.pdf.

Butler, Judith. 1990. *Gender Trouble: Feminism and the Subversion of Identity*. New York: Routledge.

Cabiria, Jonathan. 2008. Virtual World and Real World Permeability: Transference of Positive Benefits for Marginalized Gay and Lesbian Populations. *Journal For Virtual Worlds Research* 1 (1): 1–13.

Caillois, Roger. 1961. *Man, Play and Games*. New York, NY: The Free Press.

Chang, Edmond Y. 2015. Love Is in the Air: Queer (Im)Possibility and Straightwashing in FrontierVille and World of Warcraft. *QED: A Journal of GLBTQ Worldmaking* 2 (2): 6–31.

Condis, Megan. 2015. No Homosexuals in *Star Wars*? BioWare, 'Gamer' Identity, and the Politics of Privilege in a Convergence Culture. *Convergence: The International Journal of Research into New Media Technologies* 21 (2): 198–212.

Consalvo, Mia. 2003. Hot Dates and Fairy-Tale Romances: Studying Sexuality in Video Games. In *The Video Game Theory Reader*, ed. Mark J.P. Wolf and Bernard Perron, 171–194. New York, NY: Routledge.

Eskelinen, Markku. 2001. The Gaming Situation. *Game Studies* 1 (1). http://www. gamestudies.org/0101/eskelinen/.

Frasca, Gonzalo. 2003a. Ludologists Love Stories, Too: Notes from a Debate That Never Took Place. In *Level Up: Digital Games Research Conference Proceedings*, ed. Marinka Copier and Joost Raessens, 92–99. Utrecht: Utrecht University.

———. 2003b. Simulation Versus Narrative: Introduction to Ludology. In *The Video Game Theory Reader*, ed. Mark J.P. Wolf and Bernard Perron, 221–236. New York, NY: Routledge.

Gee, James Paul. 2007. *What Video Games Have to Teach Us About Learning and Literacy*. 2nd ed. New York, NY: Palgrave Macmillan.

Glassie, Summer. 2015. 'Embraced Eternity Lately?' Mislabeling and Subversion of Sexuality Labels Through Asari in the *Mass Effect* Trilogy. In *Rated M for Mature: Sex and Sexuality in Video Games*, ed. Matthew Wysocki and Evan W. Lauteria, 161–174. New York, NY: Bloomsbury Academic.

Harper, Todd. 2011. *Gay-for-Play: Addressing the Challenge of Relevant Gay Game Content*. Paper presented at the 12th Annual Meeting of the Association of Internet Researchers, October 13, Seattle, WA.

Huizinga, Johan. 1955. *Homo Ludens*. Boston, MA: Beacon Press.

Jenkins, Henry. 2004. Game Design as Narrative Architecture. In *The Game Design Reader: A Rules of Play Anthology*, ed. Katie Salen and Eric Zimmerman, 670–689. Cambridge, MA: The MIT Press.

Juul, Jesper. 2003. The Game, the Player, the World: Looking for a Heart of Gameness. In *Level Up: Digital Games Research Conference Proceedings*, ed. Marinka Copier and Joost Raessens, 30–45. Utrecht: Utrecht University.

———. 2005. *Half-Real: Video Games Between Real Rules and Fictional Worlds*. Cambridge, MA: MIT Press.

Kennedy, Helen. 2002. Lara Croft: Feminist Icon or Cyberbimbo? On the Limits of Textual Analysis. *Game Studies* 2 (2). http://www.gamestudies.org/0202/kennedy/.

Kryzwinska, Tanya. 2015. The Strange Case of the Misappearance of Sex in Videogames. In *Rated M for Mature: Sex and Sexuality in Video Games*, ed. Matthew Wysocki and Evan W. Lauteria, 105–118. New York, NY: Bloomsbury Academic.

Lauteria, Evan W. 2012. Ga(y)mer Theory: Queer Modding as Resistance. *Reconstruction* 12 (2). Games and/as Resistance (Special Issue). http://reconstruction.eserver.org/122/Lauteria_Evan.shtml.

———. 2015. Assuring Quality: Early 1990s Nintendo Censorship and the Regulation of Queer Sexuality and Gender. In *Rated M for Mature: Sex and Sexuality in Video Games*, ed. Matthew Wysocki and Evan W. Lauteria, 42–59. New York, NY: Bloomsbury Academic.

———. 2016. Affective Structuring and the Role of Race and Nation in *XCOM*. *Analog Game Studies* III (I). http://analoggamestudies.org/2016/01/affective-structuring-and-the-role-of-race-and-nation-in-xcom/.

McLelland, Mark J. 2004. From the Stage to the Clinic: Changing Transgender Identities in Post-War Japan. *Japan Forum* 16 (1): 1–20.

Navarro-Remesal, Victor, and Shaila García-Catalán. 2015. Let's Play Master and Servant: BDSM and Directed Freedom in Game Design. In *Rated M for Mature: Sex and Sexuality in Video Games*, ed. Matthew Wysocki and Evan W. Lauteria, 119–132. New York, NY: Bloomsbury Academic.

Ouellette, Marc A. 2013. Gay for Play: Theorizing LGBTQ Characters in Game Studies. In *The Game Culture Reader*, ed. Jason C. Thompson and Marc A. Ouellette, 47–65.

Phillips, Amanda. 2017. Welcome to MY Fantasy Zone: *Bayonetta* and Queer Femme Disturbance. In *Queer Game Studies*, ed. Bonnie Ruberg and Adrienne Shaw, 109–123. Minneapolis, MN: University of Minnesota Press.

Pozo, Diana. 2015. Countergaming's Porn Parodies, Hard-Core and Soft. In *Rated M for Mature: Sex and Sexuality in Video Games*, ed. Matthew Wysocki and Evan W. Lauteria, 133–146. New York, NY: Bloomsbury Academic.

Ruberg, Bonnie. 2015. No Fun: The Queer Potential of Video Games That Annoy, Anger, Disappoint, Sadden, and Hurt. *QED: A Journal in GLBTQ Worldmaking* 2 (2): 108–124.

Schmieder, Christian. 2009. World of Maskcraft vs. World of Queercraft? Communication, Sex and Gender in the Online Role-Playing Game World of Warcraft. *Journal of Gaming and Virtual Worlds* 1 (1): 5–21.

Sedgwick, Eve Kosofsky. 1985. *Between Men: English Literature and Male Homosocial Desire*. New York, NY: Columbia University Press.

Shaw, Adrienne. 2009. Putting the Gay in Games: Cultural Production and GLBT Content in Video Games. *Games and Culture* 4 (3): 228–253.

———. 2012. Do You Identify as a Gamer? Gender, Race, Sexuality, and Gamer Identity. *New Media and Society* 14 (1): 25–41.

———. 2014. Representation Matters (?): When, How and If Representation Matters to Marginalized Game Audiences. In *Challenging Communication Research*, ed. Leah A. Lievrouw, 105–120. New York: Peter Lang.

———. 2015. *Gaming at the Edge: Sexuality and Gender at the Margins of Gamer Culture*. Minneapolis, MN: University of Minnesota Press.

Sherlock, Lee. 2013. What Happens in Goldshire Stays in Goldshire: Rhetorics of Queer Sexualities, Role-Playing, and Fandom in World of Warcraft. In *Rhetoric/Composition/Play Through Video Games*, ed. R. Colby, M.S.S. Johnson, and R.S. Colby, 161–174. New York, NY: Palgrave Macmillan.

Sicart, Miguel. 2003. *Family Values: Ideology, Computer Games & The Sims*. Level Up Conference Proceedings, University of Utrecht, Utrecht.

Suits, Bernard. 1978. *The Grasshopper: Games, Life and Utopia*. Toronto, ON: University of Toronto Press.

Thompson, Nathan James A. 2014. Queer/ing Game Space: Sexual Play in *World of Warcraft*. *Media Fields Journal* 8. http://www.mediafieldsjournal.org/queering-game-space/.

Wolf, Mark J.P. 2001. *The Medium of the Video Game*. Austin, TX: University of Texas Press.

Youngblood, Jordan. 2013. C'mon! Make Me a Man!: *Persona 4*, Digital Bodies, and Queer Potentiality. *Ada: A Journal of Gender, New Media, and Technology* (2). http://adanewmedia.org/2013/06/issue2-youngblood/.

———. 2015. Climbing the Heterosexual Maze: *Catherine* and Queering Spatiality in Gaming. In *Rated M for Mature: Sex and Sexuality in Video Games*, ed. Matthew Wysocki and Evan W. Lauteria, 240–252. New York, NY: Bloomsbury Academic.

Part II

Representing Queerness

4

The Representation (or the Lack of It) of Same-Sex Relationships in Digital Games

Yowei Kang and Kenneth C. C. Yang

Recent data on the global digital game market shows that sales have grown to $6.2 billion as of February 2016 (SuperData Research 2016). The global diffusion of digital gaming platforms has led to exponential growth of global gamer populations (Soper 2013). According to the same industry report by *GPIL Gamers, a publicly traded company on gaming-related properties*, there are 1.2 billion gamers around the world. In the US alone, almost half the population now plays digital games as an important leisure activity (Entertainment Software Association 2015). PricewaterhouseCoopers LLP (2015) has estimated that global digital games revenue will continuously grow to reach an estimate of US$93.18 billion by 2019.

Overall, the rising economic importance of digital gaming has contributed to its ascendance as a promising domain of scholarly exploration (Wolf and Perron 2003). Raessens' and Goldstein (2005) divides digital game research into five major areas of investigation: design, aesthetic, reception, cultural, and social issues. Related to this chapter are two macro-level perspectives, which consider gaming as a cultural phenomenon (Richard and Zaremba 2005; Shaw 2009) and as a social phenomenon (Goldstein 2005; Griffiths and Davies 2005; Rushkoff 2005; Schleiner 2005).

Y. Kang (✉)
National Taiwan Ocean University, Keelung, Republic of China

K. C. C. Yang
University of Texas, El Paso, TX, USA

© The Author(s) 2018
T. Harper et al. (eds.), *Queerness in Play*, Palgrave Games in Context,
https://doi.org/10.1007/978-3-319-90542-6_4

This chapter, situated within the social and cultural aspects of digital game research, explores the representation of same-sex relationships in digital games. The authors were motivated to explore this issue after reading news about Nintendo's *Tomodachi Life*, a popular 3DS life simulator game. The company received complaints from its gay, lesbian, bisexual, and transgender (henceforth, GLBT) players because the game does not allow *Miis* (i.e., personalized avatars of players) of the same gender to have romantic relationships (*Malta Today* 2014; Starr 2014). Nintendo apologized to gay activists and planned to introduce gay relationship options and same-sex avatars in its later version (Funaro 2014).

Controversies Surrounding Same-Sex Relationships in Nintendo's *Tomodachi Life*

To contextualize our analysis, the authors first provide an overview of Nintendo's *Tomodachi Life* controversy surrounding the inclusion of same-sex relationships in this popular game. *Tomodachi Life* was launched in May 2014 and easily sold 1.85 million copies in Japan; its English version was released in the US and Europe one month later (Ivory 2006). Within the game, there is a strong emphasis on relationships between players and their personalized avatars, known as *Miis* (Walton 2014). In this relationship game, players' *Miis* flourish when taking part in various social activities and engaging with other avatars in the virtual social space (Ko and Lau 2014). This is as the name of the game implies: *tomodachi* means "friend" in the Japanese language (Maume 2014). *Tomodachi Life* embeds five types of relationships among players and their *Miis*, such as becoming friends/family/siblings, best friend, sweetheart, spouse, ex-sweethearts/ex-spouses. Different colors are also used to represent various stages of the relationships from dark green/highest to blue/lowest (see Fig. 4.1).

In *Tomodachi Life*'s European and Oceania versions, there are slightly more complicated relationship categories that range from friend, best friend, special someone, married couple, ex/divorced, parent/child, and sibling (see Fig. 4.2).

After a player's *Mii* is created, it must then be fed, dressed, and pleased by players in order to interact with other *Miis* and establish relationships in a virtual island they live (Maume 2014; Walton 2014) (see Fig. 4.3).

Unlike the representations of GLBT characters/avatars in conventional digital games, *Tomodachi Life* has a unique design feature by embedding relationship rules as an indispensable part of players' game experiences. The rela-

Category	Dark green	Green	Yellow green	Orange	Red	Purple	Blue
Friends/Family/Siblings	Best bud	Good buddy	Great pal	Good pal	Getting along OK	Kinda getting along	Not getting along
Best Friend	BFF	Bestie	Trust completely	Trustworthy			
Sweetheart	Let's get married!	Super in love	Totally in love	Very much in love			
Spouse	Soul mate	Super happy	Totally happy	Very happy			
Ex-Sweethearts/Ex-Spouses	Still friends	Great memories	For the best	No hard feelings	Not speaking	Try to avoid	Want to forget

Fig. 4.1 Types of relationships in *Tomodachi Life*

Category	Dark Green	Green	Yellow Green	Orange	Red	Purple	Blue
Friend	Most enjoyable	Great fun	A lot of fun	Fun	Mostly fun	Not much fun...	Not a great match...
Best Friend	Best friend forever	Trust completely	Trust a lot	Trustworthy	Fairly trustworthy	Trust a little	Really a best friend?
Special Someone	Want to get married	Completely in love	Very much in love	In love	Only just in love	Slightly unhappy	Unhappy
Married Couple	One in a million	Completely happy	Very happy	Happy	Fairly happy	Slightly unhappy	Unhappy
Ex/Divorced	Can still be friends?	Good memories	Wounds have healed	Sad	Painful	Just want to forget...	Never want to see again...
Parent/Child	One in a million	Completely happy	Very happy	Happy	Fairly happy	Slightly strained	Strained
Sibling	One in a million	Completely happy	Very happy	Happy	Fairly happy	Slightly strained	Strained

Fig. 4.2 Types of relationships in *Tomodachi Life*, Europe/Oceania

Fig. 4.3 Geographical setting of *Tomodachi Life*

tionships are not constrained between players and their *Miis* (such as asking for relationship advice) but among *Miis* interacting with each other socially (Cacho 2014). Walton (2014) clearly describes how relationship rules have become a vital part of players' experiences below:

> Tomodachi Life revolves around relationships, be they romantic or otherwise. Happy islanders ask to make friends, want to introduce people, or declare their undying love for a friend with alarming regularity. They don't always hit it off, particularly if you give them bad advice in the small-talk department, but once friends, they're often at each other's apartment hanging out. You do have the option of telling a Mii not to make friends with another, but expect the dark rain clouds of depression to be (literally) floating over their heads while they get over it.

Research Questions

This chapter employed a combination of both procedural rhetoric (Bogost 2007, 2008) and media representation theory to discuss the representation of same-sex relationships in digital games in general and Nintendo's *Tomodachi Life* in particular. Through a textual analysis of players' discourses collected from a popular gaming community forum, the authors sought to answer the following questions:

Research Question #1:   What are emerging themes in gaymers' discourses related to same-sex relationships in digital games?

Research Question #2:   How will theories of procedural rhetoric and media representation account for the representation (or lack of it) of same-sex relationships in digital games?

Representation of Same-Sex Relationships in Digital Games

Representation of GLBT characters and same-sex relationships has been a highly contentious issue and widely debated among digital game researchers (Beasley and Standley 2002; Monson 2012; Pulos 2013; Shaw 2009; Williams et al. 2009). In a widely publicized 2006 incident on the popular *World of Warcraft*, Sara Andrews advertised her GLBT-friendly guild in a public forum, which caused Blizzard to suspend her account for violating its anti-sexual harassment policy (Shaw 2012). Blizzard stated that a GLBT-friendly guild would create a negative gaming environment, because it would cause harassment from homophobic players to attack GLBT players. Shaw observes that, due to increased pressure from GLBT groups, Blizzard later revoked the suspension of Sara's account. Debates on whether digital games should be inclusive enough to fairly represent different social groups continue. Six years later, a YouTube clip of BioWare's *Mass Effect* 3 showing a gay relationship between a male Commander Shepherd and his same-sex teammate, Steve Cortez, led to outcry among the game's fan base (refer to Fig. 4.4) (MacKnight 2013; Totilo 2012).

Examining how various groups are represented in media has been associated with issues such as social justice, power imbalance, media effects, and stereotype formation (Williams et al. 2009). However, blaming digital game

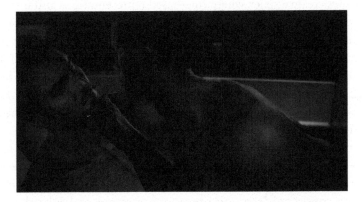

Fig. 4.4   A depiction of a same-sex relationship in BioWare's *Mass Effect*

designers for any misrepresentation of social groups is often myopic because the decision to create game content is contingent on many ecological factors, such as game designers' preference, players' role as consumers, industry's assumptions, socio-cultural-economical context, and so on. Shaw's (2009) cultural production perspective speculates that multiple stakeholders are involved in the production of GLBT representations in the digital games. These factors include the following:

> (a) the presence of motivated producers in the industry, those that are personally, politically, or commercially interested in GLBT content; (b) how the audience for a text or medium is constructed; (c) what the public backlash from both the GLBT community and conservative groups will be, as well as industry-based reprisals in the form of censorship or ratings; (d) the structure of the industry and how it is funded; and (e) how homosexuality, bisexuality, or transgender identities can be represented in the medium. (228)

Although the representation of individual GLBT players and their sexuality has been frequently studied in digital game literature (Beasley and Standley 2002; Pulos 2013; Shaw 2009), the representation of same-sex relationships remains to be a topic that has not been fully explored. In the following sections, the authors review theories of procedural rhetoric and media representation to contextualize our analysis.

Theoretical Foundation

Theory of Procedural Rhetoric

Digital games create a space where rule-based representations and interactions abound to facilitate the persuasive process during gameplay (Bogost 2007). Playing digital games is equivalent to conducting symbolic manipulations and interactions with in-game design elements (Bogost 2007; Kang 2011). Bogost points out that digital games are "an expressive medium ... represent how real and imaged system work" (1). The emphasis on the mode of "procedurality" in digital games leads Bogost to propose the theory of "procedural rhetoric."

This theory places a strong emphasis on procedures and procedurality in digital games and lends itself to studying the inclusion of same-sex relationships as a design decision through which rule-based interactions are embedded as part of gameplay experiences in *Tomodachi Life*. Procedurality in digital games often consists of "the unit operations, systems, and rules that make a game a game" (Colby 2014, 44). Bogost's theory thus implies that the process of designing digital games is equivalent to creating a set of rules governing how players will interact with each other in a virtual space. The conscious decision of rule setting by game designers reveals the many untold rules in human experiences. A designer's decision to include or exclude same-sex relationships among *Miis* is multifaceted in that this does not only represent how same-sex relationships are perceived as a relationship norm in society but also shows what gameplay experiences game designers believe *Tomodachi Life* players should be allowed to experience.

Digital game scholars employing the theory of "procedural rhetoric" have subsequently shifted their domain of research to emphasize the role of rules (procedurality) and ruled-based representations in shaping players' experiences in digital games (Thorhauge 2013). Thus, GLBT representations in digital games are created because of a set of rules to determine how these avatars would look like and how relationships can be formed.

Rules in digital games are an in-game design element (in addition to audio, visual, textual, and kinetic elements) that enable players to cogenerate their gameplay experiences (Kang 2011). These gameplay interactions include using the pre-determined in-game elements (like avatars, in-game map, relationship rules, etc.) to interact other players. Kang argues that players in some digital games allow players to choose or create their virtual self-representations (i.e., avatars), executing subsequent online interactions with other players' representations and actions to achieve gratifications once a raid or mission is successfully completed.

Analyzing public forum discussions on same-sex relationships lends support to the main thesis of this study: game designers represent and duplicate, whether intentionally or unconsciously, hegemonic heterosexual relationship rules in many digital games they have developed, though other factors often interact with these content creation decisions. Because the digital game market is highly competitive and the need to respond to players' demands is critical to its commercial success, the authors thus argue that studying representation of same-sex relationships in digital games provides an opportunity to understand the interaction of multiple sources of ecological influence in digital game design.

Theory of Representation

The study of representations has increasingly attracted digital game scholars' attention. Williams et al. (2009) speculate that the disparity of media representation in traditional mass media is likely to be replicated in digital game platforms. Based on a large content analysis of 133 digital games, their data consistently predicted imbalanced representation of gender and race: 85.23% of the game characters they examined are male, while 14.77% are female. Ethnic minorities have observably been under-represented in these digital games, even though the percentage matches approximately existing census data.

Williams et al. (2009) assume that the disparity in gender and ethnic representations in digital games is likely to reflect "underlying systematic social inequalities" (830) in the real world. They argue that game designers merely create the games to "reflect their own identity" (830) because game designers tilt toward certain demographics. Furthermore, the representational disparity of social groups is due to the assumption that players are mainly White and young males. Similarly, Monson (2012) studied racial representations in *World of Warcraft* and concluded that stereotypical imagery from real-world ethnic groups is replicated in the game. The representational variations of gender and race in digital games pose an interesting question about how game designers determine whether the virtual world should reflect the real world in digital game design. The same question arises when it comes to the representation of same-sex relationships in digital games.

The decision to represent GLBT in the creation of digital games is affected by a variety of factors in recent digital game research (MacKnight 2013). One of these factors concerns as what game designers think. Flanagan (2015) attributes the inclusion of GLBT contents and sex-same relationships in *Fallout 2* to the decision of its designer, Tim Cain, who is gay and later married in 2012. Tim Cain reflects on his decision to include gay marriage in this game below:

> We kind of liked pushing boundaries a bit. Not always with violence. We wanted a game which is full of social commentary. So [same-sex marriage] was just another thing we were doing. I don't even think anybody in the team really argued over it. We didn't think 'Oh my god, this an amazing thing.' It was just 'We're going to cover every possible base here.' And then we moved on. (Flanagan 2015)

Game designers' decisions, on the other hand, are often affected by market consideration. Kerr (2006) observes that digital game contents are often developed by the presumptions of the industry that players tend to be homophobic; therefore, they are less likely to accept gay-friendly or GLBT contents. Similarly, Shaw (2009) has interviewed digital game designers and found that market considerations are one of the main reasons to develop GLBT-friendly games.

An important ecological factor that has begun to attract the attention of digital game researchers is a player's mindset (Shaw 2012). Players as consumers can determine if a digital game will be well received in the competitive marketplace. To understand the perspective of digital game players, Shaw employed a combination of textual analysis and in-depth interview methods to examine if GLBT groups consider their representations in digital games essential to their game experiences. Contradictory to what an identity politics perspective would assume, many GLBT players interviewed have voiced that gay content in games would be a plus, but it is not a requirement for them to consider purchasing the product. Shaw also speculates that GLBT players are more tolerant of the underrepresentations of their sexuality since games are fantasy. However, since *Tomodachi Life* has placed a very strong emphasis on relationship development among players' avatars, it is likely the deprivation of relationship building with other avatars actually would diminish the players' experiences.

Research Method

Method Selection

The authors employed a textual analysis method to scrutinize how digital game players perceive same-sex relationships in digital games. Content analyzing digital games has been a widely used research method to examine race, gender, and GLBT representation (Hou 2012; Waddell et al. 2014; Williams et al. 2009). However, while a large-scale quantitative content analysis of digital games provides a glimpse of how various social groups are represented in games, it did not address how players perceive and respond to this issue. Therefore, a textual analysis method of players' discourses has gained its popularity among digital game scholars (MacKnight 2013; Shaw 2007, 2012).

Sampling Textual Data

Textual data were collected within a two-week period ending on April 1, 2016 from a popular discussion forum, *r/Gaymers*, that currently has 44,752 subscribers and is "a community for LGBT and straight alliance redditors" (https://www.reddit.com/r/gaymers/). As a source of textual data, *r/Gaymers* does not merely include players' direct responses and thoughts, but points (or *karma*) are used via up- or down-vote functions to indicate popularity or agreement among the community participants about the submitted statements (MacKnight 2013; Reddit n.d.)

Following MacKnight's (2013) approach, the selection of extra-game communities, such as *r/Gaymers*, also has the benefit of providing thoughts and responses from players in a more deliberate and permanent manner. In addition, players' responses are also more "immediate," "reactive," and "transitory" (65–66). Despite these benefits, the authors acknowledge the short duration of data collection, demography of the players and their comments, and representativeness of the textual data as some of its methodological limitations.

Three search keywords—"Tomodachi Life," "same-sex relationships," and "gay relationships"—were used to retrieve players' discussions from *r/Gaymers*. All the comments are now archived and provided complete historical records to examine how players were discussing these issues. Results from the "Tomodachi Life" keyword sequence to search *r/Gaymer* generated 2 out of 83 threads (see Table 4.1). Within each thread, multiple comments in a series of response chains are available.

Another keyword phrase, "same sex relationships," was used to search *r/Gaymers* and identified the following 12 out of 42 threads after removing those not related to same-sex relationships in digital games. A total of 364 comments are available for analysis (see Table 4.2).

"Gay relationship" as a keyword sequence ultimately generated the following 11 out of 161 threads after removing threads not related to same-sex relationships and two duplicate entries in digital games. A total of 252 responses are available for analysis (see Table 4.3).

Table 4.1 Search results using "Tomadachi Life" as a search phrase

Thread titles	URL [Number of comments]
1 TotalBiscuit, popular gaming YouTuber, talks about LGBT characters in reference to the recent Tomadachi Life controversy (starts at 14:48)	https://www.reddit.com/r/gaymers/comments/25d68w/totalbiscuit_popular_gaming_youtuber_talks_about/ [25 comments]
2 John Oliver on the Tomadachi Life controversy	https://www.reddit.com/r/gaming/comments/25zbtn/john_oliver_on_the_tomadachi_life_controversy/ [0 comment]

Table 4.2 Search results using "same-sex relationship" as a search phrase

Thread titles	URL [Number of comments]
3 Same-sex relationship options in video games through time	https://www.reddit.com/r/gaymers/comments/1z38aa/samesex_relationship_options_in_video_games/ [88 comments]
4 Nintendo apologizes for not including same-sex relationships in TC; promises to do better in future installments	https://www.reddit.com/r/gaymers/comments/255pag/nintendo_apologizes_for_not_including_samesex/ [76 comments]
5 How The Sims got its same-sex relationships	https://www.reddit.com/r/gaymers/comments/1ju28z/how_the_sims_got_its_samesex_relationships/ [20 comments]
6 New Fire Emblems to feature same-sex relationships!	https://www.reddit.com/r/gaymers/comments/3awn70/new_fire_emblems_to_feature_samesex_relationships/ [27 comments]
7 The Sims 4 tells users to 'be proud' with showcase of same-sex relationships	https://www.reddit.com/r/gaymers/comments/29imuw/the_sims_4_tells_users_to_be_proud_with_showcase/ [28 comments]
8 Star Wars: The Old Republic To Offer Same-Sex Relationships In New Expansion	https://www.reddit.com/r/gaymers/comments/165er7/star_wars_the_old_republic_to_offer_samesex/ [18 comments]
9 Bioware is sooooooooooo far ahead of everyone else	https://www.reddit.com/r/gaymers/comments/3hn6fr/bioware_is_sooooooooooo_far_ahead_of_everyone_else/ [51 comments]
10 Dragon Age 3 Announced!	https://www.reddit.com/r/gaymers/comments/102sjz/dragon_age_3_announced/ [9 comments]
11 Has anyone else given up on "equality" in video games?	https://www.reddit.com/r/gaymers/comments/16ml7f/has_anyone_else_given_up_on_equality_in_video/ [22 comments]
12 Activist group attacks Star Wars: The Old Republic for plans to allow same sex relationships (x-post r/swtor)	https://www.reddit.com/r/gaymers/comments/p3yn0/activist_group_attacks_star_wars_the_old_republic/ [5 comments]
13 [Spoilers!] Fallout 4 Romantic Experience	https://www.reddit.com/r/gaymers/comments/430mxc/spoilers_fallout_4_romantic_experience/ [9 comments]
14 Nintendo to 'fix' bug which allowed male same-sex relationships in computer game	https://www.reddit.com/r/gaymers/comments/1eelqg/nintendo_to_fix_bug_which_allowed_male_samesex/

Table 4.3 Search results using "gay relationship" as a search phrase

Thread titles	URL [Number of comments]
15 Nintendo on Gay relationships (Fire Emblem Awakening) (X-post from/r/ nintendo)	[11 comments] https://www.reddit.com/r/gaymers/ comments/18262l/nintendo_on_ gay_relationships_fire_emblem/ [41 comments]
16 We may not all like Origin or EA, but let's all agree here: Mass Effect 3 did gay relationships right.	https://www.reddit.com/r/gaymers/ comments/qqh5d/we_may_not_all_ like_origin_or_ea_but_lets_all/ [35 comments]
17 Nintendo's rejection of gay relationships gives fans a lot to be angry about | Technology	https://www.reddit.com/r/gaymers/ comments/251pd4/nintendos_ rejection_of_gay_relationships_ gives/ [43 comments]
18 A straight gamer's take on gay relationships in Dragon Age II	https://www.reddit.com/r/gaymers/ comments/jj1sw/a_straight_ gamers_take_on_gay_ relationships_in/ [7 comments]
19 So casual mentions in Borderlands 2 of gay relationships and stuff (like when a character says "his husband") and stuff like that, I'm okay with that. <3	https://www.reddit.com/r/gaymers/ comments/10t5za/so_casual_ mentions_in_borderlands_2_of_ gay/ [24 comments]
20 Nintendo: Why We Patched Gay Relationships in Tomodachi Life	https://www.reddit.com/r/gaymers/ comments/22t7xj/nintendo_why_ we_patched_gay_relationships_in/ [9 comments]
21 Gay Content Coming to Fallout 4!	https://www.reddit.com/r/gaymers/ comments/3lnm28/gay_content_ coming_to_fallout_4/ [38 comments]
22 We get gay relationships in Massive Chalice! Either gay couples adopt, or they get bonuses other than children. Not quite sure how he'll handle it.	https://www.reddit.com/r/gaymers/ comments/1fw2g1/we_get_gay_ relationships_in_massive_chalice/ [9 comments]
23 Homosexuality in games (x-post from/r/ Games)	https://www.reddit.com/r/gaymers/ comments/siz7s/homosexuality_in_ games_xpost_from_rgames/ [26 comments]
24 Star Wars: The Old Republic Will Allow Gay Relationships	https://www.reddit.com/r/gaymers/ comments/kgvtg/star_wars_the_ old_republic_will_allow_gay/ [5 comments]
25 Tales of Zestiria: First official gay couple in the series!	https://www.reddit.com/r/gaymers/ comments/3qnpck/tales_of_zestiria_ first_official_gay_couple_in/

Findings and Discussion

Emerging Themes in Players' Discourses

Theme 1: Awareness of the Interaction Between Procedurality and Representation in the Digital Game Design Process

One popular post by "MoreNerdThanHipster" (9 points, 1 year ago) offers one procedural possibility to include same-sex relationships in digital games without offending other heterosexual players:

> You don't even need a "sperm donor" mechanic or whatever to explain raising a kid. You can literally have a romance, blank the screen, and then, wow, the couple in love has a baby. You don't need to code gay people having sex then going to an adoption agency. LOL

The subsequent responses to this game design recommendation by another participant who has deleted or removed their account ("username deleted," 1 point, 1 year ago) agree with the inclusion of same-sex relationships represented subtly to deal with the romance-marriage-family-relocation (out of the virtual island) rules embedded in *Tomodachi Life* as seen below:

> I thought this. To be honest, in a game which is probably child-friendly in nature, the "where babies come from" part never needs to be seen. Romance and then, poof, baby would suffice.

Participants of this response chain (Thread #1) are fully aware that game designers have the complete procedural authorship in determining how GLBT representation can be included in digital games. Another well-liked posting by "scratchmellotron" [6 points, 1 year ago] begins a new response chain by expanding the discussion to *BioWare* to talk about how same-sex relationships are designed into the digital games:

> Knew I liked him for a reason.
> Not sure I agree with there being a problem with Bioware's approach to gay characters, but I guess I might have low standards considering we're starved for them.

One of the players, "HeadCrabK" [0 points, 1 year ago], takes a procedural perspective by pointing out that by making all characters "bisexual" is a "cheap" solution to address the representation issues in digital games, in spite of designers' good intention:

> The Bioware approach really is cheap, like "What we do about homosexual play-
> ers who wants to date characters from the same sex? Just make all the characters
> bisexual".

Interestingly, this participant's initial post has generated heated debates
among forum participants as seen in the response chain. Texts from *r/Gaymers*
participants, GLBT or straight, indicate that they are fully aware of the game
design process as a process that needs to weigh both pros and cons. "scratchmellotron" [7 points, 1 year ago] agrees that having a bisexual character is
better than none.

> Yeah I don't personally have an issue with that. I see your point though.
>   I'd rather have bisexual characters than be annoyed at not being able to
> romance the one I want. Like Alistair in Dragon Age Origins.

Another participant, "ksypl" [2 points, 1 year ago] concurs with the viewpoint of "scratchmellotron." "ksypl" clearly notes the procedurality of same-
sex relationships as part of game rules can be embedded by offering interaction
options to allow gay romance in the game:

> I wouldn't have a problem with everyone being bi, but what tends to happen
> instead is that everyone is straight except for the "romance options," who give
> every indication of being straight except that they can be romanced by the pro-
> tagonist regardless of their gender. For example, I don't remember the first two
> Dragon Age games mentioning any same-sex relationships among minor char-
> acters, and most of the bi characters either made it clear that they generally
> preferred opposite-sex partners, or were at least far more shy about discussing
> same-sex relationships than opposite-sex ones.

The inclusion of GLBT characters and same-sex relationships in digital
games is equivalent to embedding nonnormative rules into the digital games
that pose challenges to the dominant heterosexual assumptions of how digital
games should be experienced (Bogost 2007). While the in-game representation of GLBTs have clearly shown the incremental progress of the digital game
industry to become more inclusive, allowing same-sex relationships (such as
dating, romance, or marriage) carries more significant meanings from the perspectives of digital game research.

First, although digital games have allowed various forms of same-sex relationships since the 1990s, the omission of this relationship option in
Tomodachi Life is an intentional and purposeful design decision to create "a
playful alternate world." Apparently, Nintendo's defense of their initial

exclusion is based on a ludic dimension of how *Tomodachi Life* should be designed in which game design and mechanics are integrated into its present format (Harper 2011). However, Nintendo fails to realize the intersection between these game design elements and players' experiences when GLBT players are deprived of the opportunities to fulfill same-sex relationships.

Bogost (2007) states "procedural rhetoric entails persuasion—to change opinion or action. Following the contemporary model, procedural rhetoric entails expression—to convey ideas effectively" (29). The exclusion of same-sex relationships in a relationship-heavy *Tomodachi Life* not only fails to effectively persuade players to engage in the game but is likely to make a social statement that certain behavioral rules are less worthy to be written into the game. Marini says, "excluding same-sex relationships from your virtual world, when the real world is becoming increasingly relaxed about them, is about as direct a piece of social commentary as it's possible to imagine" (Maume 2014).

Theme 2: Awareness That Multiple Ecological Factors Affects the Digital Game Design Process

Williams et al. (2009) found that the digital game industry tends to assume that all players are young, White males, which ultimately affects the content creation process in the development of digital games. Another *r/Gaymers* participant, "ObjectiveTits" [1 point, 1 year ago], seems to agree re the relationship between industry assumptions and content creation process:

> I see what you're saying and the way they handle gay characters definitely needs work, but I feel like people never give bioware credit for being one of the first triple A companies to cater to us in so many triple A games. The problem with them specializing plot or cutscenes for same sex romance-able npcs is you get the hoards of insecure gamer dudebros that complain about it "shoving gayness in their face" then you get gay people complaining that the gay character isn't the exact niche archetype that they wanted and no matter how it's done it's all just a ploy for game companies to cash in on that sweet gay money. Overall I've given up trying to convince everyone on the debate. You just can't please people. I'd rather have a whole party of people with their own personalities and fully realized roles that all happen to be bi than just one or two characters who's main personality trait is "I'm the gay option". But I do understand what you're saying I really do. Games and society in general just have to mature more before we can reasonably expect something good.

In Thread #4 (posted by "KeatonKaifei"), 76 comments were generated in response. Cross-national variation in GLBT rights, another ecological factor, has been acknowledged and agreed-upon among many *r/Gaymers* participants. "Jonvox" [23 points, 1 year ago] received overall favorable karma points in identifying Japan's unique GLBT policy, which affected the decision to exclude same-sex relationships in *Tomodachi Life*:

> They don't actually understand the situation.
> This is true, but I wouldn't expect that of a Japanese company. I'm really not an expert in the matter so correct me if I'm wrong, but from what I've heard, LGBTQ rights aren't really up to snuff in Japan like they are in the Western world. So it's really encouraging for me to see them stumble by thinking they've made the right decision, then realize their faults and apologize.

However, some participants disagree that Nintendo should be allowed to use cross-national ignorance of GLBT rights as an excuse if *Tomodachi Life* will be released in the North American and European markets, where sexual minorities are more protected than in Japan. "monkey_sage" [5 points, 1 year ago] takes the same stance:

> Nintendo is an international company that has been active in America and Europe for decades, with a strong presence. I *do* expect that of them. I expect a lot better. I think it's lazy to fall back on, "Well, that's just how it is in Japan."

Similarly, another participant, "Gentleman_Jimmy," concurs with "monkey_sage":

> Seriously, this.
> If I hear one more person say, "well, they *are* a Japanese company" or "that's the way it is over there".
> Like they have no interaction with any other cultures whatsoever, and they're this whimsically ignorant self-contained community, living in a bubble in the deepest forest of Japan.
> FFS.

Furthermore, the study of how same-sex relationships are represented in digital games can also shed light on the emergence of the gaming industry as a "global production network" (Johns 2006, 151) when cross-national norms need to be integrated into better meeting the demands of players from different countries. The controversy surrounding *Tomadachi Life* (Cacho 2014) is caused by the fact that, despite the global nature of digital games, designers of the games may not be responsive to variations in terms of cultures, values, customs, and laws in different countries. For example, while same-sex relationships are widely accepted in the US and several European countries, Nintendo's Japanese designers may still be influenced by the current lack of protection of gay relationships in Japan (Maume 2014). An in-depth analysis of the game design process and the rationale behind such a process is likely to reveal many other ecological factors affecting the representation of same-sex relationships in these digital games. The intersection between culture and GLBT representation should be understood through Shaw's discussion on how these factors could affect digital game design. Shaw argues that stakeholders, in determining the GLBT representations in games, are influenced by the industry structure, socio-economic-cultural factors, and fans/players.

Theme 3: Representations of GLBT Individuals and Same-Sex Relationships in Digital Games as a Social Commentary Stance

A common theme found in the threads on same-sex relationships is to what extent digital game companies should include less represented social groups, if at all. While Nintendo's initial response to the exclusion of same-sex relationships is based on whether a virtual gaming space should represent all social groups, many critics argue that the exclusivity decision in itself makes a social commentary stance that some social groups should not be included in the game (Maume 2014).

One of the *r/Gamers* participants, "orangewaxlion" [3 points, 1 year ago], addressed this in a statement representative of the stance of many critics:

> I'm not sure that the first one was really remotely more "PC." This one spells out "yeah, we just can't recode this on a whim but *will* deal with it in any sequels."
>
> The other one just seemed slightly weasely and in a patronizing way whether how this "playful alternate world" automatically looks at the existence of LGBT people as "social commentary."

However, this does not mean that all participants agree that the lack of same-sex relationships in *Tomodachi Life* indicates that Nintendo is homophobic or is making a social commentary to be anti-homosexuality. Many participants acknowledge the complicated process of digital game design. This comment from "SoberPandaren" [8 points, 1 year ago] garnered some support from the community:

I don't think it was ever their intent. More like they never thought there would be an entire issue over it since the game was already released for over a year and no one said anything about it. It wasn't social commentary to them until people started to apply their terms of what social commentary.

One commentator ([deleted], 3 points, 1 year ago) has suggested critics are "gay rights Nazis":

Not really. They simply stated they didn't want to make a political situation out of it. By including gay characters/relationships, it would have been.
    Although, by not doing it, the gay rights nazis have turned it into a political issue. It's pretty sad that we have to have fairness and equality injected into every goddamn thing that exists nowadays.

Theme 4: Awareness of the Role of Players in Shaping How Digital Games Are Designed

Participants agreed that players actually exert their power in shaping the design of digital games, if they mobilize to express their concerns and if digital game companies are responsive to consumers. The optimism as expressed by many participants was generally indicated by favorable karma points associated with such responses. For example, "DantesInfernape" [23 points, 1 year ago] perceived Nintendo's subsequent response to be more inclusive in future versions of *Tomodachi Life*:

I appreciate how they don't skirt around the issue to avoid social politics; they acknowledge that including same-sex relationships is something that they want to do and should have done, and that they were wrong in not doing it. It's refreshing to see that type of directness from a company on an issue that is unfortunately still so controversial, and I think it says a lot about how far the LGBTQ rights movement has come in the past 20 years.

The same favorable sentiment is expressed by "blasianFMA" [20 points, 1 year ago] who also expressed a similar opinion on how important it is for players to be active and aware of their role.

Nintendo heard the concerns and listened. They said they'll be more inclusive in the future. That's what I and people who were complaining like me wanted. Had we NOT spoken up, this would not have happened. So to anybody reading this who might be on the fence about making a fuss when they feel slighted, remember this: A close mouth doesn't get fed. Now if ALL of the people that were being discriminated against would understand that this wasn't just some petty BS and they'd start being more serious about issues and paying attention to the world, then, perhaps it wouldn't take as long as it is taking for the laws surrounding LGBT discrimination to be struck down/passed etc.

Conclusion

As the importance of "gaymers" grows, the digital game industry has increasingly placed more emphasis on meeting their demands (Soller 2014). As shown in this controversy, the representation of same-sex relationships in digital games points to an important question for examining the intense contestation of rules, representation, and content creation in digital games to meet the demands of a global game population.

The examination of the same-sex relationship representation has far more important theoretical implications than existing research on GLBT avatar representations for several reasons. First, the establishment of same-sex relationships in digital games demonstrates that a digital game has procedurally enabled the presence of GLBT players to express and to share their sexuality with other players. This chapter aims to contribute to the discussion of GLBT representation from a procedural rhetorical perspective, in addition to the dominant social justice approach in existing queer literature (Eaklor 2008; Ivory et al. 2009; Walters 2001).

Secondly, from the procedural rhetorical perspective, the inclusion of same-sex relationship options further indicates that this relationship type can be treated equally as acceptable behavioral norms among players in the virtual gaming space. Relationship building with other *Miis* in *Tomodachi Life* is also essential to players' in-game performance, avatar statistics, and ultimate gameplay experiences. Sundén (2009) confirms the effects of rule transgression in digital games by including the rule of same-sex relationships. In this ethnographic research, GLBT players take part in digital games through what she calls "transgressive game," in which pre-existing cultural norms of an ideal player with pre-determined sexuality are part of the game design, but adapted to shape an online game community. Sundén thus argues that, when GLBT players adopt pre-determined straight and male characters in digital games to interact with other players, their gameplay has been affected, to some extent, as to how the game is played and how to shape the gaming community as a result.

Interestingly, Starr (2014) describes a rule transgression strategy to bypass the current exclusion of same-sex relationships in *Tomodachi Life*. To enable a same-sex relationship among *Miis* of the same gender, Starr (2014) tested a strategy to create a male *Mii* with female facial features, makeup, name, voice, hairstyle, and clothes. Such a strategy demonstrates how game designers' rules can be altered and contested by players' ingenuity to address the representation of GLBTs in digital games.

Limitations and Future Research Directions

Studying digital games as a stand-alone object does not properly address the design of digital games and their contents is affected by ecological factors ranging from market consideration, cultural and social norms, players, game designers, advocacy groups, and so on. Existing research also fails to explore the intersection between rules, representations, and gameplay experiences. Therefore, a triangulation method (Shaw 2012) is urgently needed to adequately study the intense interactions among representation of same-sex relationships, procedurality by game designers, players' perceptions of these relationship rules in digital games. A more thorough understanding of the representation decisions is made possible after situating players' discourses within a large ecology of the digital game industry.

Future research should expand to other digital game forums (such as *r/gayming*, *r/transgamers*, *r/GuildWars2Gaymers*, *r/HaloGaymers*, etc.), social media outlets, and comments under YouTube content to better understand what players would think to ensure a representative textual sample of players' opinions and perceptions. The authors acknowledge the current demographics of Reddit community forums are slightly tilted toward male participants (with 53% are male while 47% are female) (Reddit 2015). However, more thorough demographic data is not available on Reddit to further estimate the gender distribution in *r/Gaymers* and to assess potential impacts on textual data. The authors therefore caution the interpretation of present findings and recommend future research to assess whether participants' gender is likely to pose variations in their comments. Given the volume of textual data, a mixed method of both quantitative and qualitative data processing will help better interpret the results.

Bibliography

Beasley, Berrin, and Tracy Collins Standley. 2002. Shirts Vs Skins: Clothing as an Indicator of Gender Role Stereotyping in Video Games. *Mass Communication and Society* 5: 279–293.

Bogost, Ian. 2007. *Persuasive Games: The Expressive Power of Videogames*. Cambridge, MA: MIT Press.

———. 2008. The Rhetoric of Video Games. In *Digital Media: The John D and Catherine T Macarthur Foundation Series on Digital Media and Learning*, ed. Katie Salen, 117–139. Cambridge, MA: MIT Press.

Cacho, Gieson. 2014. Review: Problems with 'Tomodachi Life' Go Beyond Gay Controversy. *San Jose Mercury News*, June 4. http://www.mercurynews.com/entertainment/ci_25896814/review-problems-tomodachi-life-go-beyond-gay-controversy. Accessed August 16, 2016.

Colby, Richard. 2014. Writing and Assessing Procedural Rhetoric in Student-Produced Video Games. *Computer and Writing* 31: 43–52.

Eaklor, Vicki L. 2008. *Queer America: A GLBT History of the 20th Century*. Westport, CT: Greenwood Press.

Entertainment Software Association (ESA). 2015. *Video Games: The New Social Setting*. Washington, DC: Entertainment Software Association (ESA). http://www.theesa.com/wp-content/uploads/15/04/Essential-Facts-15-Infographic.pdf. Accessed April 3, 2016.

Flanagan, Jack. 2015. The Complete History of Lgbt Video Game Characters. *The Daily Dot*, May 18. http://www.dailydot.com/geek/gay-characters-video-games-history/. Accessed April 26, 2016.

Funaro, Vincent. 2014. Nintendo Pledges to Include Gay Marriage in Next Tomodachi Game. *The Christian Post*, May 19. https://www.christianpost.com/news/nintendo-pledges-to-include-gay-marriage-in-next-tomodachi-game-120004/. Accessed July 1, 2016.

Goldstein, Jeffrey. 2005. Violent Video Games. In *Handbook of Computer Game Studies*, ed. Joost Raessens and Jeffrey Goldstein, 341–357. Cambridge, MA: The MIT Press.

Griffiths, Mark, and Mark N.O. Davies. 2005. Does Video Game Addiction Exist? In *Handbook of Computer Game Studies*, ed. Joost Raessens and Jeffrey Goldstein, 359–369. Cambridge, MA: The MIT Press.

Harper, Todd. 2011. Rules, Rhetoric, Andgenre: Procedural rhetoric in Persona 3. *Games and Culture* 6 (5): 395–413.

Hou, C.-I. 2012. Gendered Avatars: Representation of Gender Differences Between Cartoons and Simulated Online Role Playing Games in Taiwan. *China Media Research* 8 (3): 81–91.

Ivory, James D. 2006. Still a Man's Game: Gender Representation in Online Reviews of Video Games. *Mass Communication and Society* 9 (1): 103–114.

Ivory, Adrienne Holz, Rhonda Gibson, and James D. Ivory. 2009. Gendered Relationships on Television: Portrayals of Same-Sex and Heterosexual Couples. *Mass Communication & Society* 12 (2): 170–192.

Johns, Jennifer. 2006. Video Games Production Networks: Value Capture, Power Relations and Embeddedness. *Journal of Economic Geography* 6 (2): 151–180.

Kang, Yowei. 2011. *Hybrid Interactive Rhetoric Engagements in Massively Multiplayer Online Role-Playing Games (MMORPGS): Examining the Role of Rhetors and Audiences in Generative Rhetorical Discourses.* El Paso: The University of Texas.

Kerr, Aphra. 2006. *The Business and Culture of Digital Games: Gamework/Gameplay.* London: Sage Publications.

Ko, J., and D. Lau. 2014, July. From Creativity to Creative Industries: A Curly Road That Education Can Contribute. *Journal of Youth Studies* 17 (2): 35–39.

MacKnight, M. William. 2013. *Saving Prince of Peach: A Study of "Gaymers" and Digital LGBT/Gaming Rhetorics.* Kingston: University of Rhode Island.

Maume, C. 2014. Not Super, Mario; Video Games Nintendo's Refusal to Allow Gay Characters in Its New Release Has Sparked Upset – Not Least Because Gaming Has Traditionally Promoted Tolerance, Says Chris Maume. *The Independent* (London), May 9.

Monson, Melissa J. 2012. Race-Based Fantasy Realm: Essentialism in the World of Warcraft. *Games and Culture* 7 (1): 48–71.

PricewaterhouseCoopers LLP. 2015. *Video Games: Key Insights at a Glance (2).* PricewaterhouseCoopers LLP. http://www.pwccn.com/webmedia/doc/6357368 93052930844_em_games2_2.pdf. Accessed April 1, 2016.

Pulos, Alexis. 2013, March. Confronting Heteronormativity in Online Games: A Critical Discourse Analysis of LGBTQ Sexuality in World of Warcraft. *Games and Culture* 8 (2): 77–97.

Reddit. 2015, December. *Reddit Help: Audience and Demographics.* https://reddit.zendesk.com/hc/en-us/articles/205183225-Audience-and-Demographics. Accessed August 15, 2016.

———. n.d. *Frequently Asked Questions: How Is a Submission's Score Determined?* https://www.reddit.com/wiki/faq. Accessed April 27, 2016.

Richard, Birgit, and Jutta Zaremba. 2005. Gaming with Girls: Looking for Sheroes in Computer Games. In *Handbook of Computer Game Studies,* ed. Joost Raessens and Jeffrey Goldstein, 283–300. Cambridge, MA: The MIT Press.

Rushkoff, Douglas. 2005. Renaissance Now! The Gamers' Perspective. In *Handbook of Computer Game Studies,* ed. Joost Raessens and Jeffrey Goldstein, 415–421. Cambridge, MA: The MIT Press.

Schleiner, Anne-Marie. 2005. Game Reconstruction Workshop: Demolishing and Evolving Pc Games and Gamer Culture. In *Handbook of Computer Game Studies,* ed. Joost Raessens and Jeffrey Goldstein, 405–414. Cambridge, MA: The MIT Press.

Shaw, Adrienne. 2007. *In-Gayme Representation? Media Representation, Online Communities, Identities and Gayming.* Chicago, IL: National Communication Association Annual Conference.

————. 2009, July. Putting the Gay in Games: Cultural Production and GLBT Content in Video Games. *Games and Culture* 4 (3): 228–253.

————. 2012, October. Talking to Gaymers: Questioning Identity, Community and Media Representation. *Westiminster Papers* 9 (1): 69–89.

Soller, Kurt. 2014. Rise of the Gaymers. *Bloomberg*, February 20. http://www.bloomberg.com/news/articles/14-02-20/gay-gamers-gain-influence-industry-support. Accessed August 16, 2016.

Soper, Taylor. 2013. Study: 1.2 Billion People Are Playing Games Worldwide; 700m of Them Are Online. *GeekWire*, November 25. http://www.geekwire.com/13/gaming- report-12-billion-people-playing-games-worldwide/. Accessed July 4, 2015.

Starr, Michelle. 2014. How to Have Same-Sex Relationships in Tomodachi Life. *CNet*, May 28. https://www.cnet.com/news/how-to-have-same-sex-relationships-in-tomodachi-life/. Accessed July 1, 2016.

Sundén, Jenny. 2009. *Play as Transgression: An Ethnographic Approach to Queer Game Cultures.* Paper presented at the 4th Digital Games Research Association International Conference: Breaking New Ground: Innovation in Games, Play, Practice and Theory, London.

SuperData Research. 2016. *Worldwide Digital Games Market*, February. https://www.superdataresearch.com/blog/us-digital-games-market/. Accessed April 3, 2016.

Thorhauge, Anne Mette. 2013. The Rules of the Game—the Rules of the Player. *Games and Culture* 8 (6): 371–391.

Totilo, Stephen. 2012. Youtube Users Are Currently Mostly Hating Mass Effect 3's Gay Male Sex Scene. *Kotaku*, March 1. http://kotaku.com/5889801/youtube-users-are-currently-mostly-hating-mass-effect-3s-gay-male-sex-scene. Accessed April 27, 2016.

Waddell, T. Franklin, James D. Ivory, Rommelyn Conde, Courtney Long, and Rachel McDonnell. 2014, May. White Man's Virtual World: A Systematic Content Analysis of Gender and Race in Massively Multiplayer Online Games. *Journal of Virtual Worlds Research* 7 (2). https://journals.tdl.org/jvwr/index.php/jvwr/article/view/7096.

Walters, S.D. 2001. *All the Rage: The Story of Gay Visibility in America.* Chicago: University of Chicago Press.

Walton, Mark. 2014. *Tomodachi Life Review*, June 6. http://www.gamespot.com/reviews/tomodachi-life-review/1900-6415783/. Accessed April 26, 2016.

Williams, Dmitri, Nicole Martins, Mia Consalvo, and James D. Ivory. 2009. The Virtual Census: Representations of Gender, Race and Age in Video Games. *New Media & Society* 11 (5): 815–834.

Wolf, Mark J.P., and Bernard Perron. 2003. Introduction. In *The Video Game Theory Reader*, ed. Mark J.P. Wolf and Bernard Perron, 1–24. New York, NY: Routledge.

5

Affliction or Affection: The Inclusion of a Same-Sex Relationship in *The Last of Us*

Daniel Sipocz

In the summer of 2013, video game developer Naughty Dog released the game *The Last of Us* on the Playstation 3 console. The game struck a chord with its audience immediately, winning more than 200 Game-of-the-Year awards and selling more than 7 million copies in its initial release (Dunning 2014). The success spawned a stand-alone downloadable content game entitled *The Last of Us: Left Behind* as a prequel, which was released in February 2014. More importantly, the franchise included a gay male character and a same-sex relationship between two teenage girls. The inclusion of LGBTQ characters, while not new in the video game industry, is somewhat rare.

This study considers video games as a relevant and significant part of popular culture, as evidenced from a 2014 Bloomberg report that video game sales were expected to exceed $560 million, earning more revenue than Hollywood (Basak 2014). Mortensen (2008) noted that the study and analysis of digital worlds, such as those in video games, "can teach us something about human behavior, innovations, deviance" (203). This is particularly important, as identities are shaped and influenced by the cultural institutions people come in contact with. According to Greer (2013), "Our own identities are not simply self-authored but exist through the (re)iteration of existing norms that determine acceptable and culturally intelligible configurations of sex, gender and sexuality" (6). Consequently, the ways in which women and their sexuality are represented in the media—especially their identity and agency—can

D. Sipocz (✉)
Berry College, Mt. Berry, GA, USA

© The Author(s) 2018
T. Harper et al. (eds.), *Queerness in Play*, Palgrave Games in Context,
https://doi.org/10.1007/978-3-319-90542-6_5

shape, reinforce, or challenge an individual or society's beliefs about sexuality (Behm-Morawitz and Mastro 2009; Dill and Thill 2007).

According to Vargas (2008) the industry is perceived to be the domain of young heterosexual men, and that games cater to the male demographic, creating and reinforcing normative definitions of sexual orientation and relationships. Murray (2006) argued that video games are a powerful mechanism conveying cultural values and myths and also act as markers of the status quo. Rich's (2003) compulsory heterosexuality, a cornerstone of queer theory, illustrates how most societal structures lead individuals to believe that heterosexuality is the norm, which other people who do not fit this belief or assumption. Consalvo and Perron (2003) assert that virtual worlds, via video games, operate under an initial assumption of heteronormativity. This study will engage with Rich and Consalvo's work by analyzing the *The Last of Us* franchise's representation of gay characters and their same-sex relationships through textual analysis and paratext, borrowing from Pinckard's (2003) elements of genderspace.

One cannot examine sexuality without a discussion of gender (Karl 2007). Summers and Miller (2014) found that in the past 20 years, the role of women in video games has shifted from the damsel in distress to sexual object. Ivory (2006) argued that female video game characters are overall under-represented and that as playable characters they are hyper sexualized. This contributes to misogynistic behavior by gamers who reject non-gender conforming roles, as characters in such roles are less desirable to this type of gamer. Alternatively, video game developers reinforce compulsory heteronormativity and the male gaze by focusing on heteronormative sexual orientations. This occurs frequently because the industry has an aversion to risk in regard to sexual orientation and gay characters, which are only alluded to and rarely presented explicitly as LGBTQ (Consalvo and Perron 2003; MacKnight 2013; Vargas 2008; Williams et al. 2009). The industry's risk aversion stems from the potential fiscal and regulatory ramifications if non-heteronormative sexuality were included and not palatable to the general public (Shaw 2009). For example, video game developer Rockstar Games, best known as the publisher of the *Grand Theft Auto* franchise, faced backlash when it released the game *Bully* in 2006. The main character, Jimmy, was able to pursue relationships with both male and female characters in the game, including an optional gay kiss. Jack Thompson, an attorney and video game legislation advocate, criticized the game receiving an ESRB rating of Teen rather than Mature rating because of the optional gay kiss (Sliwinski 2006). Game developers are careful with less palatable content, such as Jimmy's gay kiss, to avoid a backlash that may include negative publicity and financial losses (Shaw 2009).

Method

This chapter seeks to go beyond affirmation or rejection of non-heteronormative identities through textual analysis and paratext. According to McKee (2003), textual analysis is a way for researchers to gather information about how others make sense of the world, and the text is something researchers make meaning from. The analysis borrows from Hall's reading theory (1993) to examine the relationship between characters, dialogue, societal norms, the creator's intent, and the context the game was released into to discuss the franchise's relationship with social change, particularly in regard to LGBTQ inclusion. Hall's reading theory calls for a close reading of a text in three categorized ways: (1) a dominant reading, in which an individual's social situation is supported. (2) A negotiated reading, in which an individual's social situation is partially supported. (3) An oppositional reading, in which an individual's social situation comes in direct conflict with the message of the text. The researcher considered all three of Hall's readings as he played through the text. Interpretation of scenes and dialogue began with the dominant meaning, what reinforces cultural beliefs about sexuality, sexual orientation, and relationships. Once the researcher established dominant meanings, he began to interpret other readings based upon a lens of queer theory and compulsory heterosexuality (Rich 2003), to examine the inclusion of non-heteronormative identities and their social standing in *The Last of Us* video game franchise.

Pinckard (2003) argued that games must be looked at holistically in order to make sense of their representations. This study uses three of Pickard's four aspects of "genderspace" in games as elements of analysis: (1) the environment surrounding characters outside of the game; (2) the aesthetics of the character, particularly, its movements, actions, voice performances; (3) the programmatic qualities of the character that players have no control over, such as the character's choices, other character's reactions, and the biases from the video game creators. These genderspace elements were used to assist the researcher in interpreting the three different readings of characters, scenes, and dialogue to examine what meanings the text creates about sexuality, sexual orientation, and relationships. Using compulsory heteronormativity and genderspace, this chapter seeks to address four research questions:

RQ1: To what extent are LGBTQ characters included?
RQ2: How are these characters portrayed?
RQ3: How is the same-sex relationship depicted and does its characterization challenge heteronormative assumptions?

RQ4: What was the game developer's intent regarding the inclusion of LGBTQ characters and a same-sex relationship?

Analysis

Environment Around Gay Characters Outside the Game and Character Aesthetics

Ellie

When *The Last of Us* was released, Naughty Dog included a character description of Ellie on their website:

> A brave, 14 year old girl, Ellie has grown up in this harsh world and it is all she has ever known. She's an orphan who was raised in a boarding school run by the military within the bounds of the quarantine zone. Naïve and curious about the outside world, she is wise beyond her years and highly capable of taking care of herself and those around her. Obsessed with comic books, CDs, and other pop culture, her knowledge base is filled by the remnants of a world that no longer exists. (n.p.)

In addition to the character description, box art of the first-run release of *The Last of Us* sets the tone for what to expect with Ellie. The box art shows Ellie in the foreground with a serious expression as she glares into the distance with a rifle on her back and Joel in the background. Joel is the other lead character who accompanies Ellie on a journey to find an anti-government faction, the Fireflies. Players are introduced to him through his tragic backstory, in which his daughter dies during the initial outbreak of a zombie infection; players learn that in the 20 years since then, Joel is no longer the caring father figure he once was.

Ellie stands in water up to her knees, wearing blue jeans and a red t-shirt over a black long sleeve shirt. Her location in the foreground indicates that she is an important character in the game but also establishes her as a subject to the male gaze with her attractive aesthetics as a young, teenage girl. Consequently, the developers created an air of mystery surrounding Ellie in promotion, which would carry over into the game as players learned relatively little about Ellie's backstory, including her sexual orientation. Players quickly learn that Ellie has a foul mouth, quirky but witty sense of humor, and maintains a stereotypical teenage attitude about authority and the rules. Ellie's behavior exemplifies these traits when she first meets Joel: when a wounded friend stumbles through a door, she threatens Joel with a knife, demanding he back away.

Riley

Players meet Riley Abel for the first time in *The Last of Us: Left Behind*, the downloadable content prequel game. Riley is African American but her race is not a point of overt discussion at all. She is roughly the same age as Ellie. Riley appears to be brave, brash, inconsiderate, and selfish based on her actions at the beginning of *Left Behind*. However, Riley is later shown to have a good heart, desiring to make Ellie happy.

Players could potentially encounter Riley earlier, through a five-part comic book story in which Riley comes to Ellie's aid when bullies gang up on her. After a rough start between the two, when they decide to escape the military school together, Riley reveals desires of joining the Fireflies. The two even meet the Firefly leader Marlene. Shortly after, Riley leaves without notice to join the Fireflies. Her absence deeply affects Ellie emotionally; she believes that Riley is dead at the beginning of *Left Behind* when Riley sneaks into Ellie's room in the middle of the night, waking her.

Bill

Players encounter Bill partway through the game. Bill, a lone survivor in an abandoned city near Boston, is gay. For the game's creative director, Neil Druckmann, the decision to include Bill as gay was about creating a strong narrative. Druckmann explained to Gaygamer.net that Bill was intentionally written to be gay:

> And then in writing the character, I was like 'oh well, it's much more interesting to say ok, here's this guy who vocalizes all these concerns and says you should never care for someone else but actually deep inside he's the opposite of that, where he's yearning to have a partnership, someone to be with him.' So then the idea became that he had a partner that he was living with; they kind of looked out for each other; someone he cared for and someone he failed in protecting... 'And that's how he became a gay character.' (Einhorn 2013)

At first players are made aware that Bill is different from everyone else. Joel describes Bill as paranoid and unfriendly in a way that makes Bill sound crazy. Joel's description of Bill immediately places him into another category—an

Other, something different. Players encounter bombs and traps that Bill set up to keep both zombies and humans out of his city prior to meeting him. Once the player meets Bill, they learn about his partner. The word choice of "partner" drops a subtle clue that Bill is gay but is ambiguous enough to be interpreted as a co-worker, leaving ambiguity about Bill's sexuality.

There are other visual clues about Bill's orientation, however. Bill is coded as a husky, foul-mouthed, angry and paranoid, tough-talking middle-aged man with a thick beard. Some of these traits fit into the "bear" stereotype of a gay man who is big, burly, masculine, and hairy (Hennen 2005). Bill's unfriendly, paranoid, and tough-talking traits serve to hide the pain of losing his partner Frank, first when he abandons Bill offscreen, and later when Bill finds Frank dead. Despite the negative connotations Naughty Dog built with its portrayal of Bill, GLAAD still praised Bill's inclusion into the game: "Bill is as deeply flawed but wholly unique a gay character found in any storytelling medium this year" (The Most Intriguing para. 6). Bill's complexity demonstrates there is more to just good or bad representation. It is crucial to consider the purpose of the stereotypes employed and what the creator's intent is to determine the value of the representation published. The stereotypes demarcate Bill as different, particularly in comparison to Ellie, who is forced into heteronormativity and not revealed to be gay until much later. Players are not primed to think of Ellie as queer because she is not stereotyped and othered in the way Bill is.

Scripted Choices of Characters Outside the Player's Control

Ellie's Reaction to Bill

After Bill reluctantly helps Joel and Ellie get a truck working to escape, the players receive confirmation of Bill's sexual orientation. Ellie sits in the back seat of the truck, revealing that she stole a dirty magazine from Bill's stash in his bunker of supplies, where he explicitly told Ellie not to touch anything. The magazine contains a nude male centerfold, which becomes a tool to further reinforce Ellie's heteronormativity. Ellie giggles like a stereotypical teenage girl encountering sexuality, indicating she is more aware of sexuality than one would think, in addition to messing with Joel. Ellie then makes Bill the butt of a joke, telling Joel, "Oh, I'm sure 'your friend' will be missing this tonight. Light on the reading, but its got some interesting photos ... oh, why are these all stuck together? I'm just fucking with you." Although the scene is intended to lighten the mood in a serious game, the scene treats Bill's sexuality as a joke, which not only stigmatizes homosexuality but marginalizes it as well. According to Vargas (2008), video games treat homosexuality more as a joke than a way of life. By making such a joke about gay porn, and by extension Bill's sexuality, Ellie implies—intended or not—that being gay is inferior to being heterosexual. These implications reveal societal beliefs about homosexuality that it is perceived as a joke.

The joke about Bill conflicts with Druckmann's story of how Bill came to be a gay character. As Dyer (1993) noted, the way people are represented in media is the way they are treated in real life. That Bill is made the butt of a joke, which marginalized him and made him inferior to heterosexuals, reflects how LGBTQ people are often treated in society. More than that, the creators missed an opportunity to explore Ellie's sexuality. Druckmann said Ellie's sexuality was not explored because it did not play into the story (Einhorn 2013). Despite this, her encounter with Bill was a moment that could have led to introspection. At the very least, Joel could have chided Ellie for her cruel joke. Instead, the jokes are used to bolster Ellie's heteronormativity. At this point, Ellie was outside of Boston for the first time in her life, exploring how to live in new surroundings. This exploration could have been an adept metaphor for exploring herself and who she is as she was no longer trapped inside a quarantine zone. She could have begun to signal her sexual orientation a bit.

Beyond Bill

The belief that Ellie's sexuality did not play into the story further feeds into heteronormativity where Rich (2003) argues, "The ideology of heterosexual romance, beamed at her [the average female] from childhood out of fairy tales, television, films, advertising, popular songs, wedding pageantry, is a tool" (24). Druckmann and Naughty Dog draw upon these assumptions in how Ellie is portrayed. In a heteronormative social context, Ellie is forced into compulsory heteronormativity because she is assumed straight unless specified explicitly otherwise, the player drawing on that context to make sense of *The Last of Us*'s universe. The power of compulsory heteronormativity is strengthened because it goes unquestioned. Wittig (1992) argued, "even if they, if we, do not consent, we cannot think outside the mental categories of heterosexuality. Heterosexuality is always already there within all mental categories" (43). Consequently, there is more that must be considered than whether or not a character is heterosexual, such as creator intent with the character, its design and aesthetics and how the stereotypes are used must be taken into consideration. Authorial intent in the video game industry usually prevents characters from being presented explicitly as LGBTQ (Shaw 2009). The reasons why and when Druckmann and Naughty Dog presented Bill and Ellie as gay is significant to the game's use of compulsory heteronormativity. The representation of Bill is good, bad, messy, and complex just like the individuals that created the game and the individuals that play the game, whereas Ellie's sexuality is somewhat commodified in *Left Behind*.

Ellie continues to be depicted as straight throughout the entirety of the first game, notably by a lack of addressing her sexuality at all, even when encountering Bill. Later on, Ellie is shown potentially having feelings for an African American boy named Sam, whom she and Joel befriend. Ellie and Sam, roughly the same age—an age in which romance is not out of the question—flirt awkwardly, exchanging puns as they explore a neighborhood of houses. Although this could be seen as casual conversation, evidence of potential feelings is shown when she tries to give Sam a Transformers-like toy, one he wanted but was forced by his older brother to leave behind. Ellie even confides in Sam about the things she fears, which occurs not long after their meeting. This confession stands out because it is the opposite of how Ellie acted when she met Joel and Bill. The trust to confide in someone seems to indicate feelings of affection toward Sam on some level beyond a travel companion who she just met. However, Sam becomes infected and promptly written out of the script. Sam is only referenced once more in the game, when Ellie leaves the toy on a grave, indicating she was thinking of him. By referencing Sam here, Ellie appears to be heterosexual, showing interest in a lost potential love interest. In this way, Ellie and Sam's interaction together make him a convenient prop to further reinforce Ellie's compulsory heteronormativity.

The first explicit hint of Ellie's more accurate sexual orientation is not shared until the final scene of the 2013 game. In the final scene, Ellie shares lingering concerns with Joel with the knowledge that Joel sacrificed a potential cure for humankind to save her. The final dialogue between the two seems innocuous, vaguely insinuating that Ellie's best friend may have been more than just a best friend. Ellie says to Joel:

Ellie: "Back in Boston. Back when I was bitten. I wasn't alone. My best friend was there. And she got bit too. We didn't know what to do. So ... She says 'Let's just wait it out. Y'know, we can be all poetic and just lose our minds together.' I'm still waiting for my turn. Her name was Riley and she was the first to die. Then Tess. And Sam."
Joel: "None of that is on you."
Ellie: "You don't understand."

The words, "You don't understand" seem innocuous, almost like a throw-away line. She is struggling with the loss of a loved one, Riley, who is presented as her best friend in this case. Riley died after becoming infected in a story told in the prequel *Left Behind* whereas Ellie somehow survived becoming infected.

Ellie and Riley in Left Behind

Left Behind's plot is driven by the narrative structure of a typical teenager date at the mall as seen in movies and television shows where the couple explores stores and the arcade and take photos in a photo booth. Instead of the date taking place between a male and female, overtly reinforcing heteronormativity, the date takes place between two females and eventually confirms that that Ellie and Riley's relationship is romantic in nature. According to Rich (2003), female friendship has been set aside from the erotic, marking distinct differences between friendship and romantic involvement. In *Left Behind*, there are signs of compulsory heterosexuality being forced upon Ellie and Riley, who exhibit friendship more clearly than a romantic relationship (the erotic) for half of the game.

After turning the power on in an abandoned mall, the two girls explore a Halloween costume shop, playing dress up. Ellie tries on different masks, as if she were trying on different versions of herself, exploring which one is the real her. The masks provide a different identity and exploration for Ellie as if she were exploring her sexuality as well. They set the stage to differentiate Ellie and Riley's relationship from "a sexual commodity to be consumed by males" (Rich 2003, 20) by demonstrating emotional context and connection, which are not components of the male gaze.

The displays of emotional context and connection between Ellie and Riley begin in a photo booth, and it drives home the two girls' romantic involvement. The player can choose between options such as "friends," "cool," or "love," by hitting the assigned button on the controller. Regardless of the choice the player makes, the sequence of poses Riley and Ellie strike is the same. That the choice does not affect the poses is significant, as it does not create a hierarchy of importance of one over the other. It also creates ambiguousness about the nature of the girl's relationship. Once the photos are taken, Ellie and Riley accidentally break the machine when it reports an error preventing the photos from being printed. It is then when Ellie and Riley begin to make intense eye contact and move closer to each other until their bodies are pressed against each other. Ellie and Riley are not looking at each other or speaking, letting the tension grow before making intense eye contact. This interaction raises questions about what matters: *If this is not a date, why does this scene matter? Where is the narrative taking us? And why is this so tense and sexually charged?* These implied questions tell the players this is a date and the girls may love each other. These scenes would not exist otherwise. Druckmann explained in a 2014 Reddit Ask Me Anything (AMA) that:

> Their [Ellie and Riley] characters needed somewhere else to go. If it was just about friendship, their arc would be over as soon as Ellie forgave Riley for leaving (in the Halloween store) and they were friends again. By having a romantic relationship, it has another layer of subtext to the performances and allowed the story to still evolve as *Left Behind* went on. (Druckmann and Straley 2014, n.p.)

Left Behind humanizes same-sex relationships by showcasing Ellie and Riley as real representations of people interacting in spaces that are not necessarily labeled as part of LGBTQ culture. The existence of the date is significant, particularly because Ellie's sexuality was not overtly tackled in the franchise until this point. Players saw her evolve and become a more complex character. She was also spared of becoming a joke like Bill was. After enjoying a few puns from the pun book Riley gives to Ellie, the two all but confirm they are a couple during a fight when Ellie asks if they are done talking.

Ellie: "You don't get to be pissed off at me. I'm pissed off at you."
Riley: "For what? Asking you what you think?"
Ellie: "When have you ever cared about what I think? We were good. We were better than good. Then you told me to fuck off. And then you just up and vanish. This whole day ... you feel guilty? You want an out? I'm. I'm giving it to you."
Riley: "I'm supposed to be holed up on the other side of town. I get caught as a Firefly I'm dead. *Guilt didn't make me cross a city full of soldiers Ellie.* And yeah. I did some shit I don't know how to take back but I'm trying."

The player is never told what happened between the two leading up to Riley's disappearance or the entire history between Ellie and Riley. The language used, "giving her [Riley] an out" and Riley's "Guilt didn't make me cross a city full of soldiers" present significant opportunities to interpret the relationship as a romantic one that went bad.

The penultimate scene shows the girls begin dancing awkwardly to "I Got You Babe." Ellie and Riley dance at opposite ends of a jewelry display case when the mood changes abruptly and Ellie stops dancing. Biting her lower lip and glancing at Riley, the two make eye contact warning the player something significant is about to happen. After Riley asks her what is wrong, Ellie steps toward Riley, shaking her head slightly. Ellie appears to be nervous or heartbroken. Her voice barely reaches a whisper, pleading with Riley to stay and not go on a Firefly mission.

There is silence for seven real-time seconds between the two, with the music blocked out so the focus is on Ellie and Riley. The two continue to eye each other. Riley suddenly rips off her dog tags and Ellie kisses her. The kiss is a short one, but when Ellie pulls away, smirking, Riley is smiling wide. Ellie apologizes and Riley asks what she is apologizing for. According to Rich (2003), "If we think of heterosexuality as *the* natural emotional and sensual inclination for women, lives as these are seen as deviant, as pathological, or as emotionally and sensually deprived" (30). However, through the buildup of the date, from the dorm room and Halloween store to the photo booth and the kiss, throughout *Left Behind* Ellie and Riley are shown as girls, not devoid or deprived of emotional and sensual connection. Before either of the girls can figure out what their next step is, zombies attack. The two are bitten after getting cornered not far from the exit to complete their escape. Druckmann said, "[The scene] was written with the idea that it's the first time they reveal that they like each other romantically" (Druckmann and Straley 2014, n.p.). The reveal, leading up to and following the kiss, is constructed in a nuanced way that queer on screen relationships in games don't often exhibit (Shaw 2009). For this reason, the representation of Ellie and Riley's same-sex relationship is neither good nor bad but complex and multilayered.

Discussion

The Last of Us franchise includes three queered characters (Ellie, Bill, and Riley) within its universe. Overall, the characters are portrayed in a mostly positive light. All three characters are complex individuals with layered backstories to why they behave, speak, and dress the way they do. In 2013, GLAAD recognized Naughty Dog for creating Bill as a compelling, complex LGBTQ character that was not just for token representation (The Most Intriguing 2013) despite Ellie making jokes about him. Ellie and Riley, however, were more significant figures in the franchise as their same-sex relationship was at the heart of *Left Behind*'s plot. IGN video game critic Keza MacDonald (2014) noted that Ellie and Riley's relationship is "not just significant because it's about the kind of relationship other games are terrified to explore, either—

it's significant because it does it *so well*" (para. 8). Regardless of the flaws in Ellie, Riley, and Bill, Druckmann's Naughty Dog team created characters with depth, complexity, emotion, and most importantly, humanity, which is a rarity for a post-apocalyptic world.

Despite the positive portrayals of Ellie and Riley and their same-sex relationship, the *Left Behind* release date and some cast interviews weaken more charitable interpretations of Druckmann's intentions and motives for including Ellie and Riley's same-sex relationship in the game. Ashley Johnson, who played Ellie, and W. Earl Brown, who played Bill, both insisted their characters be left open to interpretation. In an interview with Youtube show *Up At Noon*, 10 days after *Left Behind*'s release, Johnson said:

> Neil and I have talked about it so much… I know this is kind of a terrible answer, but it kind of doesn't matter. I guess she is. No, maybe she isn't. I think in the sort of world they're living in, it's not something they're even thinking about. I think it's just when you make a connection with somebody, that's the only thing you have in the world, so regardless of it being male or female, that's what's important. For Ellie, Riley meant everything for her… At the end of the day I don't think it really matters. Sorry guys. (Miller 2014)

However, Ellie's sexual orientation *does* matter and not just because *Left Behind* is centered on a date between two females. According to Shaw (2010), "The inclusion, and even exclusion of traditionally under or over misrepresented groups in games, requires active reflection and thought by developers" (13). Naughty Dog would not have invested all that time and money in developing a story for Ellie and Riley that did not mean anything. Ellie, Riley, their sexuality, and relationship were commodified by Naughty Dog and Sony when *Left Behind* was released on Valentine's Day. Releasing the game on Valentine's Day was an opportunity to sell more copies of the game and generate more buzz by spotlighting two attractive teenage girls as the agents of non-heteronormative love. Naughty Dog would not have released a similar game featuring Bill in a same-sex relationship with his partner Frank. Female same-sex relationships are more palatable to society than male same-sex relationships (Shaw 2009). If Naughty Dog had released a game featuring Bill, it would have likely received the same negative reaction that Rockstar earned with *Bully* did with an optional gay kiss.

Conclusion

The success and cultural significance of *The Last of Us* franchise can be measured by the more than 8 million copies sold. It expresses that sexuality in the video game industry does not have to focus solely on heterosexuality and that players do not have to assume compulsory heterosexuality, either. Players seemed to appreciate the diversity in *The Last of Us* characters, as evidenced by a gamer's only score of 9.1 out of 10 on Metacritic (The Last of Us 2013), which is separate from critics scores and reviews. That Ellie, as a female and LGBTQ character, was a playable character in a game that featured her as the main protagonist was significant. There are very few female lead characters in video games, especially those who carry the bulk of the story, much less confirmed LGBTQ female characters in gaming, which makes Ellie's presence notable in multiple levels.

The release and success of *The Last of Us* also coincided with a time in which society's view of same-sex relationships was growing more favorable. A year after *The Last of Us* was released, the US Supreme Court ruled in favor of legalizing same-sex marriage, indicating some degree of social change. In response to the ruling, Ashley Johnson then tweeted a photo of Ellie and Riley from the photo booth scene in *Left Behind* (see Fig. 5.1). Johnson's tweet is even more notable because she had argued against labeling Ellie as queer in her interview on the YouTube show *Up at Noon* (Miller 2014).

The tweet showed further that pop culture artifacts, such as video games, do not have to be solely heterosexual and that characters do not have to be stuck performing compulsory heterosexuality to be successful. If anything, the popularity of Ellie and *The Last of Us* franchise could spur other game

Fig. 5.1 "Love Wins" tweet by Ashley Johnson

developers to include more LGBTQ characters in their games. Developers will have to take on this task in much of the same Naughty Dog did: with precision and focus on the story and limiting the commodification of the LGBTQ characters. There's plenty of room for improvement on how characters can be presented. The lack of discussion surrounding Ellie's orientation, particularly at moments when she's interacting with Bill, is problematic if we are to believe Ellie as a queer character. Naughty Dog continuously built up her heterosexuality before doubling back in the later released prequel. Game developers need more commitment to presenting queer characters transparently, as Naughty Dog did with Bill. Doing so will not only continue to increase the quantity of LGBTQ characters but to also improve the quality of how these characters are presented and included in the plot of games.

Bibliography

Basak, Sonali. 2014. U.S. Video-Game Industry Sales Increase 8% on Consoles. *Bloomberg Business*, September 11. bloomberg.com/news/articles/2014-09-11/u-s-video-.

Behm-Morawitz, Elizabeth, and Dana Mastro. 2009. The Effects of the Sexualization of Female Video Game Characters on Gender Stereotyping and Female Self-Concept. *Sex Roles* 61 (11/12): 808–823. https://doi.org/10.1007/s11199-009-9683-8.

Consalvo, Mia, and Bernard Perron. 2003. Hot Dates and Fairy-Tales Romances: Studying Sexuality in Video Games. In *The Video Game Theory Reader*, ed. Mark J.P. Wolf, 171–194. London: Rutledge.

Dill, Karen E., and Kathryn P. Thill. 2007. Video Game Characters and the Socialization of Gender Roles: Young People's Perceptions Mirror Sexist Media Depictions. *Sex Roles* 57 (11/12): 851–864. https://doi.org/10.1007/s11199-007-9278-1.

Druckmann, Neil, and Bruce Straley. 2014. Hi, We're Neil Druckmann (Creative Director) and Bruce Straley (Game Director) of The Last of Us and The Last of Us: Left Behind at Naughty Dog. *Reddit*, February 21. www.reddit.com/r/IAmA/comments/1ykno8/hi_were_neil_druckmann_creative_director_and/.

Dunning, Jason. 2014. The Last of Us Sales Figures Cross 7 Million, New PS3/PS4 DLC Incoming. *Playstation LifeStyle*, February 16. http://www.playstationlifestyle.net/2014/07/16/the-last-of-us-sales-figures-cross-7-million-sold-new-dlc-incoming/.

Dyer, Richard. 1993. Seen to be Believed: Problems in the Representation of Gay People as Typical. In *The Matter of Images: Essays on Representations*, ed. Dyer Richard, 19–51. London: Routledge.

Einhorn, Sam. 2013. On Bill: An Interview with Neil Druckmann of Naughty Dog. *GayGamer*, September 27. www.gaygamer.net/2013/09/on-bill-an-interview-with-neil-druckmann-of-naughty-dog.

Greer, Stephen. 2013. Playing Queer: Affordances for Sexuality in Fable and Dragon Age. *Journal of Gaming & Virtual Worlds* 5 (1): 3–21.

Hall, Stuart. 1993. Encoding, Decoding. In *The Cultural Studies Reader*, ed. Simon During, 90–103. New York: Routledge.

Hennen, Peter. 2005. Bear Bodies, Bear Masculinity: Recuperation, Resistance, or Retreat? *Gender and Society* 19 (1): 25–43.

Ivory, James D. 2006. Still a Man's Game: Gender Representation in Online Reviews of Video Games. *Mass Communication and Society* 9 (1): 103–114.

Karl, Irmi. 2007. On-/Online: Gender, Sexuality, & the Techno-Politics of Everyday Life. In *Queer Online: Media, Technology and Sexuality*, 45–64. New York, NY: Peter Lang Publishing.

MacDonald, Keza. 2014. The Significance of The Last of Us: Left Behind – IGN. *IGN*, February 19. http://www.ign.com/articles/2014/02/19/the-significance-of-the-last-of-us-left-behind.

MacKnight, William M. 2013. *Saving Prince Peach: A Study of 'Gaymers' and Digital LGBT Gaming Rhetorics*. Open Access Dissertations. Paper 135.

McKee, Alan. 2003. *Textual Analysis: A Beginner's Guide*. London: Sage Publications.

Miller, Greg. 2014. Reinventing The Last of Us' Ellie, Reinventing Thief – Up at Noon. *YouTube*, February 24. http://www.youtube.com/watch?v=e0HA6JRMmLw.

Mortensen, Torill Elvira. 2008. Humans Playing World of Warcraft: Or Deviant Strategies. In *Digital Culture, Play, and Identity: A World of Warcraft Reader*, ed. Hilde Corneliussen and Jill Walker Rettberg, 203–224. Cambridge, MA: MIT Press.

Murray, Janet H. 2006. Toward a Cultural Theory of Gaming: Digital Games & the Co-evolution of Media, Mind and Culture. *Popular Communication* 4 (3): 185–202.

Pinckard, Jane. 2003. Genderplay: Successes and Failures in Character Designs for Videogames. *Game Girl Advance*, April 16. www.gamegirladvance.com/archives/2003/04/16/genderplay_successes_and_failures_in_character_designs_for_videogames.html.

Rich, Adrienne Cecile. 2003. Compulsory Heterosexuality and Lesbian Existence (1980). *Journal of Women's History* 15 (3): 11–48. https://doi.org/10.1353/jowh.2003.0079.

Shaw, Adrienne. 2009. Putting the Gay in Games: Cultural Production and GLBT Content in Video Games. *Games and Culture* 4 (3): 228–253.

———. 2010. *Identity, Identification, and Media Representation in Video Game Play: An Audience Reception Study*. Publicly Accessible Penn Dissertation, Paper 286.

Sliwinski, Alexander. 2006. Warm Tea: The Bully Boy-on-Boy Kiss Goes Mainstream. *Engadget*, October 28. http://www.engadget.com/2006/10/28/warm-tea-the-bully-boy-on-boy-kiss-goes-mainstream/.

Summers, Alicia, and Monica K. Miller. 2014. From Damsels in Distress to Sexy Superheroes. *Feminist Media Studies* 14 (6): 1028–1040. *Communication Source*.

The Last of Us. 2013. *Metacritic*, June 14. http://www.metacritic.com/game/playstation-3/the-last-of-us.

The Most Intriguing New LGBT Characters of 2013. 2013. *GLAAD*, December 26. http://www.glaad.org/blog/most-intriguing-new-lgbt-characters-2013.

Vargas, Jose Antonio. 2008. Video Games. Edited by David M. Haugen. Detroit: Greenhaven Press/Thomson Gale.

Williams, Dimitri, Nichole Martins, Mia Consalvo, and James D. Ivory. 2009. The Virtual Census: Representations of Gender, Race and Age in Video Games. *New Media & Society* 11 (5): 815–834.

Wittig, Monique. 1992. *The Straight Mind and Other Essays*. Boston: Beacon.

6

What If Zelda Wasn't a Girl? Problematizing *Ocarina of Time*'s Great Gender Debate

Chris Lawrence

Introduction

The Legend of Zelda: Ocarina of Time (Nintendo 1998a) introduced the series' first ambiguously gendered character: Sheik, a ninja-like companion of Link and alterego of the Princess Zelda. Since *Ocarina*'s release, a vigorous and ongoing debate has erupted concerning Sheik's gender—with very little momentum awarded to any position outside of the male/female binary. Participants in the debate are largely separated into two camps: those who believe that Zelda physically transforms into what they imagine as a male body, and those who believe that Zelda is simply in disguise and remains what they consider to be female.

I have no interest in arguing for a specific set of pronouns to assign to Sheik and will refrain from using any throughout this discussion. Instead, my argument is that in their fixation on an imagined body, fan debates have largely overlooked an imperfect but nonetheless uncharacteristically subversive examination of gender identity offered by Nintendo in their 1998 best seller. A close reading of Sheik's depiction in the game, grounded by the theory of gender performance and an analysis of gender normativity within the game world, reveals a character whose representation eludes tidy gender-based categorization within the hegemonic order of the game world, undermining a strictly binary approach to determining the character's gender identity. I move

C. Lawrence (✉)
University of Waterloo, Waterloo, ON, Canada

© The Author(s) 2018
T. Harper et al. (eds.), *Queerness in Play*, Palgrave Games in Context,
https://doi.org/10.1007/978-3-319-90542-6_6

away from the debate about Sheik's imagined body and instead argue that the character's performance constitutes a site of alternative masculinity—which is to say, a masculinity that exists as separate and distinct from the character's body, in spite of (and even because of) fan efforts to reinterpret that body along the gender binary. Moving beyond *Ocarina*, I examine the gradual shifts in the character's depiction in subsequent games in the series: in all media appearances of Sheik since *Ocarina*, the character has been more explicitly feminized both in visual depiction as well as in the assignment of pronouns.

My research in this chapter will use the fan debates as a springboard into an examination of what is in many ways a watershed video game character who doesn't fit into a neat box. Though I will be addressing how the character's depiction has shifted in subsequent works, I will be looking principally at the original 1998 release of *The Legend of Zelda: Ocarina of Time* on the Nintendo 64 in order to offer a sense of the character as originally depicted by the designers.

Overview of *Ocarina*

As universal as its critical acclaim and as enduring as its legacy may be, *The Legend of Zelda: Ocarina of Time* is nonetheless, as of this writing, nearly two decades old, and so those parts of the game relevant to my discussion warrant a brief summary. Like most games in the long-running *Zelda* series, *Ocarina of Time* puts the player in the boots of the protagonist Link, who is tasked with saving the fantasy kingdom of Hyrule from the villainous Ganon. As is usual in the series, the game's titular character Zelda is a princess who must be saved by Link from the clutches of evil before the game's end. One of the particular narrative conceits in *Ocarina* is an extended diversion from this conventional damsel-in-distress routine: before Zelda is inevitably captured near the game's end, she spends a substantial portion of the game operating under an alternative, considerably more active alterego: the ninja-like persona Sheik. The point of this disguise is nominally to allow Zelda to evade capture by Ganon, who seeks to acquire her piece of the omnipotent wish-granting Triforce. Throughout the second half of the game, which follows Link's exploits in late adolescence after a seven-year time skip, Sheik plays a supporting role, shadowing Link's footsteps across the kingdom to dispense wisdom and assistance at timely junctures. Throughout this part of the game, Sheik rarely interacts with anyone but Link, whose thoughts as a silent protagonist are unknown. Sheik is, however, identified by one other character as explicitly male. Describing an offscreen rescue, the princess of the merfolk Zora race,

Fig. 6.1 Zelda

Ruto, says that "A young man named Sheik saved me." Later in the game she asks of Link, "If you see Sheik, please give him my thanks, OK?" In both of these instances, Sheik's masculinity is taken as a matter of fact.

Conspicuously, however, Sheik never self-identifies with a specific set of pronouns. The Princess Zelda is depicted with a lithe, feminine regality—complete with floor-length dress, makeup, jewelry, long hair, and a pronounced bust (see Fig. 6.1). Other adult female characters in the game, such as Ruto, Malon, and Nabooru, echo these patterns with designs that emphasize feminine curves. Sheik, on the other hand, is in many ways presented as overtly masculine, with a wiry, muscular physique, flat chest, square hips, shorter hair, and a lower-pitched voice (see Fig. 6.2)—literally, in this case, a downpitched recording of the same actress who voices Zelda, Jun Mizusawa (Wikipedia 2015).

The game's presentation of Sheik's gender is an ambiguous one for reasons spanning the technological (i.e. the simplistic polygon rendering capabilities of the Nintendo 64 hardware limit the fidelity with which bodies of any kind can be visually approximated), to the narrative (Sheik encounters few characters other than Link, whose thoughts are not revealed to the player), to the performative (the combination of Sheik's appearance and behavior resist strict categorization). This has created enough room for interpretation to fuel long-running and vigorous debates in online Zelda fandom about the categorization of Sheik's imagined gender, with fans leveling arguments at one another running the gamut from "Sheik is a woman" (*Zelda Universe* 2010) to "Sheik is a male" (Ibid.). In short, Sheik's depiction in *Ocarina of Time* represents an uncommon space of gender fluidity for a mainstream game of the time, and fans have responded to that fluidity by attempting to police it, placing Sheik into a more conventional gender binary.

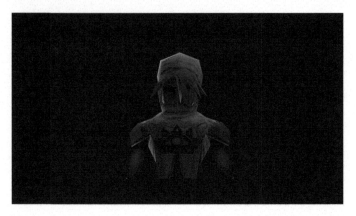

Fig. 6.2 Sheik

The result is what some media outlets later came to call the "Sheik Gender Debate," where fans assembled on Zelda-focused forums to debate Sheik's place on one end or the other of a conventional gender binary. Two opposing sides came to dominate the conversation: those who believed that Zelda was merely cross-dressing and preserved a female gender identity, and those who believed that Zelda physically transformed herself and assumed a male gender identity using magic (Riendeau 2014). Fans on either side of this conflict often take their viewpoint as a matter of fact and do not perceive the character with any ambiguity in the first place: "Well obviously she's a girl because she's ZELDA in disguise!" (*Zelda Dungeon* 2010) offers one fan on the *Zelda Dungeon* forums. Another fan posting in the same thread makes a similarly concise show of support for the other side: "I have noticed that Sheik had a male voice when he made a sound, so I would assume that because of this, Sheik is a boy" (Ibid.) Some fans attempt to distinguish between Zelda as a baseline persona and Sheik as a "character" conceived by Zelda as a disguise, but the debate inevitably remains focused on the discussion of Sheik's body.

Immediate and obvious problems arise in any attempt to prove anything about Sheik's body with evidence from the game alone. Any such attempt stumbles immediately over the question of what actually constitutes a "body" for a character like Sheik. In the strictest sense, Sheik does not have a "human" body at all; instead, the character's avatar is a textured polygon model—and a fairly primitive one at that, by today's standards. The design of this model may be informed by real-world constructions of an imagined gendered body and in turn may inspire players to project their own constructions of the same upon it, but beyond a vague exterior resemblance there is nothing biologically human about this body. It has no blood, no muscle, and no organs—reproductive or otherwise.

The irony here is that zealous defense of *either* of the prevailing fan positions—Sheik as male or Sheik as female—to the exclusion of the other misses the point, bypassing virtually everything that is novel or interesting about the Sheik character in the first place. Worse still, these arguments erroneously presuppose that Sheik's gender is contingent upon one of two imagined configurations of the character's body. Either one of these configurations—or neither of them—*might* be technically true (albeit impossible to prove), but the compulsion to "decide" an imagined gender for Sheik one way or the other is simultaneously indicative that Sheik's ambiguity disrupts cisgender hegemony and dooms the ensuing attempt to reassert the very hegemony that Sheik flouts.

Theorizing Sheik's Gender Performance

In order to move the conversation away from a fruitless and unproductive scrutiny of Sheik's imagined body, I will draw upon a framework of theorists who emphasize the performative aspects of gender over the bodily. In her landmark essay "Performative Acts and Gender Constitution: An Essay in Phenomenology and Feminist Theory," Judith Butler (1988) argues for such a performative theory of gender identity, summarizing that "the body becomes its gender through a series of acts which are renewed, revised, and consolidated through time" (523). This is critical for our reading of Sheik, who we understand from the story to be an alternative persona of the feminine-coded Princess Zelda but who differs sharply from the latter in both visual presentation and public behavior. Most notably, this destabilizes the argument—recurring in the fandom—that Sheik cannot be masculine simply because Sheik is a character being played by Zelda; if all gender identity constitutes a series of mediated and performed acts, then "Sheik" as a performance is no more or less real than gender as a performance.

Butler (1990) refines this argument in her book *Gender Trouble*. She dissolves the sex-gender binary entirely, writing that "if gender is the cultural meanings that the sexed body assumes, then a gender cannot be said to follow from a sex in any one way. Taken to its logical limit, the sex/gender distinction suggests a radical discontinuity between sexed bodies and culturally constructed genders" (6). To turn back toward Sheik, then, the fact that Zelda and Sheik are the same person has no bearing on the sex(es) or gender(s) of *either* identity. Instead, "gender is always a doing, though not a doing by a subject who might be said to preexist the deed" (Butler 1990, 25). Butler cautions that this doing is never a simple choice made by an individual in a vacuum and is instead informed and regulated by social practice: "A political genealogy of gender ontologies, if it is successful, will deconstruct the substantive appearance of gender into its constitutive acts and locate and account for those acts within the compulsory frames set by the various forces that police the social appearance of gender" (33). Butler's theory thus accounts for Sheik doubly. First, Sheik's body, however fans choose to imagine it, does not in any way constrain or restrict the character's performed gender. Second, that imagined body and the gender which is done to it are in fact mediated by the very fan debate that calls them into question.

Butler, however, only takes us halfway there. We cannot arrive at a conclusive treatment for Sheik solely by accepting Butler's assessment of gender as performative. Fortunately, Jack Halberstam's (1998) work on the subject of female and alternative masculinities is a useful starting point here for my specific discussion of the ambiguously gendered space occupied by Sheik. In *Female Masculinity*, Halberstam begins from the premise that biological maleness and masculinity can be separated but that alternative masculinities are habitually overshadowed and obscured by the reflexive cultural reaffirmation of a hegemonic white-male masculinity (2). As he elaborates, "Ambiguous gender, when and where it does appear, is inevitably transformed into deviance, thirdness, or a blurred version of either male or female" (20). Given Halberstam's emphasis of a deliberately practiced cultural blindness toward alternative gender identities and alternative masculinities, it's no surprise that the online gender debate concerning Sheik practices a similar blindness, focusing on an imagined body and largely bypassing the possibility of Sheik performing what amounts to a culturally invisible alternative masculinity. In many ways *Ocarina* enforces the gender binary both in and out of universe quite aggressively; interested parties need look no further than a North American 30-second commercial for the game hinging upon the tagline "Willst thou get the girl?/Or play like one?" (Nintendo 1998b). If the ad is to be taken literally, then it follows that in 1998 the very act of a female-identified person playing *Ocarina*—at least competently—was already an act of gender deviance or, to put it more positively, a site of alternative masculinity.

It is in *Female Masculinity* that Halberstam (1998) identifies the now-famous "bathroom problem," where interactions within a public space demonstrate how gender is explicitly segregated and policed (20). When Halberstam frames the problem by rhetorically asking "why do we still operate in a world that assumes that people who are not male are female, and people who are not female are male (and even that people who are not male are not people!)" (Ibid.), the accompanying commentary on the presumptions underlying the Sheik gender debate seems almost to write itself. Beyond the specific example of the bathroom as "an arena for the enforcement of gender conformity" (24), Halberstam asks "what makes femininity so approximate and masculinity so precise?" (28). Sheik, then, is policed so rigorously specifically because the character is presented imprecisely—with no actual body to give a semblance of "proof" to those who seek to preserve the binary. Indeed, if we step away from the public bathroom to observe how Sheik is policed in the public forum, inserting the character into Halberstam's own discourse, it might go something like this: "[Sheik] first appears as not-woman ... but then [Sheik] appears as something actually even more scary, not-man" (21).

This reading fits comfortably here, but Halberstam is writing about the struggles of real-life human beings while Sheik, at the end of the day, is a video game character. This caveat also has implications for our application of Butler's model of gender as a socially directed and reaffirmed performance. Indeed, how can we, given the technological and narrative constraints of *Ocarina* as a game and story world, even begin to approach a gender performance of any kind by any character in this game? What do any of these characters actually *do* that might be called a performance of their gender? The Halberstam bathroom problem is challenging on the face of it to apply to *Ocarina's* game world, where there are so few actual interactions between characters, to say nothing of policing those interactions. What constitutes a public space in Hyrule when the non-player characters cannot be said to have any actual awareness of one another?

The solution is to acknowledge that the game world is *written* in a way which has been informed in many ways by real-world cisgender hegemony but that it nonetheless *operates* under a different set of rules and constraints dictating what a character can and can't do regardless of their gender. Rather than simply transposing our own knowledge of gender norms, performativity, and policing wholesale onto Hyrule, we need to examine the game on its own terms to arrive at a better-informed sense of what it actually means to be masculine, feminine, or neither in the fantasy kingdom.

Gender Roles in Hyrule

In terms of behavior, Sheik is certainly a more dynamic, action-oriented persona than Zelda. In fact, this points to an identifiable facet of gender roles in Hyrule: masculinity is defined by mobility and action, while femininity is defined by immobility and helplessness. To frame this idea in Butler's (1988) terms, immobility is a socially prescribed set of acts (or in this case, non-acts) which constitutes a sense of "doing" a female gender in Hyrule, while mobility and activity do the same for a male gender. During the childhood phase of the game, the Princess Zelda remains in Hyrule Castle. Rather than acting directly in the interests of the kingdom, she dispatches Link on a quest to gather the spiritual stones hidden throughout the land. Only when her personal safety is threatened does she leave the castle, and even then she is literally carried out by her bodyguard Impa on horseback (more on Impa shortly).

Players are offered one clue that the childhood incarnation of Zelda performs her gender in any way other than feminine-immobile. A secret gossip stone, when spoken to with the correct item, will communicate the following: "They say that contrary to her elegant image, Princess Zelda of Hyrule Castle is, in fact, a tomboy!" Tomboyism, which Halberstam (1998) defines as "an extended childhood period of female masculinity" (5), ultimately proves to have no direct bearing on the childhood representation of the princess in-game. Instead, the line proves to be doubly prophetic, both of Zelda's future time living as Sheik and of her eventual reversion back to her feminine-coded princess identity. As Halberstam (1998) observes, "We could say that tomboyism remains tolerated as long as the child remains prepubescent; as soon as puberty begins, however, the full force of gender conformity descends on the girl" (6). Correspondingly, Sheik proves in the end to be a temporary identity.

The adult incarnation of Princess Zelda is similarly immobile to what we see of her childhood analogue, in spite of her extended time as the more action-oriented Sheik. Near the end of the game, Sheik meets Link in the Temple of Time and uses the Triforce of Wisdom to return to the Zelda persona. After she advances the plot and her expository use is at an end, Zelda is immediately found by Ganondorf and captured. Of note in this scene is the nature of Zelda's capture: she is literally trapped in a giant pink crystal in the shape of a rupee—the currency of Hyrule. The scene borders on comical in its absurdity but also gestures pointedly to one of the main ideas in Gayle Rubin's (1975) landmark essay "The Traffic in Women," wherein she invokes Marx to argue that the sex/gender system in capitalist society frames women largely as vessels for a capital-driven sexual exchange between patriarchal familial units. Zelda in her female persona, then, is literally commoditized and immobilized within a giant crystalline coin and waits out the rest of the game to be rescued by Link. After he does so, she accompanies him out of the crumbling castle, unlocking doors with her magic along the way, until the pair is confronted by Ganondorf once more, who transforms at last into the beastly Ganon. During this fight, Zelda assumes a support role, using her magic while standing outside the arena to immobilize and seal Ganon after Link bests him at actual swordplay. The last we see of Zelda, she is standing still once more, seemingly in the clouds, as she sends Link back to his own timeline.

In her YouTube series *Tropes vs. Women in Video Games*, Anita Sarkeesian (2013) highlights the dichotomy between Sheik's more active role and Zelda's comparative helplessness by placing her in a subset of her Damsel in Distress trope called the "Helpful Damsel." Sarkeesian notes that Zelda is "at her best" in the series when assuming the Sheik persona but reiterates that even this role is bookended by the immobile and helpless Zelda role. Sheik's independent value as a transgressive character is nonetheless upheld with Sarkeesian's reminder that "the Damsel in Distress as a plot device is something that happens *to* a female character."

This also serves as a reminder of Butler's (1988) idea that gender, even theoretically framed as a performance, is not something done freely by the individual, but rather negotiated by social practice. Butler states that it is "clearly unfortunate grammar to claim that there is a 'we' or an 'I' that does its body" (521) and instead cautions that "the body is always an embodying *of* possibilities both conditioned and circumscribed by historical convention" (Ibid.). Susan Bordo (1993) takes up a similar thread when discussing the evolution of the "politics of the body" in feminist discourse, observing that "feminism imagined the human *body* as itself a politically inscribed entity, its physiology and morphology shaped and marked by histories and practices of containment and control" (188). Zelda's femininity, then, is demonstrated not only by her own actions but by the actions done to her both in and out of the game world, as evidenced by the historical processes that lead Ganondorf to commoditize Zelda and render her helpless. Likewise, Sheik's masculinity cannot be undermined by the actions done to Zelda but is identified as non-normative and thus ironically queered by fan efforts to police the character's gender.

Zelda's literal immobility points to a broader characterization of female characters in *Ocarina* as static, inactive characters. The other princess in the game, the Zora Ruto, refuses for a portion of the game to walk under her own power and must literally be carried through a dungeon by Link, who uses her to solve puzzles along the way. Other examples of conspicuously immobile female characters include a woman in Kakariko Village who needs her cuckoos rounded up and defers to Link for the task, citing a skin allergy, the rancher Malon who is blackmailed midway through the game by an insubordinate farmhand and placidly waits to be rescued by Link, and an unnamed resident of Hyrule Castle Town who sends a ten-year-old Link out after dark to fetch her prized dog rather than risk venturing outdoors herself.

Attentive readers have been readying a solid counter-argument to all this for several paragraphs: gameplay mechanics, rather than narrative conventions, are at the root of much of this state of affairs. Even in 1998 *Zelda* had already established itself as a formulaic series where a kingdom goes to rot and *all* of its citizens sit at home waiting to be saved by Link, who often appears to be the only one who does anything or goes anywhere. By this reading then, all of the characters discussed above are immobile not to satisfy Hylian gender norms but to satisfy gameplay conventions as quest givers and quest objects.

The problem with this dismissal is that while the majority of characters in *Ocarina* are immobile regardless of their gender, there are still a number of more active NPCs, and they are predominantly male. Here I use the word active quite literally; in contrast with the immobile women discussed previously who may as well be welded to the spot, all of these men actually move about the game world. These characters include the Running Man who circles Hyrule Field and will challenge Link to unwinnable footraces, the quartet of carpenters who roam aimlessly around town (and eventually even attempt to join the Gerudo tribe), the guards who patrol Hyrule Castle and must be stealthily avoided, the ghostly gravekeeper who races with Link through his own crypt, and certain members of the all-masculine Goron tribe who despite their slow manner of speech can roll around their city at a brisk clip. We can also count Ganondorf, who is depicted on horseback three times, chases after Zelda and Impa during their escape, and confronts Link as a boss twice, among the ranks of masculine-active characters in the game.

There are two major exceptions to this rule of feminine-immobile characters in *Ocarina*: the aforementioned Impa and the almost-all-feminine Gerudo tribe. Impa is presented as the last surviving member of the Sheikah tribe and is an active character similar to Sheik. Without fellow tribe members to compare (excepting Sheik, who assumes a Sheikah identity), we don't have enough information in the game to determine whether Sheikah gender roles differ from the Hylian mainstream. Indeed, Impa's last-of-her-tribe status establishes her as an "other" who already exists outside of hegemony before we even broach the topic of gender. Within the game's text, Impa is referred to with female pronouns four times, and one resident of Kakariko Village describes her as "a great woman." Impa further presents a unique case in the game by having a character model which is both feminine-coded (with highly pronounced breasts and hips) and overtly muscular; no other female character in the game presents such an imposing physique (see Fig. 6.3). While this, as well as her active role, may suggest that Impa is "doing" her gender incorrectly by Hylian standards, her position as Zelda's confidant and protector demonstrates that Impa holds an obvious place of trust in the kingdom. It is possible that the kingdom tolerates gender disruptions on an individual basis. After all, as a loyal servant to the crown as well as the lone survivor of a culture bordering on extinction, Impa poses little immediate threat to the hegemony.

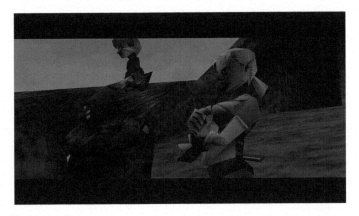

Fig. 6.3 Impa

The Gerudo, on the other hand, who appear in the game with force of numbers, are less fortunate. Most of them behave identically to the castle guards, patrolling their desert fortress with the player being tasked with staying out of their line of sight. Four of them actually serve as mini-bosses and fight Link directly with paired scimitars, while two of them, Koume and Kotake, collectively serve as a full-fledged dungeon boss with a developed backstory.

In the end, however, the Gerudo only serve to reinforce Hylian gender normativity, because their status as an all-female tribe of warriors exacerbates their otherness to the kingdom's other denizens. As Butler (1988) observes, "Discrete genders are part of what 'humanizes' individuals within contemporary culture; indeed, those who fail to do their gender right are regularly punished" (522). Based on the patterns we have identified for gender identities in Hyrule, the Gerudo are performing their gender incorrectly en masse and so are punished by the wider society of the kingdom.

Furthermore, the gender performance of the Gerudo in Hyrule is complicated by their racist depiction. In her video "Not Your Exotic Fantasy," Sarkeesian (2017) traces the phenomenon of exotification in games, observing that "Harmful, ignorant, racist stereotypes have been used in the design of supporting characters and enemies in games for decades, and often the result is female characters who are both sexualized and exotified." The Gerudo, who are the darkest-skinned characters in the game and evoke Middle Eastern stereotypes in the design of their clothing, weaponry, and architecture, are regarded by other characters in the game with a level of mistrust bordering on racism and are presented to the player in an almost-entirely adversarial capacity. In contrast with the castle guards, with whom the only possible interaction is to be caught and ejected from the castle, the Gerudo guards can be snuck up on and "stunned" by the player with projectiles or even the sword. The castle guards, who enforce the law of the hegemony, are untouchable, while by contrast the game encourages the player to perform violence upon the Gerudo guards, who are gender-deviant women of color.

But what about the most active citizen in Hyrule of all: the player character? Link's depiction in the game corresponds uncannily with Halberstam's (1998) reading of James Bond's representation of masculinity in the film *GoldenEye*. Halberstam writes that "Masculinity ... has little if anything to do with biological maleness and signifies more often as a technical special effect" (3). Zeroing in on Bond, Halberstam continues: "When you take his toys away, Bond has very little propping up his performance of masculinity. Without the slick suit, the half-smile, the cigarette lighter that transforms into a laser gun, our James is a hero without the action or the adventure" (4). Link, by comparison, leans heavily on his enormous arsenal of tools, weapons, and accessories, and his own "slick suit" becomes an heirloom passed down to future heroes in subsequent games of the series. He certainly seems to need a lot more help getting around than a certain ninja.

Sheik's Alternative Masculinity

This at long last brings us back to Sheik. More important than Link's reliance on toys is the subversion of his overt male masculinity in the game to Sheik's alternative masculinity. Halberstam (1998) writes, "In Goldeneye is it M who most convincingly performs masculinity, and she does so partly by exposing the sham of Bond's own performance" (4). This reading lends itself easily to Sheik, who guides Link about the kingdom, always keeps two steps ahead of him, does so without the benefit of any visible gadgets excepting smoke bombs and a harp, and even warns the hero off from confrontation where he is out of his depth.

In comparison to the feminine-immobile role played by Zelda, Sheik assumes a comparatively masculine-active role. The ninja appears to follow Link all over the kingdom, confronting him at the entryway to each of the six temples in order to offer advice and teach him an Ocarina song. It doesn't matter how remote or dangerous the temple grounds are, nor how long the player struggles in real time to get to these locations: Sheik is always there first and always leaves first. Most of these encounters conclude with Link attempting to get closer to Sheik, only for the latter to depart with a mixture of physical agility and smoke bombs.

During a mid-game encounter in Kakariko, Sheik enters the fray in earnest. Warning Link to keep back in a bid to protect him, Sheik fights the revenant Bongo Bongo but is violently thrown around by the invisible monster. As if to dispel any notion that the leading man might do better, Link is dispatched in identical fashion and indeed remains incapacitated for longer, as he wakes up with Sheik looking down at him.

Based on our foundation for what constitutes masculine and feminine behavior in Hyrule, Sheik is most definitely "doing" male gender, regardless of how the disguise is maintained or how deep it goes beneath the outfit. Based on the conditions of gender normativity observed in the fantasy world of the game, Sheik is certainly practicing *a* masculinity; furthermore, the very act of questioning whether or not this is a male masculinity or a female masculinity ensures that at the very least this is an alternative masculinity whether the answer is either, both, or neither. Likewise, Zelda is "doing" a female gender, and as Sarkeesian (2013) might frame it, in turn has the female-coded damsel role "done" to her.

What, then, are the consequences of Sheik's ambiguous, alternative masculinity for a game that otherwise polices the gender binary in a very conventional way and for a community which in turn polices Sheik in an effort to force the character into that binary? The answer is that regardless of the other issues in the game of racism and sexism, the out-of-date gender representations in the game's marketing, or even authorial intent, Sheik's ambiguous and alternative performance of masculinity constitutes a subversive act which undermines the gender binary. The very fact that fans have been willing to split into binary-driven either-or camps and argue about imaginary bodies for the better part of two decades proves conclusively that Sheik is a disruptive force that destabilizes the gender binary in games. It is here, outside the narrative confines of the game and within the public discourse of online fandom, that Butler's (1988) theory of gender performativity carries the most weight for the character. Her words about how those who fail to perform their genders are punished (522) ring especially true here. The online fandom, then, punishes and dehumanizes Sheik for failing to do "gender" correctly, ultimately reaffirming that Sheik's character within *Ocarina* is subversive.

Beyond *Ocarina*

While I have argued thus far for a subversive reading of Sheik as a character who deliberately flouts the gender binary, it's worth considering that this is not the only—or even the first—instance of Nintendo toying with the gender identity of its characters. Looking back, many players can recount the by-now almost mythical tale of how the original North American release of *Metroid* for the Nintendo Entertainment System came with packaging and instructional materials referring to its newcomer protagonist Samus Aran as a "he." Brianna Wu and Ellen McGrody (2015) even argue for Samus as a transgender woman, citing a 1994 interview where one of Samus' original character designers, Hirofumi Matsuoka, refers to Samus as "not a woman" but instead "newhalf" (a Japanese term, sometimes used pejoratively, which has been used to describe everything from people of mixed race to pre-transition transgender individuals). It's hardly ironclad, but that's not at all the point Wu and McGrody set out to make; instead they are showcasing that even in popular mainstream titles—and even when associated developers give potentially harmful takes on their own work—it is possible to position established characters like Samus as positive sites of disruption. In such a context, it becomes a lot more plausible that Sheik can be positioned to serve similarly subversive goals.

On the other hand, fans have also quoted Nintendo in an effort to foreclose gender debates. When *Polygon* reached out to Nintendo for comment on the "Sheik Gender Debate" in 2014, senior product manager Bill Trinen answered the call and gave an official statement: "The definitive answer is that Sheik is a woman—simply Zelda in a different outfit" (Riendeau 2014). Though many fans take this statement as tantamount to the word of God, as evidenced by the long thread of comments on the same *Polygon* article expressing relief that the debate is finally "over," this is in fact no more conclusive an argument than the quote from Matsuoka about Samus.

In defense of Trinen's position, we can point to the steady feminization of Sheik in the character's subsequent appearances in other Nintendo games. In successive entries of the *Super Smash Bros.* series, Sheik's visual depiction as a playable character has involved a widening of the hips and bust, evoking a more overtly feminine body (see Fig. 6.4). Trophy descriptions for the character in these games also refer to the character universally as "she." *Hyrule Warriors*, released in 2014 for the Wii U, hedges its bets more carefully. The game specifically avoids using any pronouns whatsoever in relation to Sheik, but in a Nintendo Direct online video presentation showcasing the game prior to its release, a specific pronoun is used: "Much like Impa, she's a remaining survivor of the Sheikah" (Nintendo 2014a). Additionally, the in-game character retains a more feminized design consistent with recent depictions, seemingly solidifying Nintendo's contemporary perspective that Sheik is a woman. Furthermore, the next alterego that Princess Zelda canonically assumes after *Ocarina* is her identity as the pirate captain Tetra in 2003's *The Legend of Zelda: The Wind Waker*. Though Tetra herself is a subversive charac-

Fig. 6.4   Sheik as depicted in *Super Smash Bros. for Wii U* (Nintendo 2014b)

ter with a high degree of agency and autonomy, she is referred to in-game exclusively by female pronouns and no corresponding debate has emerged regarding that character's imagined body.

This, however, does not constitute direct proof of Sheik's gender identity in the original 1998 *Ocarina*, and indeed we can point to a recent act of *deliberate* gender-bending by Nintendo in the form of Linkle, a female version of Link debuting in *Hyrule Warriors Legends* for Nintendo 3DS. 2017's *The Legend of Zelda: Breath of the Wild* even allows Link to obtain Sheik's mask and dress up as the character, though the game problematically also requires Link to cross-dress in a separate instance in order to infiltrate the Gerudo Village, thoughtlessly preying upon the anxieties Halberstam (1998) associates with the bathroom problem 20 years prior.

When Sheik is more explicitly feminized, this can be interpreted as a retcon of the original character. Nintendo, for their part, have demonstrated that they are aware of the waves that ripple through their online fandom, as evidenced by their recent responses to controversies surrounding *Tomodachi Life* and *Fire Emblem Fates*. In both cases we see a public response—an apology on Nintendo's part for insensitivity regarding same-sex relationships, either through omission in *Tomodachi Life* (Schreier 2014) or conversion to heterosexual normativity in *Fire Emblem Fates* (Frank 2016). Framed through this context, we might wonder at Nintendo's view of the online gender debate with Sheik. Nintendo has indeed dodged the question for years by retconning the character and introducing less androgynous versions which avoid inciting further debate. Trinen's "definitive" answer thus arrives only after years of presenting the public with "revised" versions of Sheik who by their very design attempt to foreclose the debate altogether.

Conclusion

"What if Zelda was a girl?" reads a humorous t-shirt (Shirtoid 2014) which satirizes the potential confusion over the fact that the series is named after its princess rather than its protagonist. The t-shirt features a gender-swapped (and rather curvaceous) artistic rendering of Link, further adding to the joke, a joke which has come true with the introduction of the official gender-swapped Linkle in *Hyrule Warriors Legends*. Though the shirt is sold and marketed for laughs, it nonetheless gestures quite earnestly toward an instability of the gender binary in the series, an instability which has at times elicited forceful responses from the fandom and has nowhere raised tempers so high as it has with Sheik. The subversive act of Sheik's character implies an opposite question to that of the shirt: "What if Zelda wasn't a girl?"

To the disappointment of the fandom and contrary to Nintendo's belated official response, there is no meaningful answer to either of these questions which arrives at any definitive conclusion about Sheik's imagined body. Sheik has no body. Any imagined body projected onto Sheik, whether by fans or Nintendo executives, is nothing more than an act of policing: an attempt by the hegemony to reassert its dominance by moving Sheik away from a position that disrupts the gender binary. What Sheik *is* is a site of alternative masculinity, a masculinity which is performed and maintained independently of the character's (nonexistent) body.

As Sarkeesian points to throughout her work, bodies in games, as in all popular media, are used to reinforce heteronormative discourses of sexism, racism, and ableism. On one hand, a digital "body," which can be quantified and studied, is a thing of certainty, with known observable properties. But none of those observable properties actually constitute gender. A polygon mesh has no gender until some other aspect of the game identifies it as having one. The impulse to assign a gender to an imagined digital body is an import from the heteronormative anxieties of the material world; the digital body is itself perfectly ambiguous. Ambiguity is thus Sheik's ethos and endures as *The Legend of Zelda: Ocarina of Time*'s most significant contribution to gender representation in games.

Bibliography

Bordo, Susan. 1993. Feminism, Foucault and the Politics of the Body. In *Up Against Foucault: Explorations of Some Tensions Between Foucault and Feminism*, ed. Caroline Ramazanoglu, 179–202. Hove: Psychology Press.

Butler, Judith. 1988. Performative Acts and Gender Constitution: An Essay in Phenomenology and Feminist Theory. *Theatre Journal* 40 (4): 519–531.

———. 1990. *Gender Trouble: Feminism and the Subversion of Identity*. New York: Routledge.

Frank, Allegra. 2016. Nintendo Changes Controversial *Fire Emblem Fates* Scene for Western Launch. *Polygon*. Last Modified January 21, 2016. http://www.polygon. com/2016/1/21/10810944/fire-emblem-fates-nintendo-drugging-scene.

Halberstam, Judith. 1998. *Female Masculinity*. Durham: Duke University Press.

Jun Mizusawa. 2015. *Wikipedia*. Last Modified November 9, 2015. https://en.wiki-pedia.org/wiki/Jun_Mizusawa.

Nintendo. 1998a. *The Legend of Zelda: Ocarina of Time*. Nintendo 64 Game.

———. 1998b. *Zelda: Ocarina of Time Commercial*. YouTube Video, 0:30. Posted December 31, 2007. https://www.youtube.com/watch?v=gY4I31YpVqk.

———. 2003. *The Legend of Zelda: The Wind Waker*. Nintendo GameCube Game.

———. 2014a. *Hyrule Warriors Direct 8.4.2014*. Filmed August 4. YouTube Video, 26:22. Posted August 4, 2014. https://www.youtube.com/watch?v=3_DZtTR3zu0#t=527.

———. 2014b. *Super Smash Bros. for Wii U*. Wii U Game.

———. 2017. *The Legend of Zelda: Breath of the Wild*. Nintendo Switch Game.

Riendeau, Danielle. 2014. Zelda Fans Debate Sheik's Gender, But Here's Nintendo's Final Word. *Polygon*. Last Modified August 5, 2014. http://www.polygon. com/2014/8/5/5948989/zelda-nintendo-sheik-gender-cosplay.

Rubin, Gayle. 1975. *The Traffic in Women*. New York: Monthly Review Press.

Sarkeesian, Anita. 2013. *Damsel in Distress: Part 1 – Tropes vs. Women in Video Games*. YouTube Video, 23:34. Posted March 7, 2013. https://www.youtube.com/watch?v=X6p5AZp7r_Q.

———. 2017. *Not Your Exotic Fantasy – Tropes vs. Women in Video Games*. YouTube Video, 12.12. Posted January 31, 2017. https://www.youtube.com/watch?v=K2hYdBxxTTM.

Schreier, Jason. 2014. Nintendo Apologizes For Not Putting Gay Marriage In *Tomodachi Life*. *Kotaku*. Last Modified May 9, 2014. http://kotaku.com/nin-tendo-apologizes-for-not-putting-gay-marriage-in-tom-1574185262.

Sheik Gender Discussion. 2010. *Zelda Dungeon*. Last Modified June 13, 2010. http://zeldadungeon.net/forum/threads/sheik-gender-discussion.9681/.

Sheik's Gender. 2010. *Zelda Universe*. Last Modified September 15, 2010. http://zeldauniverse.net/forums/Thread/102163-Sheik-s-gender/?pageNo=1.

What If Zelda Was a Girl? 2014. *Shirtoid*. http://shirtoid.com/109093/what-if-zelda-was-a-girl/.

Wu, Brianna, and Ellen McGrody. 2015. *Metroid's* Samus Aran Is a Transgender Woman. Deal With It. *The Mary Sue*. Last Modified September 1, 2015. http://www.themarysue.com/metroids-samus-aran-transgender-woman/.

7

Maidens and Muscleheads, White Mages and Wimps, from the Light Warriors to *Lightning Returns*

Mark Filipowich

Heroes flee a burning town on the outskirts of a peaceful republic; a lone cyber punk leaps into action somewhere in an industrial cityscape: there have been enough permutations in the *Final Fantasy* formula that by now the tropes the series pioneered circled back from clichés. The *Final Fantasy* series has enjoyed a rare staying power in videogames, a medium not only compelled by technology's narrative of progress but burdened with a cost and time-intensive production process with little room for self-reflection. Each new *Final Fantasy* is connected, with rare but noteworthy exceptions, only by vague thematic and tropic commonalities and a slowly mutating set of game rules. Released in 1987 by Squaresoft, the original *Final Fantasy*, along with rival-turned-merger partner Enix's *Dragon Quest*, formed the archetypal Japanese role-playing game (JRPG). Though there is considerable cross-pollination between Japanese and Western RPGs, a number of characteristics have distinguished the JRPG from the outset, as described by Matt Fox (2013):

> Unlike Western RPGs where you usually create a character from scratch, JRPGs tend to cast you as a pre-established character—in Dragon Quest you are the descendant of the mighty Erdrick—and rather than simply slaying and looting you are given an emotional hook, in this case it's your relationship as rescuer and companion to the Princess Gwaelin. Because of the fewer control options JRPGs also tend to play more as "stop start" affairs than their western counterparts. The exploring is frequently broken up with menu selections, inventory tweaking,

M. Filipowich (✉)
Concordia University, Montreal, QC, Canada

© The Author(s) 2018
T. Harper et al. (eds.), *Queerness in Play*, Palgrave Games in Context,
https://doi.org/10.1007/978-3-319-90542-6_7

turn-based battles with enemies, and conversations between party members or NPCs [non-playable characters]. It's a gameplay style that's attuned to the Japanese way of doing things. It doesn't rush the player, rather it allows the story to resonate and for all strategies to be considered. (87)

The distinction between WRPGs and JRPGs is less based on a geography of production than of content. Significantly, Fox's description of *Dragon Quest*—which he claims to be the first JRPG (86)—is guided by the premise of a classically gendered tale of a heroic knight rescuing and falling in love with a damsel in distress. Indeed, gender dynamics remain as important to the genre now as in its beginning. Yet as the legacy of classical gendered and sexed narratives remains entrenched in JRPGs such as *Final Fantasy*, gendered and sexed representations are more complicated than a knight's pursuit of a princess. Although *Final Fantasy* often upholds heteronormative gender roles and narratives, throughout the series there are numerous instances of "queering" the narrative in particular figures and events. Such moments of nonnormative gender and sexuality do not "counter-balance" the otherwise regulatory gender narratives, but they do expose the performativity of gender and empower subjects outside traditional gender norms. Moreover, as globalized texts, *Final Fantasy*'s gender roles must negotiate within the norms of very different cultures. As a result, the "queering" of a figure to one audience may be normative to another which highlights not only gender's fluidity but the extent to which social factors author its scripts.

The narrative analysis I present here should not be taken as a comprehensive approach to the whole series, nor do I wish to argue that it constitutes some emancipation from gender oppression. Indeed, because *Final Fantasy* is created to net profit from a global audience, its challenges to hegemonic scripts like gender will always remain within the bounds of mainstream acceptability. Still, there are several textual moments in various *Final Fantasy* titles that stress the performative nature of gender and "queer" heroism and power. While I don't wish to discount work into how game production and consumption is gendered, my scope here is limited to a textual analysis of games in the series because the JRPG—a genre that not merely includes but indeed has been shaped by over two decades of *Final Fantasy* entries—is a far more narratively oriented genre than many other genres. Furthermore, the capacity to interpret and compose narratives is central to cognitive and social development (Genereux and McKeough 2007), and play has long assisted in guiding girls to embody domestic qualities (Lazzaro 2008). The narrative tropes typically at play in the *Final Fantasy* series provide useful tools for analyzing the dynamics of power working to both maintain and disrupt globalized and gendered hegemonies.

Before engaging with the texts themselves, it is important to recognize the cultural conditions that produced *Final Fantasy*. Since the late 1990s, the English-speaking world has been engaged in what Sugiura Tsutomu calls a "third-generation Japanism," distinct from the turn of the century and post-war generations in that this latest permutation both holds mainstream appeal—particularly for young people—and that "through the personalities and lifestyles of the characters featured in these media ... young people around the world are exposed to, and may come to know, the soul and cultures of Japanese people..." (2008, 134). During this period, Japanese domestic revenue from cultural products remained stable, even though output increased. The spike in productivity was aimed to meet growing demand abroad, and creative industries maintained a particularly "Japanese" voice (unlike the previous generations of Japanism) (Tsutomu, 137–142). *Final Fantasy*, along with animation and comics, reached Europe and America in the late 1980s and doubtlessly had a role in nurturing the development of third-generation Japanism. At this time, Japanese cultural products emphasize their culture of origin, but they do so to appeal internationally. While no text should be propped up as a perfect representation of any cultural time or place, *Final Fantasy* is an especially powerful combination of local and global gender scripts. So although *Final Fantasy* is certainly a product of Japanese culture, it is important to note its development during a time of the country's heightened international activity. *Final Fantasy*, by design, speaks as much to young console owners in America, Brazil, or Germany as to those in Japan. Thus a critique of *Final Fantasy*'s gender representations must address the gender roles around its production without tokenizing Japanese culture while also addressing a globalized narrative of heteronormativity without appropriating the voices that created it.

In turning to third-generation Japanism's milieu, it is important to acknowledge the shifting gender and sex dynamics occurring in Japan at the time. Though media in Japan, like elsewhere, targets audiences along pre-established gender lines, discerning what material is acceptable for whom is not as strictly policed in Japan as in western cultures (Ito 2008) and the content of this media has maintained a much more fluid gender binary than the west (Ligman 2014). Although gender roles in both the consumption and content of Japanese popular fiction are different than elsewhere, it is still the case that manga (comics) and anime (cartoons) supported a burgeoning subculture in the 1980s United States, which in turn developed global mainstream appeal in the 1990s. Through manga, anime, and, eventually, videogames, Japanese popular fiction has become a globalized cultural phenomenon that shapes the ideological self-image of audiences in North America, Europe, Southeast Asia, and elsewhere (McKevitt 2010). Significantly *Final Fantasy*'s tenure overlaps with the proliferation of Japanese pop fiction abroad, and thus the gender codes represented therein—while still a product of Japanese game developers—also provide a space for non-Japanese players to explore alternative gender scripts and restructure those of their domestic culture.

Exposure to alternative gender scripts affects the capacity to offer one's own cultural norms:

> I think that the high level of involvement in which we perceive our bodies and identities: this is what I call *inner-actions*, following Elvira Mortensen's definition of inner-action (1996) as the mental activity activated by the game, in which the player creates an understanding of an action and, consequently, an understanding of his/her identity. (Fantone 2003)

Recall that a focus on start-stop narrative is, along with the location of production, the key generic criterion for the JRPG, so if acting is identifying, then *Final Fantasy* impels its player to inner-act according to a gender script that is at once Japanese in that these games are developed within a specific culture and international in that *Final Fantasy*, like much Japanese culture created during the decades of its existence, is designed with an international audience in mind. Thus *Final Fantasy* must offer its player a recognizable gender script, yet also provides space for alternatives. The demand to both conform to and permit deviance from encultured gender scripts is a rare duality, and even among videogames it seems that only JRPGs are so consistently structured to treat the player as at once the subjective participant and objective audience in the drama. It is most certainly the case that *Final Fantasy*'s fiction is maintained by the balance:

> In terms of its interactive function, then, [*Final Fantasy VII*] is not only offering a narrative statement but telling the player to do something—in effect, telling the player to insert herself into the transitivity system of the game. (Burn and Schott 2004)

As the player must identify *as* the avatar and recognize the distinct identity *of* the avatar, so too must their implicit understanding of gender norms accept those presented in the game while in turn restructuring according to the representations of gender in the game. This is especially pertinent as Japanese popular culture, both at home and abroad, has a complex recent history of regulating and disrupting gender expectations.

For instance, early internationally successful anime such as *Space Battleship Yamato* in 1977 negotiated a masculine war fantasy in the context of postwar Japan's constitutional prohibition from organized armament:

> By eliminating the American presence from the anime and by casting Japanese men as the protectors, *Yamato* presents a counternarrative to the "foundational narrative," a fantasy against the dominant narrative of the past and present of postwar Japan. This is not just postwar Japan's fantasy: it is a male fantasy.
>
> Masculinity is not a fixed attribute of the male body but a constantly negotiated social construction... Japanese masculinity is no exception. (Mizuno 2007)

Likewise, anime since the 1960s has represented femininity with similar ambivalence, such as the "magical girl" subgenre's empowerment of female figures that paradoxically directs them to roles accepted within traditional patriarchies:

> The magical girl as a genre consciously takes advantage of the oxymoronic rhetoric of "magic," a semantic tool that provides different, often opposite, meanings about women's duties, power, and sexuality. It is not an exaggeration to say that the genre's progress corresponds to the development of the visual and narrative rhetoric that skillfully encompasses the conservative agenda of the genre. (Saito 2014)

So gender in Japanese popular media expresses a national identification with pacifism—a feminine-coded trait—while offering some mode of masculine empowerment to hyper-feminized figures, each of which are directed toward securing a conservative imagined gender binary.

Yet, this gender binary remains equivocal, especially as Japanese popular fiction reached out to international audiences and fans developed communities and fan fictions based on well-known stories (Saito). Meanwhile, outside of these aesthetic movements, feminist organizations in Japan developed cultural and political initiatives. The study of gender in Japan arose congruently with American second-wave feminism, though not, as is commonly believed, contingently, as Ueno Chizuko explains:

> There are several reasons why we decided to call the anthology "Feminism in Japan." First, we wanted to dispel the prejudice that Japanese feminism is a "Western Import": and prove that it has its own raise-d'etre and its own original voices and discourses. Second, we wanted to work against the myth of one ethnic Japanese nation and to emphasize that among these voices, there have been important contributions made by non-Japanese, such as Korean women living in Japan. (1996)

Japanese feminism is often framed as a derivative of English-speaking gender movements, even by conservative groups within Japan. Thus, the context of *Final Fantasy*'s development is colored both by a globalized aesthetic that negotiates its own gendered anxieties and desires and the country's engagement with women's rights and research. Like many other artifacts of Japan's postwar culture, *Final Fantasy* is replete with the tensions of traditional gender scripts under the duress of an ever-changing modernity:

> The idealized traditional roles of women associated with the images of mother, wife and *geisha* persist in the psyche of the Japanese simultaneously with social change and trends that produce another set of expectations, pressures and practices that are in turn reproducing culture and altering the lives of women and men in Japan. (Chizuko)

Final Fantasy is caught directly in this cultural ebb and flow; as tempting as it is to declare *Final Fantasy* as either a purely domestic product or as an entirely postmodern global text subject only to reader response, the interplay of domestic and global aesthetic movements must be considered in analyzing how *Final Fantasy* represents and resists gendered performance.

With some notable exceptions the *Final Fantasy* games feature mostly male playable characters, with women playable characters generally falling into the category of either a mother, a maiden, or a child. Later installments parallel this trifecta of benevolent femininity with villainous women characters fitting into a corresponding category of shrew, whore, or brat (Welldon). Throughout the series, then, a clear gendered code is established and enforced through these characters, and while they may hold a measure of power in these roles, their first and most assertive traits are associations to their capacities as nurturers of men; particularly for those women in the "maiden" role who, unsurprisingly, are most frequently the story's main love interest. The maiden is often an object of purity, a figurehead of some power structure such as a princess, religious figure, or a mystical source of planetary renewal: the maiden is somewhat naïve, inexperienced, but shown to be caring of others and troubled by the weight of her concerns. In this way, the maiden acts as the phallus in Butler's theory of performative gender:

> [she is] the Phallus in the sense that they maintain the power to reflect or represent the "reality" of the self-grounding postures of the masculine subject, a power which, if withdrawn, would break up the foundational illusions of the masculine subject position. In order to "be" the Phallus, the reflector and guarantor of an apparent masculine subject position, women must become, must "be" (in the sense of "posture as if they were") precisely what men are not and, in their very lack, establish the essential function of men. (1990)

The maiden's emphasized femininity acts as a necessary foil to masculinity, an Other that lacks all that can be assigned to masculinity: stoicism, aggression, bravery, with particular emphasis "to the no-nonsense aspect of masculinity, to the idea that masculinity 'just is' whereas femininity reeks of the artificial" (Halberstam 1998). Femininity is earnest only to be captured by the "real man" to prove his masculinity.

The first and most emblematic maiden figure appears in the first *Final Fantasy*[1] as a minor NPC named Princess Sarah. Sarah is a beautiful, demure, and young royal kidnapped by the villain Garland to be rescued by the player's team of four playable characters. These Light Warriors, as they are called in the game, are not given any dialogue, do not demonstrate any personality traits, and are distinguishable only by their mechanical combat roles. This convention, known as the "silent protagonist" in videogames, has declined since the late 1980s but is often cited as a digital attempt to capture the self-dramatization of tabletop role-playing. It is not accurate to call the characters total blank slates, as they remain characterized in less direct ways, but the attempt is nonetheless assumed as an effort to hand authorial control to the player (Dickenson 2011). Importantly, these figures are given nonverbal personality cues, and, early on, all of the heroes are coded as male with the exception of the white mage, the healer, who is coded as female by a long flowing robe, fair hair, and softer lines. In the first three installments of the series, most characterization is silently presumed. In the first *FF*, four player-created heroes who occupied one of six strategic combat roles (these roles would later be called "jobs" and would become an aesthetic and mechanical staple in the series, its spin-offs, and many of its derivatives). The first *FF*'s character classes are generally androgynous, but the medic or healer—the white mage, as the series calls it—is coded as female in the game's many remakes and remastered releases. Indeed, throughout the whole series, aside from those games where jobs may be selected by players, very few white mages are men and the primary female characters who do occupy this role are often the "maidens" in the narrative. Of those in the series where combat jobs cannot be chosen, those in the maiden role act as white mages, and all but a few are primary love interests.

However, by *FF4*, the maiden figure, the noblewoman Rosa, is a permanent, playable, and characterized member of the main cast. While Rosa is much more complex a character than Sarah, she too is a template of later maidens in the series. Though she abandons her evil king to track down her betrothed, the knight and main character, Cecil. Rosa's adventurous exploits happen off-screen. By the time the player finds her, she is comatose and faces death without a rare flower, which the player must navigate many dungeons to find. Rosa is competent, but not so competent that she may adventure independent of her male love interest; she is desired, but only in a chaste and knightly way that motivates further male adventure. Moreover, like many maidens to follow—like Aerith (*FF7*), Rinoa (*FF8*), Garnet (*FF9*), Yuna (*FF10, FF10-2*), and Vanille (*FF13, FF13-2*)—Rosa's primary job is the party's healer. Although Rosa does exhibit characteristics that deviate from her coded gender, what the player sees and experiences of her personality is mostly subservient femininity rather than alternate expressions of gender. Yet, as we shall see, in *Final Fantasy*, gendered relationships are disrupted as often as they are maintained. This is particularly the case for the series' other two forms of emphasized femininity, the mother and the child, and for masculinized subjects.

Those who act as child figures are, if not actual children, characterized by a sprightly demeanor, a curious eccentricity, and a small physical frame. Such child characters are often as vulnerable and physically weak as maidens like Rosa, but they possess powers and mechanical utilities that extend beyond healing wounded comrades. Rydia (also from *FF4*), Relm (*FF6*), and Eiko (*FF9*) are all powerful sorceresses whose magic is an offensive asset and even Eiko, another healer, has a more rounded toolset than her maiden counterpart. Moreover, many child figures, such as Yuffie (*FF7*), Selphie (*FF8*), and Rikku (*FF10, FF10-2*) are lithe, athletic ninjas and fighters characterized as much by their agility and offensive versatility as their helplessness. Interestingly, Relm, Rydia, and Eiko are all literal children, while Yuffie, Selphie, and Rikku are in their late teens. Although mechanically child characters tend to be as fragile as maiden characters, they are not limited to healer roles and support the party as "rogue"-type classes.[2] This suggests a looser gender script for the as-yet unmarriageable female members of *Final Fantasy*'s cast. Significantly, the child role is somewhat divided by those characters who are preteens and those who are late teens; while the late teens tend to be sexualized and tend to rely less on magical powers, all who fill the role are capricious, naïve, and short-tempered. The child character emphasizes potential rather than limitation. Where the maiden is framed as sacred to the world either through the divine circumstances of their birth (Terra, Aerith, Rhinoa, Garnet, Yuna) or their social position in an aristocracy (Sarah, Rosa, Ashe), the child is in a process of self-discovery and adventures as a way to achieve a greater sense of self. Although child characters require protection, lest they fall into an enemy's trap (like Rydia) or temporarily betray the rest of the party (like Yuffie). Child figures have space to make mistakes and grow independent of male party members, unlike maidens who are frequently only permitted to develop as characters in the context of their relationship to male characters, only act in supporting roles to the rest of the cast, and are placed on a narrative pedestal as sacred and delicate objects.

Finally, maternal characters are, again, if not older women, either are care-takers to other members of the cast by offering wisdom and enforcing etiquette, usually for some comedic effect. Matronly characters in the series occupy a more diverse set of jobs and require less protection than either of the other two main figures of femininity in the series, acting either as witches or even physically powerful fighters. The first matron appears in *FF2* through Maria, and both *FF4*'s Rydia and *FF6*'s Terra become mother figures after the former is put through a magical aging process and returns as a caretaker and more mature spell caster, and the latter builds an orphanage after the villain succeeds in his apocalyptic plan halfway through the game. Similarly, *FF7*'s Tifa, *FF8*'s Quistis, *FF10*'s Lulu, *FF10-2*'s Paine, *FF12*'s Fran, and *FF13*'s Fang each distinguish themselves in their respective ensembles as motherly figures to the other party members as guides and protectors. Only Rydia and Lulu are limited to the role of fragile mage, while the rest are archers, swashbucklers, martial artists, or knights. Mother characters are rarely kidnapped, often act as a source of wisdom to the protagonist, seldom show any physical intimacy with other party members even when they are involved in a romantic subplot (such as Lulu and, possibly, Tifa). Mother characters bear some responsibility for the rest of the cast's development, especially the central protagonist, and, compared with the child, remain largely static as characters. *FF6*, perhaps unique in that it has no obvious central protagonist, is far more oriented to group dynamics and socialization (Brice, "Ensemble" 2011a) while also lacking a clear maiden figure. However, while the burden of narration falls on Terra in the game's first half and on Celes on the second (two women), these characters exist in a sort of Othered femininity through their possession of magic (Hemmann 2016). Yet both are also effective swordfighters and caretakers. In *FF6*, the closest figure to a maiden becomes a mother, and as the iteration of the series with the least firmly established protagonist, the inclusion of two mother figures allows each of them to outgrow the constraints the series typically places on maiden figures. The mechanical function of matron figures is the most diverse and consequently the most transgressive in the series, occasionally adopting male-coded science-fiction and fantasy roles. Tellingly, those entries in the series with less emphasis on an individual male journey offer more space for transgressive matron figures to flourish.

These character types and mechanical classes align with regulated gender scripts and allow the male characters to act in a much wider scope of mechanical ability and possess far more varied aesthetic and narrative purpose. The activity of these avatars—and the separation of their prescribed freedoms along gender lines—is of special importance given that these virtual activities are often assigned in rules designed by programmers and designers who are largely men and the non-virtual "rules" of life are replicated in the digital space: "In the case of gender, the strict, omnipresent environment rules in videogames serve to 'keep girls out,' intimating other prevalent logics and structures in 'life,' and other real-world environments" (Burrill 2008). As in videogames at large, *Final Fantasy* reinstitutes the gender rules in its digital fantasy. Yet, to dismiss entirely the queering potential of represented bodies in this space as repetition of familiar gender scripts ignores both the Japanese influence on these norms and the cybernetic nature of bodies in games. While cinema is certainly a curated hyperreality, and theater is certainly an abstraction of events, videogame fiction conveys meaning in heavily abstract ways: characters denote agility with impossible leaps, wisdom through obtuse puzzles, beauty through grotesquely emphasized bodies (Filipowich 2014). Players operate within and outside the diegesis, and many of the artistic embellishments that in other media are used to gloss over disruptions of meaning (cameras follow action, close-ups capture emotion, etc.) are used in games to emphasize meaning (food restores a life source depleted by injury, nameless henchmen fall by the thousand to demonstrate a hero's power) or, as Laura Fantone writes, "Most videogames are characterized by accumulation and exaggeration as the logic regulating the event the player is involved in: recurrent risk of death, apocalyptic environmental catastrophes, climactic consequences of actions which involve unusual objects that symbolize weapons, psychic energies and magical powers" (2003). Abstractions, exaggerations, and the cybernetics between player and avatar augment the already complex gender scripts embedded in the *Final Fantasy* series.

Not only are videogame cybernetics able to "widen the horizons of feminist concepts of the body because they cross genders, species and human/machine distinctions" (Fantone 2003) but in the *Final Fantasy* series, where the player must associate with and understand a separation from their avatar (Burn and Schott), gender can never adequately reflect both the avatar's and the player's gender in the same gesture. The structures of gender are maintained through constant interpellation, demanding that the subject associate themselves with an ideal they are constantly reminded of (Vint 2007). But although the masculine hero Cecil of *FF4*, for example, may be interpellated as a masculine subject, that creates tension with the feminine player who must identify with him to play the game, just as the masculine player is called to identify with Lightning, a central hero of *FF13* and its two direct sequels. The resultant tension from the cybernetic break between the player and the characters they are impelled to identify with offers play inside gender scripts. This is particularly the case for male characters in the series. While women characters, particularly those outside the maiden role, bend gender standards either for the

Japanese patriarchy under which it was created or for the global patriarchy under which it is consumed, masculinity is not only more loosely codified, but it is often an obstacle to overcome. Many male *Final Fantasy* protagonists are androgynous, and while that androgyny is the cause for duress in some internet forums, within the texts, androgynous masculinity is precisely at the core of how these male heroes grow and become powerful.

Significantly, gender nonconforming men in Japanese popular fiction—while still often subject to transphobia or to reify patriarchal relationships (Brice 2011b "Atlus")—can be celebrated for performing outside gender codes. This is particularly the case for *bishōnen* fiction, a subgenre featuring feminized and sexualized male characters. In *bishōnen*, the largely female audience enjoys the growth and exploration of male sexuality beyond heteronormative limits: "*Bishōnen* represents and aesthetic preference in Asia that is embodied in a young man whose beauty (and sexual appeal) transcends the boundary of sex" (Chen 2007). Although JRPGs are seldom as definitively *bishōnen* texts (especially those imported to the west), they are created in a media landscape that permits such male queering, and they express a particularly Japanese inflection of masculinity in *Final Fantasy*. While it could be said that much of the queer masculinity in *Final Fantasy* or Japanese fiction in general is eschewed or diminished for European and American audiences, they nonetheless offer a space for alternative, androgynous, and/or queer masculinities to signify themselves.

While some entries in the series may assume a gender of its player, many of these heavily scripted games demand a space of play to relate with the main cast. Cecil in *FF4* begins the story as an accomplished warrior for the king; his face is obscured by black, spiked armor. Although he questions his king privately, Cecil only proves that he is an adequate challenge to an oppressive king by undergoing a bodily transformation from dark knight to paladin. The mechanics of Cecil's dark knight persona pair interestingly with his costume: as a dark knight, Cecil's contribution to combat is as an aggressive strongman who becomes more powerful when he injures himself to attack. Cecil's design, a man obscured by black armor, emphasize his stoicism, loyalty, and emotional reservation while his role in battle is reduced to a self-destructive aggression. However, as a paladin, Cecil's face is exposed, his blond hair flows in curled locks past his shoulders, his eyes widen and his face softens; likewise, Cecil as a paladin has a more rounded toolset that allows him to heal his comrades and stand in front of weaker party members. Cecil's power is in abandoning the strict, obedient, violent masculinity and in becoming less overtly masculine, Cecil develops a more complete role in the game. Moreover, to make this challenge possible, Cecil's new form must do battle with his dark knight persona. To defeat the dark knight persona, the game insists that Cecil must "give up your hate" and the player can only overcome the dark knight by refusing to attack him. To transform into his higher self, Cecil must mechanically reject the violence that had to that point defined him. In exchange, Cecil's aggressive combat skills are replaced with white magic to mend injured allies. In this instance, Cecil's masculinity is undercut and guides the major personal development in his adventure.

Likewise, *FF7*'s protagonist, Cloud, leaps into the decayed urban core of Midgar as an aloof mercenary. As the journey urges Cloud and his friends onward, he recounts several experiences with his hero-turned-nemesis, Sephiroth, a world renowned super soldier created out of the remains of an unearthed extraterrestrial. Sephiroth is a kind of public vindication of masculine power: he is mysterious, individualistic, and powerful. Importantly, Sephiroth is also alien. Halfway through *FF7* it is revealed that Cloud's sense of self is constructed out of the memories of another soldier, Zack. Cloud's memories as Sephiroth's sidekick and a burgeoning war hero are his substitution of Zack's experience. Cloud's iconic weapon, the buster sword, actually belonged to Zack and in taking Zack's weapon Cloud sublimates his desire to be the masculine hero that Zack was. Importantly, in Cloud's battle stance, he holds the sword upright between his legs, literally possessing the phallus of a man he wishes he could be (Filipowich 2011). Like Cecil, Cloud's journey can only reach closure when he queers his relationship to masculinity. Cloud's emotional maturity comes with rejecting the illusion of masculinity he had thitherto maintained. Of course, much of Cloud's journey is telegraphed early on in a scene where he must dress in drag to secure access to a brothel. While several articles of clothing can improve his disguise, only a dress and wig are required to proceed. To get the dress, the player must convince a disenchanted couturier to take on the job and for the wig the player must earn it from another cross-dresser in town. The dressmaker is shocked that "a tough lookin' guy like that" would want to dress in drag while the wig's owner urges Cloud to win a squatting competition at the local gym. In both instances, Cloud's strongly coded gender traits are met with tension and reconciled, first through the dressmaker's surprise at Cloud's masculinity and the accomplishment of creating an appropriate garment for him; likewise, to earn the wig and pass as female Cloud must demonstrate his superiority in a masculine-coded activity.

FF8's main character, Squall, also begins as a severe, uptight male figure who, only upon reflecting on his childhood, recognizes that "he never turned out okay," and much of his standoffish behavior is rooted in an inability to appropriately manage his emotions (Howe 2016). Lightning in

FF13 is a woman but shows an aloofness much like Cloud and Squall; however while she is short-tempered she does not struggle with the insecurity of her earlier counterparts. Moreover, while Lightning does demonstrate a masculinized heroism, her appearance and wardrobe are highly feminized, particularly in *FF13: Lightning Returns*, where her power is tied to the costume she wears. Indeed, gender versatility is expressed through clothing in many games in the *Final Fantasy* series. While the original *FF* appears to have primarily male-coded avatars, *FF3*, *FF5*, *FF: Tactics*, *FF13: Lightning Returns*, in addition to massive multiplayer online titles, *FF11*, and *FF14* directly empower characters with a broad gender appearance. In titles where players may assign "jobs" to the cast, characters swap out thematically similar uniforms for each job, but each keep their individuality. *FF5*, one of the few to have more women in the main cast than men, follows the pattern of a maiden, child, and mother figure quite strictly (respectively, Reina, Krile, Faris), the player is never compelled to mechanically mirror their plot-based roles. Reina can don the sexualized uniform of the dancer job, the armor-clad dragoon, or the clownish geomancer. Likewise, Bartz and Galuf, the game's male characters, have a similar gendered range in their outfits. The most effective teams though consist of characters who have combined numerous jobs and skill sets. Thus, power comes only by existing in fluctuating gender expression.

Although *Final Fantasy* is rooted in a specific cultural understanding of gender norms, its global distribution and multimodal relationship with its audience places it at the cross-section of a number of gender theories. Although it regulates gender under global norms, embedded within the series is a space to play, and, in fact, such play continues to mark both the series and its genre within videogames. As consistently as it constricts its feminized characters with maiden/child/mother triads, there nonetheless remain noteworthy exceptions that provide sites of play in codes of womanhood. Similarly, masculine-coded heroes in *Final Fantasy* regularly develop outside dominant gender narratives. The interaction between local and global gender scripts in the series, whether deliberately or not, necessarily challenges one script or another in those moments where the tension between one code and another cannot be reconciled. Rather than alienate the player or diminish the narrative, these moments where gender codes are disrupted or undermined offer an opportunity to evaluate and critique the burden of gender on a cultural interpretation of gender codes.

Notes

1. Henceforth, I shall refer to specific titles in the *Final Fantasy* series with the acronymic *FF* followed by the number/subtitle where appropriate. For the series in general, I will continue to use the entire title.
2. In role-playing games, rogues occupy a mechanical position within a support and offensive spectrum, either as ranged attackers or as fast and skilled warriors. Rogues are characterized by swiftness and deception and tend to be ineffective in direct confrontation.

Bibliography

Brice, Mattie. 2011a. Women, the Ensemble, and Narrative Authority in the *Final Fantasy* Series. *Alternate Ending*, February 28.

———. 2011b. It's Time to Talk About It: Atlus, Naoto, and Transphobia. *Alternate Ending*, August 30.

Burn, Andrew, and Gareth Schott. 2004. Heavy Hero or Digital Dummy? Multimodal Player-Avatar Relations in *Final Fantasy 7*. *Visual Communication* 3 (2): 213–233.

Burrill, Derek A. 2008. *Die Tryin': Videogames, Masculinity, Culture*. New York: Peter Lang.

Butler, Judith. 1990. *Gender Trouble*. New York: Routledge.

Chen, Jin-Shiow. 2007. A Vision of Multiple Genders: Cross-Cultural Learnings in Asian Countries from the Images of *Kuan Yin* and "*Bishōnen*". *Journal of Cultural Research in Art Education* 25: 91–103.

Chizuko, Ueno. 1996. The Making of a History of Feminism in Japan. *Asian Journal of Women's Studies* 2: 170–191.

Dickenson, Kevin. 2011. Misconceptions About Silent Protagonists in Video Games. *PopMatters*, February 7.

Fantone, Laura. 2003. Final Fantasies: Virtual Women's Bodies. *Feminist Theory* 4 (1): 51–72.

Filipowich, Mark. 2011. A Profile of Cloud Strife. *bigtallwords*, November 17.

———. 2014. The Narration and Abstraction of Bodies in Games. *bigtallwords*, March 5.

Fox, Matt. 2013. *The Video Games Guide: 1000+ Arcade, Console and Computer Games, 1962–2012*. 2nd ed. Jefferson, NC: McFarland & Company, Inc.

Genereux, Randy, and Anne McKeough. 2007. Developing Narrative Interpretation: Structural and Content Analyses. *The British Journal of Educational Psychology* 77 (4): 849–872.

Halberstam, Jack. 1998. *Female Masculinity*. London: Duke University Press.

Hemmann, Kathryn. 2016. Magic and Gender in *Final Fantasy VI*. *Kill Screen*, August 16.

Howe, Austin. 2016. '*I Didn't Turn Out Ok at All': Interrogations of Masculinity in Late Final Fantasy*. Presentation at the Oregon Game Studies Conference, Eugene, OR, February 4.

Ito, Mizuko. 2008. Gender Dynamics in Japanese Media Mix. In *Beyond Barbie and Mortal Kombat: New Perspectives on Gender and Gaming*, ed. Yasmin B. Kafai, Carrie Heeter, Jill Denner, and Jennifer Y. Sun, 97–110. Cambridge, MA: MIT Press.

Lazzaro, Nicole. 2008. Are Boy Games Even Necessary? In *Beyond Barbie and Mortal Kombat: New Perspectives on Gender and Gaming*, ed. Yasmin B. Kafai, Carrie Heeter, Jill Denner, and Jennifer Y. Sun, 199–216. Cambridge, MA: MIT Press.

Ligman, Kris. 2014. Queerly Anime. *Medium*, January 22.

McKevitt, Andrew. 2010. "You Are Not Alone!": Anime and the Globalizing America. *Diplomatic History* 34 (5): 893–921.

Mizuno, Hiromi. 2007. When Pacifist Japan Fights: Historicizing Desires in Anime. *Mechademia* 2 (1): 104–123.

Saito, Kumiko. 2014. Magic, *Shōjo*, and Metamorphosis: Magical Girl Anime and the Challenges of Changing Gender Identities in Japanese Society. *Journal of Asian Studies* 73 (1): 143–122.

Tsutomu, Sugiura. 2008. Japan's Creative Industries: Culture as a Source of Soft Power in the Industrial Sector. In *Soft Power Superpowers: Cultural and National Assets of Japan and the United States*, ed. Watanabe Yasushi and David L. McConnel, 128–153. Armonk, NY: East Gate.

Vint, Sherryl. 2007. *Bodies of Tomorrow: Technology, Subjectivity, Science Fiction*. Toronto: Toronto University Press.

8

The Big Reveal: Exploring (Trans)Femininity in *Metroid*

Evelyn Deshane and R. Travis Morton

Introduction

In 1986, Japanese games developer Nintendo released *Metroid* for the NES (Nintendo Entertainment System), a game about Samus Aran, an ex-soldier of the Galactic Federation turned Galactic bounty hunter. The game was a typical side-scroller with an 8-bit soundtrack and arcade-style boss fights in space. But the ending, where Samus Aran faced the player and revealed herself to be a woman, was different than most video games of the era. Samus's "big reveal" is often cited as one of the biggest shocks in video game history by fans, players, and critics alike (Game Informer 2007). Ever since Samus's reveal, she's become one of the most popular playable women characters in video games (Rougeau 2013).

Samus's gender presentation is coded and revealed to the audience in the same way transgender women in film are revealed. As Brianna Wu and Ellen McGrody write in a 2015 article for *The Mary Sue*, there is other evidence to suggest that Samus may also be a transgender woman. "It's true!" they write, "one of the most famous women in video game history also happens to be a transgender woman! It's none other than Nintendo's Samus Aran!" Both writers go on to cite Hirofumi Matsuoka, one of the designers for Super Metroid, from a 1994 strategy guidebook where he states that Samus "wasn't a woman" but instead uses the Japanese term ニューハーフ which roughly translates to "newhalf." The reveal of Samus's identity (both in and outside of the game) as

E. Deshane (✉) • R. T. Morton
University of Waterloo, Waterloo, ON, Canada

© The Author(s) 2018
T. Harper et al. (eds.), *Queerness in Play*, Palgrave Games in Context,
https://doi.org/10.1007/978-3-319-90542-6_8

a sudden plot twist not only plays on the typical understanding of video games and their audiences, but the audience's notion of gender identity.

This chapter offers a way to trace Wu and McGrody's rhetorical claim of Samus being a transgender woman by focusing on the cinematic big reveal scene often produced around images of the transgender body on screen (or in this case, video games) and how these techniques often evoke the visual equivalent of the "trapped in the wrong body" narrative associated with transgender people. Combining both transgender theory and video game studies, we also examine how reading Samus's body as trans woman can produce emotional responses in players and how that reading can affect the game-playing process, as well as the player's possible identification with character/avatar. Samus Aran, whether a cis woman or a trans woman, changed the way in which gender in video games is discussed and what to expect when a player sits down to engage.

The Big Reveal

At the end of 1986s *Metroid*, Samus Aran defeats the final boss while still wearing an orange and green exoskeleton space suit. As the ending theme music plays, Samus changes from the profile we've seen through the entire game to stare at the player face on. A message scrolls across the screen announcing peace in space and the player's victory. Samus's orange and green space suit then starts to change color rapidly, eventually disappearing. Samus, with long red hair, white skin, and pink suit and boots, steps forward. She displays typically feminine hips and breasts; as she waves, her waistline seems to get smaller (Figs. 8.1 and 8.2).

If the player manages to finish the game in under an hour, then Samus appears to the player wearing only a bra and underwear in the same shade of pixilated pink, as documented by YouTube user haikarahakuchi. After she addresses the player and waves, the ending screen comes up and "The END" flashes across a black screen.

Samus's reveal is not a new technique, and it has often been used in conjunction with transgender characters in film and/or photography. Whether it's standing in front of the mirror and undressing to expose genitals and/or the binding of breasts, or being undressed by a significant other only to incite "homosexual panic" (a term we will return to later) as genitals are discovered, or disrobed by a medical doctor for invasive tests, the transgender body has been consistently put on display for shock value. Since Samus's reveal happens at the end of the game, when the player requires no more engagement with the text-as-game, the player is exposed to Samus's secret cinematically and

Fig. 8.1 Samus, *Metroid* ending

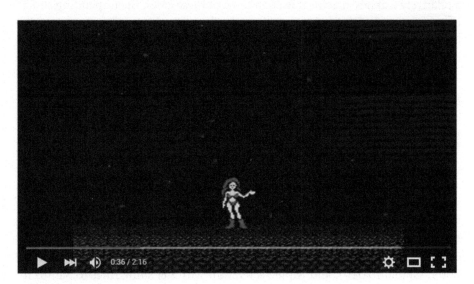

Fig. 8.2 Samus (in bikini)

narratively, rather than ludically (though we will touch on the ludic interpretation in our next section). In order to understand the history behind her reveal along with Wu and McGrody's later claim of transgender identity for this character, we explore her reveal moment in the 1986 game through a transgender-focused perspective that takes into account film studies and hermeneutics, in addition to games studies.

The deliberate staging of Samus's body turned toward the player, the stripping off of her space suit, and the following shock of her audience resemble the way in which Dil, the transgender woman in *The Crying Game* (1991), was discovered by the protagonist Fergus. Similarly, in *The Silence of the Lambs* (1991), the character Buffalo Bill reveals their tucked genitals to the audience through a song and dance routine to "Goodbye Horses" in front of a mirror. Whereas the scene from *The Silence of the Lambs* has been used again and again in popular culture as a joke, *The Crying Game* won many critical accolades and was known for its sympathetic depiction of Dil. Both examples have become standardized as the two ways in which transgender women can be viewed on screen: as the joke or sympathetically (Serano 2007).

As Jack Halberstam (2005) notes in his chapter on "The Transgender Look" in cinema, both *The Crying Game* and *Boys Don't Cry* (a film with a trans man protagonist made in 1999) contain reveal scenes that "rely on the successful solicitation of affect—whether it be revulsion, sympathy, or empathy—in order to give mainstream viewers access to a transgender gaze" (77). Because a relatively unknown actor is used in both of these cases, the impending shock of misrecognition needed to complete the "transgender gaze" or "transgender look" is compounded; a video game character like Samus, whom the audience has not experienced before, can be viewed in a similar manner.

Halberstam constructs the transgender gaze using Laura Mulvey's (1999) previous writing on the male gaze in cinema, where there is a "sexual and gendered economy of looking, watching, and identifying" and where the pleasure in the look itself is inherently gendered (Halberstam 2005, 83–84). From here, Halberstam builds off Nick Mirzoeff's idea of the "transverse look" (85) which engages in multiple viewpoints and subject positions, throwing away the one unilateral identification through the gaze itself. Indeed, this is where much of the postmodern theories on gender derive their power; the subject can experiment and play with gender roles, but not accept any of these roles as their "real-life" identity. Ellen Ripley from the *Alien* franchise is one character often evoked in this new postmodern sense of gender (Gallardo 2004; Graham 2010), and Ripley is relevant with her similarities to Samus in the sci-fi genre. But what these understandings of postmodern gender performance, and the "transgendering" of the character via the transverse look, fail to take into account is the *stability* of the cisgender body. The performance of gender exists—and *must* exist—on a stable cisgender, able-bodied, and often white person in order for it to be considered transgressive. Only when the cisgender body is assumed can it then be "flexible"; anything else becomes a threat (or a joke) since being transgender means one cannot simply opt out of being seen as "in-between" (Halberstam 2005, 84). As Halberstam (2005) notes, it's when the cisgender body is de-stabilized through a revealing of mis-matched genitals that the feelings of revulsion (or sympathy and empathy) are evoked in the viewer. Because Samus's reveal depends a surprise unveiling, she can be read (and as Wu and McGrody seem to imply in their article *must* be read) as a transgender woman through the same "transgender gaze" that Halberstam discusses. Though *Metroid* (1986) predates *The Crying Game* (1999), *The Silence of The Lambs* (1991), and *Boys Don't Cry* (1999) by several years, Samus's game-body and gender reveal mimics the way in which trans-gender women in particular have been treated on the screen for years before her 1986 debut.

Transgender author Sherilyn Connor (2010) locates the big reveal trope's origins in pornography. She describes a scene from the 1984 straight porn film *L'Amour* in which

> a neon-drenched bar which gives the film immediate value as a historical piece, straight male porn legend Harry Reems asks straight male porn demigod Jamie Gillis why women can't be more like men. It really makes no sense except to telegraph the inevitable punchline. A couple of girls identified in the credits as Ivory Essex and Rachel Whitney throw themselves at the boys (duh, it's porn) and fellatio follows. Jamie and Rachel fuck as Ivory continues to blow Harry. After a money shot in which Jamie ruins Rachel's perfectly nice black gloves, Ivory stands in front of Harry, lifts her skirt to reveal a Dirk Diggler-esque penis, and says: "And now, boys, we're going to have some real fun." (97)

Connor's essay is part cultural critique on the fragility of masculine gender roles and part personal essay about her transgender identity. She states that the main reason she likes and watches this type of pornography is because it gives her "representation. In it, I can actually see people who look like me" (98). In her essay, she walks a thin line between condemning pornography as an inher-ently flawed media and embracing pornography as a vehicle for the expression of her transgender identity. "Melodramatic reveal scenes notwithstanding," she writes, "what shemale porn taught me as a deeply closeted teenager was that a girl with a dick could be just as sexy and hot as genetic girls" (101). What Connor seems to suggest is that for transgender women, finding a place to exist was often difficult in the 1980s (and still is now), and sensationalized pornography provided a space for representation, especially for pre-op trans women like herself. But the storytelling techniques—such as the "melodra-matic reveal scenes" and the "homosexual panic" these films induced—were tired, boring, and ultimately damaging for those who were watching it/acting in it (101). Similarly, while Halberstam (2005) analyzes the transgender look in film as a transgressive medium where the body becomes "symbol par excellence for flexibility" (76–77), the tools used to do this still rely on the cisgender obsession with what's underneath the transgender person's clothing and cisgender viewers believing they have the right to access it. Revealing in this manner always functions as a way to turn the transgender body into a symbol for the cisgender producers and audience. "The transgender character will be evoked as a metaphor for subjecthood," Halberstam writes, "but will not be given a narrative in his/her own right" (84).

When Brianna Wu and Ellen McGrody (2015) examine Samus's presentation as a trans woman, they find similar issues as Connor and Halberstam. The term "newhalf" which Matsuoka uses to describe Samus in 1994 is often associated with pornography, roughly analogous to "shemale." This term, along with "tranny," is no longer accepted when referring to transgender people and only lingers in pornography, where shemale/tranny is the search term still in use. Wu writes,

> It's possible to interpret this [the term newhalf] as an ugly joke about Samus's traditionally masculine appearance, as illustrated in the 80s by Nintendo Power, where she is said to be six foot three and 198 pounds. In the uglier context, "newhalf" refers to trans women who have not had gender confirmation surgery—equivalent to Matsuoka laughing and remarking, "Yeah, Samus has a dick!"

As Wu points out, terms like shemale, tranny, and newhalf ignore the transgender woman's gender presentation and gender identity and focus solely on genitals. Trans theorist Julia Serano (2007) notes that the focus on a trans person's genitals stems from a biologically determined attitude where sex of a person is automatically and irrevocably associated with social categories and gender (i.e., that all women have vaginas) and can never become detached from these associations (i.e., only "real" women have vaginas). In order to dislodge these pervasive cultural ideas, Serano introduces something she calls "subconscious sex" into our typical categories of sex and gender; she describes the subconscious sex as an "intrinsic, self-understanding" of one's sexual embodiment and also notes that those who are cisgender "tend not to notice or appreciate their own subconscious sex because it is concordant with their physical sex (and therefore, they tend to conflate the two)" (78). In contrast, a transgender person is constantly at odds with their subconscious sex since it does not match up with their body. These feelings of disconnect often fuel the common "trapped inside a man's body" narrative as Serano explains (9), and that we will touch on later on in this chapter.

The big reveal trope is the visual equivalent of using the terms tranny or shemale since its function is to focus on genitals, which actively strips the transgender person of agency as their body is rendered as an object. The big reveal also acts as an answer to the all-too-common question asked of transgender people: Have you had the surgery? When asked by a cisgender person, the surgical question also becomes an existential one: Are you a "real" woman or are you only half-real? Is your body a biological body or something made up? This question is at the very heart of our biologically determined understanding of gender and sex.

Transgender people are constantly framed through this real/fake dichotomy. While cisgender people can embrace the flexibility of gender roles, it is because their bodies are not interrogated in the same way transgender peoples are. Moreover, when the question of desire enters in the "transgender look," it's one with ramifications to both gender *and* sexuality. The stripping of clothing in order to display the genitals (or in the video game, the underwear that conforms to genitals) hints that there is something "real" underneath that can be accessed through interrogation or through violence. As Connor notes, "the much-hyped reveal scene is followed by the ostensible hero giving the girl a bloody nose, then retching for a minute straight. All things considered, I'll take being fetishized as a sex object over being assaulted or killed as an unnatural freak" (98). When McGrody and Wu read Samus as a trans woman, they are accessing the history of cinematic treatment of transgender women, but they are also engaging with the fact that Samus has been assumed to be a man. Being unveiled as a woman, in spite of this previous assumption, parallels the same tension between the "subconscious sex" and physical sex that Serano writes about in transgender people. And it's this point—that the tension between the player's assumption and what's actually revealed when Samus takes off her suit—where her interpretation as trans is especially relevant and powerful.

What we get with Samus's big reveal scene in the video game is the *precise opposite* with the standard depiction in most cinematic big reveals: the character we thought was a man is actually a woman underneath the space suit. Since "big reveals" have been consistently used as a way to devalue the identity of the transgender player/subject/character, this reversal of interpretations actually ends up aligning with a transgender person's felt identity, where they believe themselves to be their desired gender, but no one on the outside can see it. To have a character like Samus be (mis)read for an entire game—including by the player—then take off the suit and show the "truth" of the body underneath, renders the ending a kind of coming-out scene where Samus fully becomes a woman, and we, as player, bear witness to this identity transformation. If we read her as a trans woman, then her trans identity becomes further validated through the relationship with the player—something that simply doesn't happen in cinematic reveals. Having what's underneath the space suit act as what's real (and *not* everyone's interpretation of what the space suit looks on the surface or in the player's manual) is another manifestation of the central transgender metaphor of being trapped in the wrong body. Samus, for the bulk of the first *Metroid* game, is stuck in the wrong space suit and the wrong perception of her space suit. When she comes out of it, she literally comes out—and then becomes a queer icon for those playing/watching/reading about her transformation who also identify with this transgender narrative.

It is at this point where Bob Rehak's reading of "playing and being" (104) can be especially useful to understand the queer implications of her character from a queer player's perspective, and the ways in which insecure cisgender and heterosexual characters may be baffled or offended by this reveal.

The Avatar and Game Space

Thirty years after *Metroid*, we are still asking the same questions about transgender people and framing their bodies in the same way. If a transgender body is only "half-real," what does this mean for a video game like *Metroid* and the players who interact with Samus as a character?

For game theorist Jesper Juul, the video game world is "half-real" (2005, 1). What he means by this term (which he theorized in an eponymous book) is that though the dragon the player slays is not real and the rules are for a fictional world, the event of winning or losing *is* a real event. Bob Rehak says something very similar about the player's relation to the avatar and their own identity. In "Playing at Being" (2003), he describes, through the theoretical language of French psychoanalyst Jacques Lacan, the process of identity and connection—sometimes described as "unity [and] wholeness"—the avatar evokes (104). Rehak compares the relationship shared between the player and the avatar to that of Lacan's hypothetical infant when first recognizing themselves in a mirror—Lacan's "mirror stage" of psychological development. The mirror stage is where the infant responds to this desire for unity that the reflection offers him, but this identification with the reflection means that the ego will then be split and "rendered incomplete by the very distinction that enables self-recognition" when he turns away from the mirror. From here, "the split subject goes through life alienated from itself and its needs, endlessly seeking in external resources the 'lost object' (*objet petit a*) from which it was initially severed" (106). For Rehak, the avatar seems to be the criterion for Lacan's "objet petit a" since it appears "on screen in place of the player," meaning that

> the avatar does double duty as self and other, as symbol and index. Both [self and other are] limited and freed by difference from the player, [so] they can accomplish more than the player alone; they are supernatural ambassadors of agency. (106)

The avatar can stand in for the player's self since it moves on the screen when the player tells it to move, but the avatar also acts as the "other" since it does not necessarily fit with the self the player is aware of embodying in reality. Because of these connections, Rehak notes that the player can become emotionally attached to the avatar as a site of severance between object and subject position for the player. It's this emotional attachment to the avatar/character which caused the ending of *Metroid* to be so shocking as it recalls this same severance and (possible) misrecognition.

Before we link Rehak's understanding of identity and Samus to the transgender player, we need to take up a few points about avatars, games, and gender. For one, Samus is a character, not an avatar. As Adrienne Shaw (2011) notes, an avatar implies self-representation because of the choice that goes into the character creation (where sex/gender is often one component), whereas video game characters are already pre-made and carry with them their own connotations outside of the player (4). When a player engages with a character inside a game world, the interactivity and immersion of that game world may cause a player to identify with the character more easily than in any other form of media (Wolf 2001, 3). But this interactivity does not always lend itself to identification with the player. As Shaw notes in her ethnographic study of gamers, it is difficult to parse out the identification question with any kind of definite answer since "some players think about what they are doing, not what the character is doing or what they as the character are doing" (5). Indeed, because of the ludic aspects of the game, there may be simply too much going on in the game world for a player to think much about the character. As J. Newman (2002) notes, rather than "seeing the world through their [character's] eyes, the player encounters the game by relating to everything within the gameworld simultaneously." Shaw follows this observation up by stating that "the ludic aspects of games often cause players to be too self-referential to take on the role of their character. They did not think about their relationship with the character per se, rather they thought about what they, the players, were doing" (2011, 5). Helen Kennedy and Seth Giddings

(2008) also comment on similar issues of identification in their micro-ethnographic study on game playing entitled "little jesuses and fuck-off robots: On aesthetics, cybernetics, and not being very good at Lego Star Wars" (20–25). It is therefore difficult to draw a definitive conclusion on the issue of identification, but what we do wish to comment on is how the very aspect of "doing" (Shaw 2011, 5) that may prevent the player from identifying with the avatar or character is the exact process that Rehak observes as fundamental in the identification process; the playing itself is linked to the "being" of the character, thereby making the ludic prosperities of the game part of the iden-tification. Like Kennedy and Giddings note, the game itself "forces 'identifi-cation' on the player" and it is this forced process of Samus's reveal which we will then examine (24).

When gender is invoked in the identification process, Judith Butler's theo-ries have another resonance. In *Gender Trouble* (1990), Butler writes "there is no gender identity behind the expressions of gender; that identity is perfor-matively constituted by the very 'expressions' that are said to be its results" (25). The idea that there is "no gender identity" has been debated by transgen-der authors (like Julia Serano) and taken up by many postmodern gender theorists as a way to embrace the flexibility of gender expressions. What Butler means in her analysis is that gender itself is the very "doing"; it is the "very expression that are said to be its results" (Butler 1990, 25)—meaning that what you perform *is* what you become. In this interpretation, the "subcon-scious sex" (Serano 2007) that is seemingly disregarded in the first half of her sentence is then rectified by the second half. Transgender people, who per-form something that does not quite match their body, are just as valid as the cisgender people performing their gender. The cisgender expression will be privileged, though, because they have the stabilized body on which to do this performance. Cisgender people will be considered real in their performance, while transgender people will be seen as fake—though Butler outlines that *both* are performances. Just because gender itself is a construction doesn't mean that it doesn't have validity, though, and its validity is her focus in her chapter called "Undiagnosing Gender" in her book *Undoing Gender* (2004) where she clears up the many misreadings of her first book.

On this note, while players do not necessarily consciously identify with the avatar or character they are playing, the very act of playing as that character/ avatar forms the same process of performance—and identification—that Butler discusses in her writing on gender identity. If what Shaw (2011) writes about players is true, and only "some players think about what they are *doing*, not what the character is doing or what they as the character are doing" (emphasis mine), the end result still ends up being identification in some way, because gender (or any identity marker) is a matter of that *doing*. In other words, gender is a *process*, not a thing in itself, and through game play, players experience this gendered process, one that can be divergent from their own. For trans women in real life, their gender experience is often tied up with the fact that people will continuously read them as men, even if they feel like and know they are women underneath—and this exact process is what Samus goes through during the entire game of *Metroid*. Therefore, whether the player identifies as trans or cis, they end up experiencing through game play enough of this misidentification and misrecognition to facilitate the same patterns of affects that Halberstam (2005) discusses—revulsion, empathy, and sympathy—and what Rehak notes as "being." For a brief moment in the game, they become transgender women because they are playing through a similar experience.

So far, we have argued that the shock generated by *Metroid*'s ending was deliberately sensationalized due to the ways in which prior reveal scenes have been used surrounding transgender women. Samus being a woman was meant to incite a visceral response—perhaps even physical one (as in the "retching" that Connor mentions)—since she was assumed to be a man or boy for the duration of the game. By unveiling her as a woman, the feminine identity that is formed through the act of playing must be disavowed to reaffirm masculinity of the male player to avoid—as M. Kinder notes in a 1993 study of male-identified players deliberately choosing female characters—"the risk of transgender identification" (107). Because there is no choice in playing Samus, and Samus has been coded as a man for the game, the response of a player forced into this revealing scene is similar to, but not quite the same, as the "homosexual panic" Connor (2010) notes in the pornographic reveal scenes. Whereas in pornography the man's (assumed heterosexual) desire becomes precarious due to the in-between body of the trans woman and he must reassert his heterosexual masculinity through violence, the male video gamer's identity becomes precarious. Either he acknowledges that he was playing as a woman throughout the entire game, or he finds a way to reassert his masculinity. Because the game ends as soon as Samus is revealed, the man in this scenario is unable to reassert any identity through the typical act of play. By taking away the player's ability to volunteer, the big reveal scene undermines what it sought to represent (a woman in gaming, cis or trans) in the first place and instead makes it so men and women players/characters never sympathize with one another at all. The rigid gender roles are not deconstructed through empathy, but enforced through the shock value, and subsequently, through a reassertion of the male gaze. Samus's previous queer readings disappear as her coming out becomes a striptease, one that exists for only the heterosexual male viewer's gaze and as a potential award for the player finishing the game. Being transgender through the game, and in this historical moment, is always seen as a "risk" (Kinder 1993, 107).

Rehak's main goal for his analysis of the avatar is to conjure empathy through the connection between player and avatar. The "half-real" (Juul 2005, 1) status of the video game world works at achieving a "unity and wholeness" (Rehak 2003) because the player can heal whatever is missing in the real world through the avatar (or video game character) by allowing it to represent their *objet petit a*. The *objet petit a* is important for Rehak's (and Lacan's) "split subject alienated from itself and its needs" (106). By playing in a video game, the player can heal whatever is missing in their real life, but they can also be exposed to other perspectives and broaden their experience. For the cisgender heterosexual man who plays video games, seeing Samus and having a connection with her through the act of play *should* (according to Rehak's theory) broaden the imaginative world of the game, which is fictional but also acts as a stand-in for the real world. Helen Kennedy (2002) also makes a similar point about the cisgender heterosexual men who play *Tomb Raider*, using Lara Croft as a way to enact "queer embodiment" since "the merger of the flesh of the (male) player with Lara's elaborated feminine body of pure information" can lead to potential transgender readings of the player and character alike. By creating characters like Samus and Lara, there is the possibly for gender transgression, since by simply "being there, she [Lara, but also Samus] disturbs the natural symbolism of masculine culture."

The game mechanics for *Metroid*, however, can only deliver so much. While in some ways they mimic gender as a process for transgender women, they also reassert the male gaze at the end of the game by turning the body of a woman (cis or trans) into a reward for playing the game as fast as they can. What becomes important, then, for understanding Samus as one of the most important video game characters of all time is her capacity for change as the historical moment around her game changes. The constant acts of interpretation and re-interpretation of Samus's character from Nintendo's other games, Matsuoka's 1994 interview, writers like Wu and McGrody, and the game players themselves demonstrate Samus's power as a possible emblem for change since how a particular audience ends up reading her body becomes a cipher for the social and historical moment. For a transgender player, watching Samus's big reveal scene allows them to witness the unveiling of the objet petit a: someone who was perceived as a boy for the entirety of a video game is suddenly a girl. Not only is she a woman and everyone knows it—but she has also saved the day. Wu and McGrody pick up on this interpretation in their article and publish it at exactly the right time, when the current North American culture is changing around this "transgender tipping point" (Steinmetz 2014). Though reading Samus-as-queer/trans in this original game may seem like a stretch, or at least, something that's only visible to trans or queer people later in life, many of these game mechanics and interpretations have been here all along—they only needed the right audience in order to be fully expressed.

Conclusion

After Wu and McGrody posted their article on *The Mary Sue*, they experienced a backlash against their interpretation of Samus Aran as transgender. Many fans of the game did not want to see this character as anything other than a cisgender woman, dividing gender in video games along the cis/trans dichotomy (rather than the typical male/female one). One of the more petty tactics used to disagree with their original post included several articles discussing Wu and McGrody that repeatedly misgendered Wu (Morse 2015). This tactic speaks to the mentality against which we argue in this chapter. In an attempt to keep their own interpretation of who Samus "really" was, some gamers sought to strip Wu's gender from her. By doing this, they attempt to reveal her to the world as a fake woman *and* as a fake gamer.

Halberstam (2005) notes in his work that "the exposure of a trans character whom the audience has already accepted as male or female causes the audience to reorient themselves in relation to the film's past in order to deal with the film's present and prepare themselves for the film's future" (78). Once Samus was revealed to be a woman, the entire audience had to reorient themselves in some way in order to make sense of the game they'd just played and then the rest of the series. The game designers and writers who followed the original *Metroid* reoriented themselves by adjusting her character in subsequent games. As game critic Ben Croshaw (2010) notes in his review for *The Escapist* magazine, "I always thought that after the initial shock at the end of the very first *Metroid*—that Samus' breastplate was more appropriately named than you thought—the series' position has basically been that she's a lady, just deal with it, yo. But *Other M* just can't stop banging on about it. The plot is somewhere between *Aliens* and *G.I. Jane* and has a central theme of [motherhood]." Characterizations like these serve to sever the relationship between the Samus of the original game, almost as a way to disavow the possible queer readings of the ending. In *Other M* (2010) in particular, not only are we given a perspective on the woman that is decidedly feminine, but in such a way that is reductive and crude. When Wu and McGrody view the game from a transgender player's perspective, and notice the same cinematic techniques that trans women are exposed to in films, along with the parallel visual narrative of "being trapped in the wrong body," they interpret the game through a queer narrative lens and, in doing so, offer Samus yet another reveal scene, thus making the audience go through the same reorienting that Halberstam (2005) discusses. Those who disagreed with the interpretation of Samus as trans did so by citing the subsequent *Metroid* games (such as *Metroid: Zero Mission* (2004) and *Metroid: Other M* (2010) where Samus appears as a young child who has a stereotypically feminine appearance) and asking "At what point do we see her as male?" (Wu and McGrody 2015). These questions, like the hyper-feminine *Other M* Samus, seek to look toward the future as a way to disavow the queer readings of the past.

As one commenter (who agreed with Wu and McGrody) noted, we never actually see Samus's genitals anywhere—whether in the first *Metroid* game or in any other version of *Metroid*—so she could still be transgender (Wu and McGrody 2015). Indeed, not having the final answer about Samus's genitals is a hidden blessing—as Sherilyn Connor (2010) notes that focusing on surgery in relation to transgender identity is a "path to madness" (104). By actively rejecting the notion that genitals lead to some type of inner meaning, we can broaden what it means to be feminine in a game world, so that maybe more definitions of femininity can be allowed outside of it. Whether Samus is cis or trans, she is still one of the most popular women characters in gaming, and that is something to remember and celebrate.

Bibliography

Boys Don't Cry. 1999. Directed by Kimberly Pierce. Burbank, CA: Fox Searchlight. DVD.

Butler, Judith. 1990. *Gender Trouble: Feminism and the Subversion of Identity*. New York: Routledge.

———. 2004. *Undoing Gender*. New York: Routledge.

Conner, Sherilyn. 2010. The Big Reveal. In *Gender Outlaws The Next Generation*, ed Kate Bornstein and S. Bear Bergman. New York: Seal Press.

Croshaw, Ben. 2010. Metroid Other M. *The Escapist Magazine*. http://www.escapist-magazine.com/videos/view/zero-punctuation/2015-Metroid-Other-M?fb_comment_id=10150111556328787_15747354#f24dcbd004.

Gallardo, Xiema C. 2004. *Alien Woman: The Making of Lt. Ellen Ripley*. New York: Continuum.

Game Informer. 2007. The Top 10 Video Game Twists. *Game Informer* (168): 20.

Giddings, S., and H.W. Kennedy. 2008. Little Jesuses and Fuckoff Robots: On Aesthetics, Cybernetics, and Not Being Very Good at Lego Star Wars. In *The Pleasures of Computer Gaming: Essays on Cultural History, Theory and Aesthetics*, ed. M. Swalwell and J. Wilson, 13–32. Jefferson, NC: McFarland.

Graham, Elizabeth. 2010. *Meanings of Ripley: the Alien Quadrilogy and Gender.* New York: Cambridge Scholars.

Haikarahakuchi. 2008. *Metroid Ending (Famicom Disk System Ver.).* YouTube. Online. https://www.youtube.com/watch?v=ldiDYvGvHzo.

Halberstam, Judith (Jack). 2005. *A Queer Time and Place: Transgender Bodies, Subcultural Lives.* New York: New York University Press.

Juul, Jesper. 2005. *Half-Real: Video Games Between Real Rules and Fictional Worlds.* Cambridge: MIT Press.

Kennedy, Helen W. 2002. Lara Croft: Feminist Icon or Cyberbimbo? On the Limits of Textual Analysis. *Game Studies* 2 (2).

Kinder, M. 1993. *Playing with Power In Movies, Television, and Video Games: From Muppet Babies to Teenage Mutant Ninja Turtles.* Berkeley, CA: University of California Press.

Metroid. 1986. Nintendo.

Metroid: Other M. 2010. Nintendo.

Metroid: Zero Mission. 2004. Nintendo.

Morse, Brandon. 2015. No, Samus Aran Is not a Trans Woman. *The Federalist.* http://thefederalist.com/2015/09/02/no-samus-aran-is-not-a-trans-woman/.

Mulvey, Laura. 1999. Visual Pleasure and Narrative Cinema. In *Film Theory and Criticism: Introductory Readings*, ed. Leo Braudy and Marshall Cohen, 833–844. New York: Oxford University Press.

Newman, J. 2002. The Myth of the Ergodic Videogame: Some Thoughts on Player-Character Relationships in Videogames. *Game Studies*, July. http://www.gamestudies.org/0102/newman/.

Rehak, B. 2003. Playing at Being: Psychoanalysis and the Avatar. In *The Video Game Theory Reader*, ed. M.J.P. Wolf and B. Perron. New York: Routledge.

Rougeau, Michael. 2013. 50 Greatest Heroines in Video Game History. *Complex.* http://ca.complex.com/pop-culture/2013/03/the-50-greatest-heroines-in-video-game-history/samus.

Serano, Julia. 2007. *Whipping Girl: A Transsexual Woman on Sexism and the Scapegoating of Femininity.* Berkeley: Seal Press.

Shaw, Adrienne. 2011. 'He Could Be a Bunny Rabbit for All I Care': Exploring Identification in Digital Games. Paper presented at Authors & Digital Games Research Association, DiGRA.

Steinmetz, Katy. 2014. The Transgender Tipping Point. *Time Magazine.*

The Crying Game. 1999. Directed by Neil Jordan. Burbank, CA: Palace Pictures. DVD.

The Silence of the Lambs. 1991. Directed by Jonathan Demme. Burbank, CA: Orion Pictures. DVD.

Wolf, M.J.P. 2001. Introduction. In *The Medium of the Video Game*. Austin: University of Texas Press.

Wu, Brianna, and Ellen McGrody. 2015. Metroid's Samus Aran Is a Transgender Woman. Deal With It. *The Mary Sue*. http://www.themarysue.com/metroids-samus-aran-transgender-woman/.

9

Bye, Bye, Birdo: Heroic Androgyny and Villainous Gender-Variance in Video Games

Meghan Blythe Adams

Introduction and Methodology

The pink dinosaur wearing a bow named "Birdo"—identified by the game manual as male in the 1988 game *Super Mario Bros. 2*—is probably the industry's most famous character with supposedly conflicting masculine and feminine signifiers. However, the industry is rife with such characters: what differentiates them primarily is whether this mix is portrayed as heroic androgyny or villainous gender confusion. More specifically, androgynous heroes exhibit relatively few secondary sex characteristics (such as facial hair or a large waist to hip ratio), while gender-variant characters exhibit a mix of secondary sex characteristics and social signifiers of gender, including clothing and cosmetics. This chapter explores the contrast between the tradition of androgynous player-characters like Link in *The Legend of Zelda* series and vain non-player-characters with an excess of nonnormative gender signifiers like Duvall in *Resident Evil: Dead Aim*. Often identified by the game as "really" male while attempting to emulate normative feminine dress and speech, these characters are presented by games as variously humorous, pitiable, or monstrous, and often all three.

It would be disingenuous to identify these instances of excessive, conflicting gender signifiers without acknowledging the cultural contexts that impact Western and Eastern game production differently. Additionally, while the androgynous hero appears more commonly in game series of Japanese origin,

M. B. Adams (✉)
Western University, London, ON, Canada

T. Harper et al. (eds.), *Queerness in Play*, Palgrave Games in Context,
https://doi.org/10.1007/978-3-319-90542-6_9

147

the process by which gender-variant characters are often presented by the game as transgender, even as the game discredits the legitimacy of trans and queer identity, occurs across cultural lines. However, with these acknowledgments in mind, this chapter does not deconstruct transphobia in video games: instead, this chapter aims to problematize the global game industry's acceptance of masculine-skewed androgyny as aesthetically pleasing and acceptable while portraying gender-variance as aesthetically displeasing and unacceptable. Ultimately, these differing valuations center maleness and innate masculinity as normative and present gender-variance—and implicitly femininity—as inherently wrong. This chapter uses textual analysis to contrast heroic androgyny in series like *The Legend of Zelda* and *NiGHTS* with the mixing of gendered signifiers to convey the otherness of particular NPCs in games like *Super Mario Bros. 2*, *Resident Evil: Dead Aim*, and *The Witcher 2*. Instead of offering positive alternatives to the typical use of androgyny and gender-variance in video games, this chapter aims to better understand the inherent leveraging of masculinity in heroic androgyny and villainous gender-variance in games.

The Neutral Setting: On Androgyny in Video Games

There is a specific type of androgyny presented positively in player-characters across a variety of game genres, including platforming, adventure, and role-playing. The existence of iconic androgynous heroes in some video games may seem initially beneficial because it seems to offer models of heroism that are not rooted in a static gender binary. However, I argue that this androgyny typically centers white, thin, able-bodied masculinity as the seemingly "neutral" state of being from which femininity, racial diversity, and fatness (among other identity markers) are deviations. The kind of androgyny exhibited by these protagonists is often defined by a false sense of neutrality: their bodies, faces, clothing, and actions are treated as being neither especially masculine nor feminine. However, this version of androgyny tends to represent masculinity as a neutral state from which femininity is a deviation; Carr notes in her discussion of *Abe's Oddysee* that critics ranging from Dyer to hooks have written on the power of being a neutral category and typically identified masculinity and whiteness as two hegemonic "neutral" states.[1] These critics focused primarily on the centering of masculinity or whiteness as neutral, but subsequent critics have noted particularly how some forms of androgyny reinscribe these same supposedly neutral states. Lorenzo-Cioldi identifies that the category of transcendent androgyny is characterized supposedly not by a mix of gendered signifiers but an apparent absence of them and that this transcendent model of androgyny is often "colorless, [and] uncorporeal."[2] McLaughlin refers to Lorenzo-Cioldi's definition of transcendent androgyny as a preface to claiming that the nearly bodiless transcendent androgyne "renaturalizes the white masculine liberal humanist subject."[3]

Recently, online feminist media has restated some of these arguments with a broader focus than white liberal masculinity, noting that popular conceptions of androgyny often also emphasize thin, wealthy, able bodies.[4] Scholars like Carr note the presence of masculinity as a seemingly neutral category in games, but this other tradition of critiquing androgyny's tendency to center white, thin, able-bodied masculinity has not been explored enough in game studies criticism. In the context of video games that present masculine-leaning androgyny as neutral, it becomes useful to remember that it is difficult to divorce what is neutral from what is supposed to be natural or correct. This kind of androgyny expresses Lorenzo-Cioldi's concept of androgyny as minimal, ideal, and pared down to a kind of essence that leaves no room for the messiness of the body. Signals of identity other than slim, masculine whiteness become heavy and weighted with the grossness of the body while slim, masculine whiteness is presented as ideal.

Androgynous video game heroes often lack prominent secondary sexual characteristics, which are aspects of the human body that are frequently assumed to distinguish between sexes but are not directly involved in reproduction. Secondary sexual characteristics include breasts, waist to hip ratios, the distribution or lack of pronounced facial or body hair, voice range, and the distribution of facial features. A typical androgynous hero will not exhibit breasts or facial hair, for example. Androgynous heroes often wear supposedly gender-neutral clothing and accessories, but more accurately, we should say that they tend to lack the "feminizing gendered signifiers" noted by Anita Sarkeesian in her discussion of the "Ms. Male Character": these include high heels, skirts, cosmetics, jewelry, beauty marks, and hair decorations such as bows or flowers.[5] As in Carr's reading earlier, masculinity is posed as neutral while femininity is a deviation that requires signaling. Similarly, the androgynous hero is often presented as if they possess gender-neutral (that is to say, masculine) gestures: there is no need for the "special" animation of a feminine walk, like the one some developers of *Assassin's Creed* series claim as being prohibitively expensive to code. This comment prompted disagreement by other developers, some of whom—like animator Jonathan Cooper—noted that masculine walking animations could be applied to female characters but that the reverse would result in overly effeminate gestures if applied to male characters.[6] Of course, people across the gender spectrum can exhibit different combinations of these gendered characteristics, but in mainstream video games, there is quite a stiff divide between the characteristics identified as masculine or feminine. The androgynous hero is presented as straddling that divide, but the hegemonic neutrality of masculinity in video games results in the androgynous hero being slightly masculine of center.

Consider the following incomplete collection of androgynous heroes, ranging from *Final Fantasy* protagonists to the titular hero of *NiGHTS into Dreams*. Androgynous player-characters like these often skew masculine: this skewing, like the use of the bow to indicate femininity, reifies masculinity as neutral and makes femininity abnormal. In "Androgyny: A Conceptual Critique," Kathryn Pauly Morgan cites the move from presenting androgyny as an ideal "totality through balance" of masculine and feminine to a "pluralist" ideal in which androgyny is the sum total of choice between the best of masculine and feminine but ultimately notes that both visions of androgyny are based in ideals.[7] Neither the balance nor the pluralist ideal leaves room for anything less than androgyny as perfection. The player-characters described in this section tend to lie closer to the balance ideal than the choice ideal, but that balance is, as has been described, is false and presents that ideal as light-skinned, slim-bodied masculinity. Protagonists from the *Final Fantasy* series, particularly those drawn by artist Yoshitaka Amano through the first to the sixth installment of the series have been well-known for androgyny. Androgynous main characters in the *Final Fantasy* series since Amano's departure have continued to typically be androgynous men like *Final Fantasy VII*'s Cloud Strife (1997), *VIII*'s Squall Leonhart (1999), and *XII*'s Vaan (2006). Recently, *Final Fantasy XIII* (2009) and *Lightning Returns: Final Fantasy XIII* (2014) starred androgynous female main character Lightning.[8] All of the above named characters are light-skinned and athletic. Kirby, titular protagonist of the *Kirby* series, is another iconic androgynous hero: round, pink, and soft-bodied Kirby is typically gendered as male and appeared first in *Kirby's Dream Land* in 1992. His simple character design seems to reflect his ability to copy enemies' abilities by swallowing them: his androgyny functions as a kind of blank slate in which the lack of visible gendered signifiers indicates a capacity to be written over and "filled" by the attributes of swallowed enemies. Here, his androgyny is less of an ideal blend of gender than a perceived lack of it. The fact that Kirby is not a human character contextualizes his androgyny as alien and inhuman, even as it is non-threatening and cute; this lack of signifiers underscores his difference from a human androgyne. Kirby is that much less a recognizable subject.

In contrast to this lack, more humanoid androgynous characters are often subject to "choosing" masculinity or femininity, with this decision often being made for them by subtle degrees in the alteration of their character design. As noted by Sam Leeves, female androgynous heroes are much less common than male androgynous heroes.[9] One of the most iconic examples is King from the *Art of Fighting* and *King of Fighters* series. First appearing in *Art of Fighting* in 1992, King is a woman typically identified as French, with light skin, dressed in a dress shirt, bow tie, dark pants, and cummerbund. Her body shape has been increasingly feminized since her initial appearance: her first appearance did not feature visible breasts and was more heavily muscular.[10] After this appearance, her curves were initially more obvious mostly during specific taunts or gestures as in *Art of Fighting 2* in 1994. In subsequent games, King's body shape has had an increasingly large bust and waist to hip ratio. Additionally, her initially loose trousers have become tailored to cling to her buttocks and thighs as in *King of Fighters XII* in 2010. Her voice has also become higher over time. Since her initial appearance, most games featuring King have included a feature in which when she is defeated in the final round by a certain special move, she will lose her shirt and have her bra exposed. This reveal, as well as King's increasing bodily and vocal feminization, seems to both literally and symbolically correct King's androgyny to a feminine standard.

In the tradition of Kirby, the player-character NiGHTS from *Nights into Dreams* (1996) and *NiGHTS: Journey of Dreams* (2007) is an androgynous jester with purple clothing and large eyes. Unlike Kirby and many other androgynous heroes, NiGHTS is not expressly gendered as "actually" male or female. Instead, as stated by series director Takashi Iizuka in a 2007 interview with Nintendo Life, "NiGHTS is neutral, and therefore has no gender. The impressions of the character with regards to gender are totally up to the player."[11] Iizuka suggests that NiGHTS has no intrinsic gender but that this lack of intrinsic definition invites external definition: NiGHTS' gender is rough material to be shaped by rather than defy player interpretation. Like Kirby, NiGHTS has some shape-shifting ability: both characters are non-human androgynes whose gender-neutral appearance can be interpreted by the player and whose powers are malleable. I argue that their androgyny thematically reflects their changeable abilities. Neither Kirby nor NiGHTS seem to generate the kind of fan anxiety seen in fan blogs that claim "Androgyny in Video Games (Mainly J-RPGs) ... is going overboard."[12] One possible interpretation is that because Kirby and NiGHTS are less anthropomorphic in their design, they do not cause the same anxiety of being represented onscreen by an androgynous human that makes blog author "tha pirateninja" so uncomfortable playing as Cloud Strife.[13] Similarly, the character Raiden from the *Metal Gear Solid* series has had his androgyny rehabilitated over time. In his first appearance in *Metal Gear Solid 2: Sons of Liberty* (2001), Raiden's silver hair and slight figure lead the President of the United States to grope

Raiden's genitals in an effort to confirm his sex. In his next appearance in *Metal Gear 4: Guns of the Patriots* (2008), Raiden's design is altered with a cybernetic exoskeleton, making his design bulkier. Leeves notes "the loss of Raiden's androgyny in *Metal Gear Rising: Revengeance* (2013)" in which Raiden's already-altered body is largely replaced by cybernetic parts.[14] His design is increasingly masculine across the three games as his body grows increasingly muscular and less human: like King, Raiden is forcibly normalized. Ultimately, many of the player-characters in *Final Fantasy*, along with Kirby, King, NiGHTS, and Raiden, are a small sample of androgynous heroes in video games. However, their presentation suggests that androgyny demands definition and correction at varying levels of coercive violence, even when that androgyny is, in fact, masculine-leaning.

It's Dangerous to Go Alone. Take This Gender Binary: Androgyny in *The Legend of Zelda*

Perhaps the best-known archetype of the androgynous, masculine-of-center player-character is Link from the *Legend of Zelda* series, which first appeared in 1982 and is still ongoing. There are technically many different Links in the chronology of the series, but their characterization is very consistent. Link's appearance typically includes light skin, slight or slim physical frame, a near-absence of secondary sexual characteristics, and a youthful appearance. Link is often, though not always, prepubescent, which is a state of development typically prior to the development of secondary sexual characteristics. However, even "adult" Link does not suddenly sprout a beard or curvaceous hips. Adult Link's appearance remains fairly similar to that of the young version: his vocalizations are slightly lower in tone, his height increases, and his shoulders are slightly broader. We should note, however, that Link's voice is never deep and he's neither particularly muscular nor curvaceous. At any age, Link typically has long light brown or blond hair, sharp features including pointed ears, sharp brows, and large, often blue eyes. Link's clothing typically consists of a green belted tunic, white tights, and tan boots. His resemblance to another androgynous character, Peter Pan, is intentional, according to an interview with series creator Shigeru Miyamoto and the website *Gamekult*.[15] While Miyamoto notes that the similarity was intended to suggest youthfulness, it also unavoidably suggests Peter Pan's androgyny and the pantomime-inspired tradition of his being portrayed by female actors.[16] Link also often wears small golden or silver hoop earrings that emphasize the length of his ears: while large hoop earrings are often markers of the "Ms. Male Character" identified by Anita Sarkeesian, Link's earrings are typically small: however, they often match the earrings worn by Zelda both in her princess guise and her Sheik costume.[17] Link is also able to "pass" as a woman: in the latest Zelda title *Breath of the Wild*, Link dresses in traditional Gerudo garb to pass a member of the all-female tribe in order to gain access to a city forbidden to men.[18]

One of the commonly noted elements of Link's androgyny is his physical resemblance to the Princess of Hyrule, Zelda. While the degree of their resemblance depends on the particular entry in the series, both are light-haired, slim-bodied, and have similarly pointed features. The two are primarily distinguishable most frequently through their clothing and, less frequently, their eyebrows. Zelda typically wears dresses that are often pink, purple, or white, but never green, to distinguish her from Link. Her eyebrows are often blonde and thin, while Link's are usually blonde in earlier titles (as in *Ocarina of Time* in 1998) or black (as in *Spirit Tracks* in 2009). Arguably, the darkening of Link's eyebrows can be read as a masculinizing effort. Zelda's vocalizations are often higher than Link's as well. In her guise as Sheik, Zelda and Link are basically on par in terms of masculine-centered androgyny.[19]

In contrast, Link's archenemy Ganon is often much more explicitly masculine than Link. Where Link and Zelda are paired by their mutual resemblance, Ganon is much taller and muscular than either Hylian. Ganon's depiction has differed throughout the series, ranging from a boar-like monster in the very first *The Legend of Zelda* (1986) to a tall humanoid in *Ocarina of Time* (1998), but recurring features include green or gray skin; prominent brow, nose, and eyebrows; red facial hair and eyebrows; as well as a low voice. Ganon's masculinity has been incorporated into his backstory since the introduction of the nomadic Gerudo tribe in *Ocarina of Time*: according to Gerudo leader Nabooru, a male is born once a century and destined to rule the tribe.[20] Ganon is this one-in-a-century man, embodying a culture's messianic masculine leadership gone wrong. Ganon typically appears at key plot points to kidnap Zelda or meet Link in a final battle. Often in final confrontations, Ganon transforms into a more bestial form that emphasizes his size and strength. Even at his most human, however, Ganon embodies a monstrous kind of masculinity in contrast to the more heroic Link.

At a first glance, it is tempting to think of Link's heroic androgyny positively, especially according to a certain tradition of reading androgyny as revolutionary. We can see a sample of this kind of thinking when Carolyn Heilbrun describes androgyny thusly: "This ancient Greek word—from andro (male) and gyn (female)—defines a condition under which the characteristics of the sexes, and the human impulses expressed by men and women, are not rigidly assigned. Androgyny seeks to liberate the individual from the confines of the appropriate."[21] Heilbrun reads androgyny as freeing the individual from rigid gender roles, but I argue that Link serves as a strong example of the problems posed by the mainstream androgyny Link expresses, particularly at the level of anxiety about the character's androgyny and the potentially emasculating significance of that androgyny even when it is masculine-leaning.

For some fans of the series, Link's androgyny is a potential embarrassment because, despite his masculine-leaning androgyny, he is not visibly masculine enough. This anxiety about Link's androgyny is reflected in fan response to fan speculation that an upcoming iteration of Link might be female. We can see one example in Patricia Hernandez's *Kotaku* article "Some people think Link might be a girl in the new Zelda."[22] Hernandez screenshots comments from "huge threads" on a previous Zelda-focused article titled "The New Zelda is Open World, Looks Absolutely Incredible." The comments acknowledge both Link's long-exhibited androgyny and that while some fans will be in favor of the potential change to a female version of Link, others will be very angry. Hernandez describes the clamor of fan reaction to the early footage, writing "People on forums are talking about it. There are articles about it, some of which analyze Link's figure and facial features and use it as 'evidence' of Link's gender change. Some people swear they see breasts."[23] The only thing this account directly proves is that the internet exists to enable arguments, but I would like to raise the possibility that a significant part of the discussion is fueled by fan anxiety over Link not being masculine enough, even though his androgyny is masculine of center. This reflects a valorization of increasingly extreme masculinization in video games.

Warts and All: Villainous Gender-Variance

The video game industry has a long history of villains who do not follow the gender binary or the androgyny model. This history reflects a broader context of villainous gender-non-conforming characters in media, though the conflation of villainy and gender-non-conformity in animated films lies particularly close to video games as a media form often popularly associated with children's entertainment. Previous work has on this conflation in animated films includes articles like Li-Vollmer and LaPointe's "Gender Transgression and Villainy in Animated Film," which breaks down gender signifiers ranging from facial features, physique, clothing, gesture, and speech.[24] An absence of gendered signifiers or an abundance of them, if normatively cohesive, are both part of what makes a video game hero.

In contrast, gender conflict is the realm of villains. It would be disingenuous to describe these characters as genderqueer or their practices as a kind of genderfuck; many of these are written from a perspective that does not acknowledge or respect the legitimacy of identities outside cisgender binary identity. Instead, I would group these villains under the umbrella of the gender-variant. Kathryn Pauly Morgan notes in "Androgyny: A Conceptual Critique" that proponents of androgyny tend to describe it as an ideal, rather than depict the "bumps and warts" of reality.[25] In contrast, video game depictions of gender-variance typically focus almost exclusively on these "bumps and warts." Historically, the conscious mixing of supposedly conflicting masculine and feminine signifiers that belongs largely to video game villains has almost always been negative. This trope of the gender-variant video game villain is actually fairly standardized and operates within a context that identifies certain signifiers as belonging exclusively to either men or women is deeply transphobic, has no conception of intersex people, and uses gender-variance as a sign of evil.

The typical gender-variant villain will be vain, obsessed with beauty and typically presented as "really" a man in contrast to stereotypically feminine features, clothing, speech, and interests. Often this character believes they are above the norms of gender, and this belief is portrayed as narcissistic. They often hate women. These depictions often simultaneously trade on stereotypes about transgender women and gay men: the gender-fluid villain is often thought to be attempting to masquerade as a woman as well as being a sexually voracious predator out to "trick" men into sex. Whereas the Disney villains noted by Li-Vollmer and LaPointe, as well as by Putnam, can only reference sex and gender in coded ways, video game villains tend to refer to sex more directly.[26] These depictions reveal the gender essentialist core of mainstream video game culture: supposedly conflicting gender signifiers mixed together signal otherness and villainy. Many early examples like Birdo in *Super Mario Bros.* (1988), seductive fighter Poison from *Final Fight* (1989), bullfighter Vega from *Streetfighter* (1991), magician Flea from *Chrono Trigger* (1995), and latecomer and bioterrorist Duvall from *Resident Evil: Dead Aim* (2003) come from Japanese games rather than Western games, but the trope has spread to gender-variant villains like Sander Cohen in *BioShock* (2007).

Typically, the mix of gendered signifiers is in itself depicted as unattractive, which is ironic given how often these gender villains are characterized as vain. This combination of perceived vanity and ugliness further emphasizes characters as pathetic. This irony is similar to radical feminist philosopher Mary Daly's disavowal of androgyny using a Scotch tape metaphor in her book *Gyn/ecology* in 1978. Daly writes: "The second semantic abomination, androgyny, is a confusing term which I sometimes used in attempting to describe integrity of be-ing. The word is misbegotten—conveying something like 'John Travolta and Farrah Fawcett-Majors scotch-taped together'—as I have reiterated in public recantations."[27] Daly uses the example of two popular celebrities and sex symbols, the actor John Travolta and the actress Farrah Fawcett. Separately, they are examples of ideal male and female beauty; combined, they are supposedly disgusting (to use the tenor of Daly's surrounding adjectives). The idea that feminine and masculine signifiers might be attractive separately and disgusting when combined is the core of the villainy of many of these characters. They are depicted as a perversion of proper gendered signification, but like the anxiety-provoking androgynous heroes of gaming, they can be (and often are) rehabilitated over time.

Birdo from the *Super Mario* franchise is easily the most iconic gender-variant video game villain, in part because of her rehabilitation both into an ensemble protagonist and a cisgender woman. Appearing first in *Super Mario Bros. 2* in 1988, Birdo is a pink lizard-like creature wearing a large red bow on her head. In the original guide for the game, Birdo (mistakenly named Ostro) is described by the phrase "He thinks he is a girl." Combining Birdo's feminine signifiers with the keywords "he" and "thinks" simultaneously suggests and delegitimizes Birdo's gender identity. Later depictions of Birdo have varied widely in terms of the treatment of her gender. Her trophy in the 2008 fighting game *Super Smash Brothers Brawl* describes her as "a creature of indeterminate gender," using the pronoun "it" to refer to Birdo.

In an eerie parallel to the real-life harassment and violence faced by gender-variant people and the bathroom bills popping up in North America, in the 2008 Japan-only release game *Captain Rainbow*, Birdo is arrested for entering a women's washroom. Subsequently, the player must find the "proof" that Birdo is female, which is a vibrating object hidden under her pillow, blacked out with a purple question mark, heavily implied to be a sex toy. This has obvious limitations as proof of someone's gender and relies on the false assumption that only "real" women use sex toys. Along with the player "proving" Birdo's gender in *Captain Rainbow*, Birdo has been increasingly feminized in official game art in recent years, implied to be in some way romantically partnered with green dinosaur Yoshi because of their frequent partnering in franchise sub-series installments like *Mario Party* and *Mario Kart*. Her female identity is sometimes presented without comment, as it is in *Mario Tennis*, suggesting that character's gender-non-conforming history is being erased by Nintendo in such instances, rather than that Birdo is being celebrated as trans woman.

Birdo is particularly relevant to this article because while the character's gender identity is generally held up as being feminine, different games and fan culture depict her "real" sex (based on an assumption that physiology determines identity) with varying degrees of transphobia and trans-erasure. At the same time, there has been fan resistance to Birdo being retconned as a cisgender female and celebrated instead as a gender-variant icon.[28] It remains important to remember that Birdo, like many characters who resist the gender binary, was originally a villain: her rehabilitation has followed her transition to being part of the *Mario* ensemble rather than a villain. Birdo's excess of conflicting gender signifiers sharply contrasts to non-human androgynes like Kirby: where Kirby's soft pink body is depicted as innocently free of gender, Birdo's remains at worst, threatening and at best, uncertain. Both characters are inhuman, but where Kirby embodies ideas of androgyny as cute or ethereally superior to mundane humanity, Birdo's gender transgression tends toward the earthly and monstrous. Their lack of human bodies allows their respective gender neutrality and gender transgression to take center stage: they embody androgyny as innocence and purity and gender-variance as threatening mystery.

Another Japanese-originating gender transgressor in this early style is 2003 light gun game *Resident Evil: Dead Aim*'s villain, Duvall. Duvall hits all of the characteristics of the gender-variant villain: he (and he is constantly gendered by the game as male) is arrogant and obsessed with beauty. His use of plastic surgery to maintain a youthful appearance is supposed to reinforce his narcissism. It's also notable that Duvall is hinted to have possibly had sex reassignment surgery, so his gender has a kind of shadowy, uncertain quality that the game seems to respond to by eventually transforming him into a mutated creature with heightened feminine signifiers including breasts and a gait that suggests his feet have turned into a high heel shape. Duvall seems to be punished for his surgical transformations and gender transgression; the hints of his possible SRS are implicated when he mutates, before eventually turning into a monstrous fleshy blob that explodes. His efforts to transform go out of control and literally kill him: an anti-gender-variant parable if ever there was one.

Later gender-transgressing villains from Western titles include the performer Sander Cohen from *BioShock* (2007), the minor villain Tommy from *Fable II* (2008), and the mage Dethmold in *The Witcher 2* (2011).[29] Western examples often resemble the villain-as-sissy identified by Li-Vollmer and LaPointe, which incorporates stereotypical elements of transgender identification, drag theatricality, and queerness.[30] As noted previously, gender-transgressing video game villains are often less coy than their cartoon counterparts. As a result, they can be read more directly, though they still often share a conflation of gender transgression with queerness that must be carefully read in order not to reify that conflation.

From the game *Fable II* (2008) comes Tommy, who is a very minor character whose appearance is highly suggestive of the well-worn nature of the trope of the gender-variant villain. In the side-quest "Hobbe Squatters," a person named Tommy—dressed in clothing marked for female characters—asks the player-character to go into a cave to kill the monsters inside. Tommy has a low-pitched voice, a medium frame, and a similar accent to the lower-class male NPCs but is wearing a wig often seen on upper-class female NPCs, a top similar to the female "harlot" outfit, the skirt from the lower-class female clothing set, garish make-up, and lopsided breast padding. Upon entering the cave, the player-character finds a series of journal entries that indicate Tommy has encouraged the player-character to go into the cave in the hopes the Hobbes will kill and eat them. Eventually, Tommy attacks and must be killed before the quest can be completed. The message that signals completion of the quests reads "Oakfield can sigh with relief. No longer will women's underwear disappear from laundry lines." Tommy is a fairly standard game depiction of a supposedly funny, evil man in a dress, who is both pathetic and threatening. The quest's use of the trope is snide but banal: it shows the casual ease with which the trope is used.

Finally, the mage Dethmold from *The Witcher 2* (2011) is a very recent example of the trope. His queer sexuality and mounting evil are revealed alongside one another. The character being openly acknowledged as definitively queer rather than being a vague morass of stereotypes and insinuations is in actuality fairly unusual but hardly a positive variation. While he is less broadly, "artificially" feminine than some of the other examples of this trope (like *BioShock*'s heavily made-up artist, Sander Cohen), Dethmold possesses the typical ironic vanity, sexual rapacity, and dislike of women associated with the trope.

Like the other key examples of this trope previously discussed, Dethmold is punished for his gender transgressions. The game plot offers two possibilities for the character. Both include his death. In one, he is merely decapitated offscreen, but the alternative scene depicts Dethmold being castrated and killed. In the scene in which he is killed, he is seen fussing in a mirror while a shirtless man lies in his bed. The player-character helps subdue the mage and watches as the soldier Vernon Roche cuts off Dethmold's testicles, shoves them in the mage's mouth and cuts his throat. Grisly deaths are hardly unusual in *The Witcher* series, but Dethmold's sexuality and gender (as crime) and death (as punishment) are inexorably wedded in this potential ending. A journal entry narrated by the bard Dandelion winks at the death: "Their next meeting proved to be their last, as Dethmold died at the hands of the vengeful Roche. Geralt never revealed the details of the sorcerer's demise.

I've concluded that it must have been quite savage, though I would prefer to hope that Vernon's threats had been but figures of speech..."[31] Dethmold's death is simultaneously too gruesome to describe but not too gruesome to watch or to be enacted upon Dethmold's body: this appears to be the appropriate punishment due to the gender-variant villain.

The gender-variant villain remains a common trope in games and other media and continues to combine the pathetic threat and frightening tragedy of gender-variance: this discomfort with gender fluidity is reflected in the transphobic and homophobic depictions of villains both historically in early games and in recent triple-A games. Gender-variant villains have an unlikely connection with the androgynous heroes discussed earlier in this article: their maleness is presented as their true gender, in contrast to feminine artifice. Both the masculine-leaning androgynous hero and the gender-variant villain express the assumed innate, natural masculinity of these characters as both an ideal to strive toward and a standard deviated from at their peril.

Bye, Bye, Birdo, Hello, Who?: A Call to Keyboards, Controllers, and Cardboard

Ultimately, mainstream video game production has used two seemingly revolutionary responses to gender roles—androgyny and gender-variance—to reinforce rather than challenge the strictures of gender. Androgyny and gender-variance might seem to (and sometimes well may) have anti-oppressive possibilities, but in mainstream video games, androgyny has frequently been used to reify a very specific type of largely white, thin, and able-bodied masculinity in games, and gender-variance has been used to vilify trans women and femininity more broadly. Other revolutionary uses of androgyny and gender-variance exist in games right now, but most exist on the periphery of gaming in work being done by independent developers like Dietrich Squinkifer, Christine Love, and Avery Alder.

For me, the question remains whether it is possible to embrace androgyny in video games, character design, and culture in a non-oppressive way, without needing androgyny to be a perfect gender balance or a colorless transcendent idea. Is it possible to embrace bodies, all kinds of androgynous bodies, and to code androgyny while embracing weight, size, color, and gender expressions across spectrums? Is it in fact possible to pick up the Scotch tape deplored by Daly and embrace gender excess and variance that has been used to encode villains and instead set them free?

I would like to assert one potential answer: game designers, critics, and players can approach androgyny and gender-variance thoughtfully in terms of both production and consumption. We can reject stereotypical characterizations in our own work and in work we encounter. We can offer our own creations, but we also need to recognize that representation through specific characters, which has been a major focus of this article, is only one aspect of inclusivity. We can also consider how our game environments might support or dismantle gender binaries or, as Jess Marcotte has discussed, how different approaches to game control design might be fruitfully queered.[32] It is important that we interrogate how androgyny as an esthetic can center thin, white masculinity. Progress requires that we critically engage with how beauty and ugliness, heroism and villainy interact with gender ideals and taboos in our creation and criticism. We need not only play with gender but against it, or at least against its use as a tool of oppression.

Notes

1. Diane Carr, *Computer Games: Text, Narrative and Play* (Cambridge: Polity Press, 2006), 163.
2. Fabio Lorenzo-Cioldi, "Psychological Androgyny: A Concept in Search of Lesser Substance. Towards the Understanding of the Transformation of a Social Representation," *Journal for the Theory of Social Behaviour* 26, no. 2 (1996): 145.
3. Larin McLaughlin, "Androgyny and Transcendence in Contemporary Corporate and Popular Culture," *Cultural Critique* 42 (1999): 206.
4. Lola Phoenix, "The Pursuit of Androgyny," *Medium* 20 December 2015. https://medium.com/gender-2-0/the-pursuit-of-androgyny-6a0ffa7aa1ff#. soshlkddl.
5. Anita Sarkeesian, "Ms. Male Character – Tropes vs Women in Video Games," *Youtube* 15 December 2015. https://www.youtube.com/watch?v=eYqYLfm1rWA.
6. Megan Farokhmanesh, "Animating women should take 'days,' says Assassin's Creed 3 animation director," *Polygon* 11 January 2014. http://www.polygon.com/2014/6/11/5800466/assassins-creed-unity-women-animation.
7. Kathryn Pauly Morgan, "Androgyny: A Conceptual Critique," *Social Theory and Practice* 8, no. 3 (1982): 248.
8. Elsewhere in this volume, Mark Filipowich describes androgyny in the *Final Fantasy* series in further detail.
9. Sam Leeves, "Culture Bytes: Androgyny in Video Games," *Alt:Mag*, 1 August 2014. http://www.altmaguk.net/2014/08/androgyny-in-video-games.html.
10. *Art of Fighting*, SNK (1992).

11. Mike Taylor, "Interview: Takasha Iizuka talks NiGHTS," *NintendoLife*, 5 December 2007. http://www.nintendolife.com/news/2007/12/interview_ takashi_iizuka_talks_nights.

12. Tha pirateninja, "Androgyny in Video Games (Mainly JPRGS)," 13 May 2008. http://attentionallfriends.blogspot.ca/2008/05/androgyny-in-video-games-mainly-j-rpgs.html.

13. Ibid.

14. Sam Leeves, "Culture Bytes: Androgyny in Video Games."

15. William Audureau, "Miyamoto, la Wii U et la secrete de la Triforce," *Gamekult*, 11 January 2012. http://www.gamekult.com/actu/miyamoto-la-wii-u-et-le-secret-de-la-triforce-A105550.html.

16. Bruce K. Hanson, *Peter Pan on Stage and Screen 1904–2010* (Jefferson: McFarland, 2011), 27.

17. Anita Sarkeesian, "Ms. Male Character – Tropes vs Women in Video Games."

18. *Legend of Zelda: Breath of the Wild* (2017).

19. Zelda's appearances as Sheik are discussed in further detail in Chap. 6, written by Mark Filipowich elsewhere in this volume.

20. *Ocarina of Time* (1998).

21. Carolyn Heilbrun, *Toward a Recognition of Androgyny* (Michigan: University of Michigan Press, 1973), x.

22. Patricia Hernandez, "Some people think Link might be a girl in the new *Zelda*," *Kotaku*, 11 June 2014. http://kotaku.com/some-people-think-link-might-be-a-girl-in-the-new-zelda-1589374151.

23. Ibid.

24. Meredith Li-Vollmer and Mark E. LaPointe, "Gender Transgression and Villainy in Animated Film," *Popular Communication* 1, no. 2 (2003): 89–109.

25. Kathryn Pauly Morgan, "Androgyny: A Conceptual Critique," (1982): 254.

26. Meredith Li-Vollmer and Mark E. LaPointe, "Gender Transgression and Villainy in Animated Film"; Amanda Putnam, "Mean Ladies: Transgendered Villains in Disney Films," Ed. Johnson Cheu, *Diversity in Disney Films: Critical Essays on Race, Ethnicity, Gender, Sexuality and Disability* (London: MacFarland & Co, 2015), 147–162.

27. Mary Daly, *Gyn/ecology: The Metaethics of Radical Feminism* (Boston: Beacon Press, 1973), xi.

28. Jennifer Diane Reitz, "The First Transsexual Game Character?" 2001. http://www.transsexual.org/birdo.html. np.

29. Other potential examples like Reaver from the *Fable* series have been removed from the list because they do not so closely conform to the list of attributes of the gender-variant villain.

30. Li-Vollmer and Lapointe, 103.

31. *The Witcher 2: Assassins of Kings* (2011).

32. Jess Marcotte, "Queering Game Controls" (presentation at the Annual Convention of the Canadian Game Studies Association, Toronto, ON, 31 May to 2 June 2017).

Bibliography

Andureau, William. 2012. Miyamoto, la Wii U et la secrete de la Triforce. *Gamekult*, 11 January. http://www.gamekult.com/actu/miyamoto-la-wii-u-et-le-secret-de-la-triforce-A105550.html.

Carr, Diane. 2006. *Computer Games: Text, Narrative and Play*. Cambridge: Polity Press.

Daly, Mary. 1973. *Gyn/Ecology: The Metaethics of Radical Feminism*. Boston: Beacon Press.

Farokhmanesh, Megan. 2014. Animating Women Should Take 'Days,' Says *Assassin's Creed 3* Animation Director. *Polygon*, 11 January. http://www.polygon.com/2014/6/11/5800466/assassins-creed-unity-women-animation.

Hanson, Bruce K. 2011. *Peter Pan on Stage and Screen 1904–2010*. Jefferson: McFarland.

Heilbrun, Carolyn. 1973. *Toward a Recognition of Androgyny*. Michigan: University of Michigan Press.

Hernandez, Patricia. 2014. Some People Think Link Might Be a Girl in the New *Zelda*. *Kotaku*, 11 June. http://kotaku.com/some-people-think-link-might-be-a-girl-in-the-new-zelda-1589374151.

Leeves, Sam. 2014. Culture Bytes: Androgyny in Video Games. *Alt:Mag*, 1 August. http://www.altmaguk.net/2014/08/androgyny-in-video-games.html.

Li-Vollmer, Meredith, and Mark E. LaPointe. 2003. Gender Transgression and Villainy in Animated Film. *Popular Communication* 1 (2): 89–109.

Lorenzo-Cioldi, Fabio. 1996. Psychological Androgyny: A Concept in Search of Lesser Substance. Towards the Understanding of the Transformation of a Social Representation. *Journal for the Theory of Social Behaviour* 26 (2): 137–155.

Marcotte, Jess. 2017. *Queering Game Controls*. Presentation at the Annual Convention of the Canadian Game Studies Association, Toronto, ON, May 31st to June 2nd, 2017.

McLaughlin, Larin. 1999. Androgyny and Transcendence in Contemporary Corporate Culture. *Cultural Critique* 42: 188–215.

Morgan, Kathryn Pauly. 1982. Androgyny: A Conceptual Critique. *Social Theory and Practice* 8 (3): 254–283.

Phoenix, Lola. 2015. The Pursuit of Androgyny. *Medium*, 20 December. https://medium.com/gender-2-0/the-pursuit-of-androgyny-6a0ffa7aa1ff#.soshlkddl.

Putnam, Amanda. 2015. Mean Ladies: Transgendered Villains in Disney Films. In *Diversity in Disney Films: Critical Essays on Race, Ethnicity, Gender, Sexuality and Disability*, ed. Johnson Cheu, 147–162. London: MacFarland & Co.

Reitz, Jennifer Diane. 2001. *The First Transsexual Video Game Character?* http://www.transsexual.org/birdo.html.

Sarkeesian, Anita. 2015. *Ms. Male Character – Tropes vs Women in Video Games*. Youtube, 15 December. https://www.youtube.com/watch?v=eYqYLfm1rWA.

Taylor, Mike. 2007. Interview: Takasha Iizuka Talks NiGHTS. *Nintendo Life*, 5 December. http://www.nintendolife.com/news/2007/12/interview_takashi_iizuka_ talks_nights.

tha pirateninja. 2008. *Androgyny in Video Games (Mainly JRPGS)*. 13 May. http:// attentionallfriends.blogspot.ca/2008/05/androgyny-in-video-games-mainly-j- rpgs.html.

Part III

Un-gendering Assemblages

10

Cues for Queer Play: Carving a Possibility Space for LGBTQ Role-Play

Tanja Sihvonen and Jaakko Stenros

Introduction

Games provide a possibility space governed by incentives and obstacles for inter-action. Intuitively speaking, one would assume that role-playing games have always revolved around exploring the possibilities of social interaction, alternative identities, diverging sexual orientations, and other non-mainstream constellations (hence the "role" in role-play), but from recent studies we know that has not been the case (Stenros and Sihvonen 2015; Shaw 2015a; Peterson 2012). Even though role-playing games may have incorporated sexual content and rules for erotic play (Brown 2015), there is plenty of evidence that the representations of LGBTQ—or queer—themes and characters have been scarce and only very faintly visible in games well until the 2000s (Pulos 2013; Shaw 2009).

In this chapter, we will investigate what kind of possibility spaces there are for queer play in multiplayer role-playing games. We use *queer* as an umbrella term to refer to practices that are oppositional to heteronormativity and the binary gender system, as well as non-heterosexual sexual orientations. The origins of queer are in Judith Butler's (1999) notion of the dichotomy of sexes

T. Sihvonen (✉)
University of Vaasa, Vaasa, Finland

J. Stenros
University of Tampere, Tampere, Finland

© The Author(s) 2018
T. Harper et al. (eds.), *Queerness in Play*, Palgrave Games in Context,
https://doi.org/10.1007/978-3-319-90542-6_10

167

being naturalized through performative acts, which can be made visible and even subverted through play with social norms and expectations. Since there is a specific emphasis on performance in queer studies (e.g. Stuart 2008, 80–83), we consider role-playing games a useful context for this research.

Queer is an ambivalent term that changes and challenges other concepts and connotes a specific politics of resistance (Kornak 2015, 45–46). It has a particular relationship with cultural norms, which it both embraces and abandons, persistently toying with the mainstream (Ilmonen and Juvonen 2015). First used as a derogatory insult, in the 1980s queer started to mark resistance as the term was appropriated as a means to rearticulate existing conditions in a radically different way, paving the way for its use as a mark of a new identity, sensitivity, community, and theory (Kornak 2015, 44). Queer in this text is regarded through embodied, de-essentialized, and postmodernized notions of subjectivity and types of experience. In her formulation of "transgressive play", Jenny Sundén (2009) discusses queer uses of game spaces that play with norms and expectations governing the formation of games and gaming communities, and our approach closely resembles hers. By investigating how players appropriate the affordances of the game system, how they "queer" gameplay, and "think differently", cultural norms of the ideal player can be made visible—and twisted.

Our intention in this chapter is not only to find queer characters in games and see how people play or respond to them but to locate possibilities for queer existence and interaction in the ways that some role-playing games (RPGs) function. We aim to write game-specific theory and acknowledge that representation of RPG characters works differently from, say, representation of movie characters in mainstream Hollywood film. The game industry tends to reproduce problematic or marginalizing forms of representation, and games often fail to subvert normative gender and sexuality (Shaw 2009; Shaw and Friesem 2016). Representation for us is a lens in making sense of how RPG characters and situations can be thought of in a queer way. That is why we are focused on the player's approach to play, as well as hints, allusions, and insinuations in the game-texts, in order to see how players negotiate queer affordances in games. In this chapter, we focus on representations of non-normatively gendered game characters, the ways characters express their sexuality, and the ways queer readings are possible in games.

The starting point of this chapter is the observation that in mainstream games, the traces of queerness need to be specifically tracked down. Queer spaces and possibilities do exist in games, and in subcultural contexts they may even flourish. From our perspective, a key dilemma in this area is the friction between game product and actual play experience. Some notable exceptions notwithstanding, queer experiences are rarely represented in commercial game products, and even the word gay is notoriously used negatively throughout the gaming world (Condis 2015, 201). However, the game product is only stimulus for play and thus does not determine if, when, or how queer experiences manifest in actual play. This gap between source material of a game and the game being played is at the core of this chapter.

To bridge the gap between game product and gameplay, we study role-playing games through analyzing the games as distinguished from narratives or as media and specifically through looking at how players negotiate with these games as "urtexts". Borrowing the term *urtext* from musicology, where it refers to a printed version of a work of classical music that is supposed to reproduce the original intention of the composer as faithfully as possible, we use it to denote a game "text" without the player's involvement. Considering player activities and fan fiction allows us to develop a deeper understanding of the queer possibility spaces in RPGs and the ways these transpose into actual gameplay. Our research material draws from both mainstream and niche games. We attempt to tie together materials and theory-building relevant to very different gamescapes and player cultures.

To capture the diversity of play experiences available, we have chosen to analyze three types of games and their play practices. We aim to uncover the cues for queer experiences in the following types of role-playing games: *tabletop*, *online multiplayer*, and *live-action* RPGs. We will first contextualize our analysis by looking at what role-playing entails and what kinds of role-playing games exist. We will investigate game characters and look more into detail in how the issues of representation work in the context of role-playing games. The first game type we will analyze is the analogue tradition of tabletop or pen-and-paper role-playing games. Second, we will delve into massively multiplayer online role-playing games, or MMORPGs, and third, into live-action games, or larps, which allow for diverse play styles to emerge. In the end, we will conclude the chapter by discussing under which conditions queer play may emerge and how the queering of gameplay may take place.

Role-Playing Games

Role-playing games are a subset of games where participating players create imaginary events through enacting anthropomorphic character constructs in fictional worlds. Guided by rules, these characters change and develop as the game progresses. When considering RPGs and the importance of game characters, it is essential to remember that players impact the world mainly through the characters they play. However, often the power to influence events in the game world is unevenly distributed, with a game master participant (or a digital system) having more power compared to the players. In MMORPGs, for instance, "role-playing game" refers above all to game mechanics, comprised of leveling, character classes, and the fantasy setting of the game itself, rather than the players' actions (for a more thorough discussion of the definition of role-playing games, see Montola 2008; Hitchens and Drachen 2008; Björk and Holopainen 2005, 252; MacCallum-Stewart and Parsler 2008).

The birth of role-playing games is commonly identified as the publication of *Dungeons & Dragons* (1974), which itself draws from a long history of miniature war games and strategy board games, as well as a history of play practices that feature reenactment of fictitious personas (Peterson 2012). This was the beginning of *tabletop role-playing games*. The other types of role-playing games emerged almost simultaneously from this root, although there are vital differences between the various forms and not all relevant predecessors are within the field of games. *Digital role-playing games* emerged soon after, with the first computerized version called *D&D* premiering the following year (Peterson 2012, 608–609). Digital RPGs today can be divided into two categories, single-player games (today characterized by *Fallout* and *Final Fantasy* franchises) and multiplayer online games (starting with Multi-User Dungeons and leading to the present-day massively multiplayer online games such as *World of Warcraft*, or *WoW* [Blizzard Entertainment, 2004]). Larping emerged in the late 1970s or early 1980s when players chose to physically embody their characters instead of controlling them through narration or digital representation.

An important distinction must be made between *role-playing* in games and role-playing *games* (Heliö 2004; also Mortensen 2003; Sihvonen 2011; Williams et al. 2011). The former is an attitude, a mind-set, or a style one can adopt in any activity, acting "as if" one were someone else; for instance, you can immerse yourself into the traumatized Niko Bellic in *GTA IV* or engage in larping as if your character feels strong same-sex attraction. The player's performance of a character, when acting as if, always features interpretation. Acting as if, or pretend play, is psychologically speaking a foundational play activity, the signs of which humans over the age of two exhibit (Rakocky 2007, 56; Laycock 2015, 1–2). As for the latter, role-playing games are a specific tradition of games that need not feature strong identification with the character.

For some players and RPG traditions, the activity of enacting a character through pretend play is the core of role-playing games; for others the character is but a tool. In MMORPGs the role-playing attitude is fairly rare, although the players who do engage in it easily form close and vibrant communities (Williams et al. 2011; Taylor 2006, 30; Corneliussen and Rettberg 2008). We are unaware of any studies about attitudes toward the character in tabletop RPGs, but in emic theorizing by role-players and designers, there is a division into four "stances" a player can adopt toward the character (actor, pawn, director, author) (Hardwick 1995; Edwards 2001) implying that a role-playing style is merely one of many. Similarly in larp theorizing numerous play styles have been identified (e.g. Pohjola 2004; Montola et al. 2015). Even when role-playing attitude is not central to play, players of multiplayer role-playing games do construct, maintain, and negotiate a fictional, shared social world. This co-creative world building is a key element in enabling queer play in RPGs, and thus we concentrate mainly on multiplayer forms of role-playing in this chapter.

Toward Queer Play

For a long time, games have been accused of resorting to simplistic and heteronormative character stereotypes in terms of race, ethnicity, (dis)ability, gender, and sexuality. In this context, queer characters are always quirky exceptions and "against the norm", so even if they are found in games, their representation and role in the game world cannot easily be interpreted in positive terms (e.g. Adams 2015; Condis 2015). Earlier research on role-playing games tells us that there is a scarcity of queer characters and narratives (Schröder 2008). Our analysis of tabletop RPG source material from 1974–2005 shows that when queer themes are not silenced altogether, they are met with reactions that seem humorous or extreme in hindsight. In that context we concluded that queer sexualities and situations have been either completely absent or extremely sporadic for most of the history of role-playing games (Stenros and Sihvonen 2015).

Nevertheless, digital role-playing games have been researched in the 2000s as environments for queer and other non-normative play experiences. In addition to Adrienne Shaw's groundbreaking work (2009, 2015a, b), Jordan Youngblood (2013), for instance, has studied how digital RPGs can be "queered" through engaging the player's body in transgressive gameplay in Japanese RPG *Persona 4* (Atlus Games 2008). Lee Sherlock (2013) has studied transgender player's confrontation with the heteronormative environment of *WoW*, and Jenny Sundén (2009) is doing queer-themed ethnographic research in the same game. As part of his study on gay video gamers, or "gaymers", and their online discussions on a Reddit subforum, M. William MacKnight (2013) has uncovered some queer experiences reflected in videogames in general, but his focus was not limited to role-playing games.

There is less research on larp than there is on digital or tabletop RPGs. It is therefore not surprising that queer experiences or themes have not surfaced in larp studies. However, there are some accounts of both queer larps and player experiences written by para-academics, expert hobbyists, and journalists. These texts tend to originate in the context of Nordic larp (Stenros and Montola 2010) and often relate to one of the following three larps, *Just a Little Lovin'* (Gronemann and Raasted 2013), *Mad about the Boy* (Kreil 2013; Stark 2012), or *Mellan himmel och hav* (Gerge 2004). In addition to the scarcity of research on larp, there do not seem to be that many queer larps in circulation, although the situation is changing. Recently, these topics have been addressed by American and Nordic freeform larps including *Screwing the Crew* (Nielsen and Lindahl 2013), *A Place to Fuck Each Other* (Sheep and Mcdaldno n.d.), and *Spin the Goddesses* (Edman 2016).

There are no statistics available on the number of queer role-players. Williams et al. (2011) report that people belonging to a minority group, be it related to sexuality, religious affiliation, or race/ethnicity, are more likely to engage in role-playing style of playing in online RPGs.

Numerous games do not welcome openly queer content or expression, but observation of player cultures in and around these games reveals cracks in the surface. Analyzing the representation of game characters—their looks, or even their body types and specifically gendered traits, or their behavior—is not enough to explain how queer play may come into being. There are tabletop groups comprised of all queer players playing a game with queer themes, subversive queer guilds hiding in plain sight in online worlds, indie game products and experimental larps devoted to exploring queer living, and even the occasional AAA console game that yields to queer play. Increasingly, queerness refuses to hide itself, surfacing in clashes and confrontations that concern the rules and values of game products and services. Next, we look into these affordances and see how players respond to them in the various contexts of role-playing games.

Tabletop RPGs

In our survey (Stenros and Sihvonen 2015) of queer characters in tabletop source books (the urtext in this case) from the first three decades of commercial role-playing games, we found that for almost two decades queer characters were all but nonexistent, and then they started to emerge in ways that today seem purposefully hurtful or unintentionally ludicrous. Certain publishers worked toward varied and empowering representation, while others ignored the issue altogether. Our survey ended in the year 2005 as queer themes were starting to become more commonplace.

A quick look at the source books that have been published since 2005 shows that this trend has continued. A celebrated indie teenage horror game *Monsterhearts* (Mcdaldno 2012, 42–43) advocated including queer content as it will make the story "more interesting and real", since queerness taps into the central themes of the game. The instructions are written from a self-reflexive heteronormative position, explicating how heterosexuality is constructed as normal. *Monsterhearts* is particularly relevant for this article as it motivates why including queer content makes a game more interesting; a player does not get to decide if they are attracted to a particular person (of the same sex), the dice determine that. The idea is to explore the "messy, sexy melodrama" of adolescent attraction and "the confusion that arises when your body and your social world start changing without your permission" (Ibid., 42). This is particularly interesting considering the history of tabletop RPG game mechanics for attractions, especially seduction. When same-sex attraction has been discussed in the rules, usually a character's straightness has been a defense against queer seduction attempts. *Monsterhearts* not only turns this on its head but makes surprising attraction that lies beyond the control of the player a core feature of the game system.

Inclusivity of queer representation has become mainstream in tabletop RPGs as in 2014 the fifth edition of *Dungeons & Dragons* contained a nod toward queer characters and play:

> You don't need to be confined to binary notions of sex and gender. The elf god Corellon Larethian is often seen as androgynous or hermaphroditic, for example, and some elves in the multiverse are made in Corellon's image. You could also play a female character who presents herself as a man, a man who feels trapped in a female body, or a bearded female dwarf who hates being mistaken for a male. Likewise, your character's sexual orientation is for you to decide. (Mearls and Crawford 2014, 121)

The passage, while brief and criticized both for being awkwardly worded and pandering, was relatively well received. It is a clear signal that after decades of silence, *Dungeons & Dragons* is now explicitly welcoming toward queer play.

Studies of tabletop RPG *play* are rare. While ethnographic accounts of role-playing communities exist, ones targeting specifically tabletop games are hard to find. The only work devoted to this topic specifically is Gary Alan Fine's *Shared Fantasy* (1983), and it does not address queer issues. Ashley Brown's (2013) study into erotic play in role-playing games is exceptional in this regard, for although it concentrates on online RPGs, tabletop games are also discussed extensively. Brown explores how non-normative sexual activity, such as sexual violence, is played with. She concludes that source books "simultaneously provide justification for including sexuality in role playing games and place limitations on which types of sexual expression are acceptable" (Brown 2013, 128). When players introduce elements that other participants may find problematic, they can be validated by citing specific passages in source books.

Brown's work does not focus on expressions of queer experiences or themes but on erotic play. Our aim is not to equate the sexual and the queer but the tactics used to negotiate transgressing societal norms relating to non-normative eroticism and queer existence certainly have similarities. Brown's study does mention a few gay tabletop characters, and queerness in itself does not seem to be problematic for the studied groups in any way. However, it is unclear where the cue for queer sexualities comes from: the games mentioned are based on products where queer sexualities are present in the source books (e.g. *Vampire: The Masquerade*), and the players of the group who have chosen this game also identify as queer.

Tabletop role-playing games offer a wide range of actions for players—at least in theory—since players need not just choose actions designed and implemented by game developers or other players. They can craft their own narratives. In tabletop RPGs the players and game masters can create queer characters and situations and explore queer themes if they so choose. Source books and the queer presence (or absence) they contain can provide guidelines, limits, and justifications for such inclusions, but the participants in a game session are only bound by the source books, again, if they so choose. Queer presence and hooks for identification may influence the choice of a game system. Tabletop player groups have only a handful of people, and in such microcultures shared norms can markedly differ from the mainstream. However, homegrown RPG systems notwithstanding, the source books often do function as a starting point and a framework, and when socially awkward situations arise, the books provide grounds for game-specific justification.

MMORPGs

MMORPGs combine largely predetermined fictional digital settings with the possibilities of character-based and social role-play. The boundaries of the digital system are overcome by play via text and voice chat as well as player forums, although these components are still constrained by social norms in other ways. In MMORPGs, players have very little influence over the game environment, so their main channel through which gameplay occurs is the game character. Although the development and maintenance of characters is vitally important, character creation in MMORPGs largely takes place through prefixed attributes. In *World of Warcraft*, for example, the player must first choose between the opposing factions of Alliance and Horde, after which the new character's race (such as orc, troll, human, or dwarf), gender (male or female), and class (such as mage, warrior, or priest) are defined. Although the options for character creation are detailed, there are few customization options, and heteronormative gendering of characters is especially rigorous. *WoW* is stricter in this sense than other MMORPGs, such as *Lord of the Rings Online* (2007) or *Oblivion, the Elder Scrolls* (2006).

The sexualized appearance of the female *WoW* characters has always caused commotion among the players of the game, as the disenfranchising of those disinclined to support the binary gendering of their avatars is built into the game system (MacCallum-Stewart and Parsler 2008, 230). The most common way to alter the appearance of game characters in MMORPGs is through changing their clothing: while item function is not affected by gender, appearance is. The "scanty armor" of female *WoW* characters has spawned numerous fan forum threads and even virtual beauty contests featuring the "top 10 hottest WoW characters" (pixiestixy 2011a, b). This again accentuates the difference between male and female characters and posits them unequally as erotic objects of gaze. As many have noted (e.g. MacCallum-Stewart 2008; Crowe and Watts 2014), the choice of a character's gender is mainly an aesthetic decision, although it also does affect the mode of play in some cases.

In addition to character-based role-play, or tuning up their character to match their desires, players may also engage in social role-play. MMORPGs hinge on players' cooperation and teamwork, and games like *WoW* are naturally focused on promoting intense social interaction to the point that many players are (expected to be) moving large parts of their social lives to the game world. In this context, the freedom to self-identify as queer via naming is especially important but also contested. Even though sexually themed character descriptions are not encouraged in MMORPGs, players have always found ways to circumvent the rules (Kelley 2012). It is noteworthy, then, that early 2006 there was an incident where Blizzard banned mentions of sexual orientation in player-created guild descriptions (see Pulos 2013, 78). According to Cory Doctorow's account, Blizzard moderated all LGBTQ descriptions on the grounds of anti-discrimination: they explained that if queer players were allowed to tell others about their sexual orientation, it might arouse discriminatory or unkind remarks from other players, and that would violate the anti-discrimination rules of the game (Doctorow 2006).

Although a public backlash ensued and Blizzard's decision was later reversed, there are still signs of the clash in the world of online role-playing games. Other MMORPG providers such as ArenaNet running *Guild Wars* (2005) have been implementing the policy of censoring LGBTQ words from guild descriptions and the situation with queer content in digital RPGs is improving very slowly (e.g. Shaw 2015a, 202–209). De Zwart and Humphreys (2012, 530) note that the incident brought to the surface the unfortunate fact that harassment of queers in *WoW* has always been widespread. On the other hand, it has been noted that it was the controversy with Blizzard that gave many LGBTQ people a reason to start forming their own guilds, and now they also have their own queer-friendly server in *WoW* (Archer 2014).

From the perspective of queer play, MMORPGs are tightly moderated and normative game environments, where the possibilities of transgressive play must be socially negotiated in a different way than in single-player RPGs (Sundén 2009; Kelley 2012). Yet the possibility for transgressive play, including queer and/or erotic play, exists even in *World of Warcraft*. Brown's (2013, 136–150) ethnography on erotic role-play in *WoW* finds that players may negotiate and play with content explicitly forbidden by the official rules. Furthermore, it is important to note that transgressive online role-play using a commercial MMORPG is not free-for-all but contains an additional layer of rules (imposed by, for instance, the guild and the game's developers) for how the erotic role-play should be carried out.

Larps

Larps combine elements of tabletop and multiplayer online RPGs in the sense that they provide a relatively wide range of activities that are possible, as in tabletop, but due to a (usually) larger number of players, the social norms are stricter, as in MMOs. Larps are the most ephemeral of role-playing games, since in addition to providing singular and unique play experiences, the games-as-systems in larps are less commodified. Although commercial systems (such as White Wolf's *Mind's Eye Theatre*, see e.g. Dansky 1996) exist, most larps and larp campaigns develop their own rule systems. There are different traditions at work here; in the campaign model, numerous instances of a larp are organized as part of the same longer story or in the same fictional world with slowly evolving set of rules. In the fest model, there are enormous annual larps for thousands of participants. In chamber model, there are shorter larps with a specific setting and characters that can be staged around the world based on a larp script, and in the event model, a singular larp with a particular setting and rules is staged only once (or a few times).

There are numerous larps that combine these different models, but as the different models produce different kinds of materials that can be analyzed, they help in thinking about representation in larp. The most commonly available material produced in larps are the rule sets, especially the commercially available ones and the chamber larp scripts. Campaign larps also have rule sets, but these are not as widely distributed. Event larps, especially in Northern Europe, rarely provide their larp scripts, but they are often documented via either player reports, designers' notes, or analytical pieces.

The urtext in larp, meaning the material created and curated by the larp organizers, limits what kinds of cues are found for queer play. Within those bounds the players have, at least in theory, quite a bit of leeway to introduce queer themes if they are not explicitly forbidden, if they so choose. However, larping is a social activity, and the social norms and expectations of a given player group or a tradition can act as an important limitation to queer play. Players in the relatively progressive Nordic scenes reflect on the issue:

> When you go to a larp that is not designed for queerness, and you bring up the issue and pursue queer themes, it can feel as if you are imposing your queer agenda on the game. There are not many good reasons for a person to do such a strange thing. Either you are doing it for sexual kinks or you are trying to make a point of it. Other players might not have given any thought to whether there are queer characters in the game or even in the game world. It sounds like reasonable accommodation, but it feels a lot like rocking the boat. (Paisley 2016)

> No-one told me trans* people couldn't larp. But a lot of factors—both external and internal—conspired to convince me that it just wouldn't be worth the trouble. [...] [S]ince I'm small and rather feminine, I believed that with unknown organisers and players I would have to justify my preference for and ability to portray a male character, in every game I enrolled in. Over and over again. And this thought was equally painful. So I stopped entirely, until I could grow some facial hair and no longer had breasts to hide. (Koski 2016)

Wanting to avoid a possible confrontation and ensuing awkwardness can be enough of a disincentive to not introduce queer themes or experiences if they are not discussed in the urtext. Furthermore, even if the urtext were to briefly discuss queerness, queer players may still brace for possible negative reactions from other players, who may not have read the urtext as carefully. In larp—and possibly also tabletop and online role-playing games—the local play culture has an important impact, and essays such as the two quoted above work to influence that culture.

Discussion

It has recently been said that in addition to the game industry shying away from incorporating sex in games (Gallagher 2012; Krzywinska 2012), game studies has a problematic relationship with scholarly treatises of sex and sexuality (Harviainen et al. 2016). Although present in all kinds of forms, sexual acts incorporated in the gameplay itself have not been analyzed thoroughly yet, although some examples of such investigations exist (Brown 2015; Fox et al. 2013; Stenros 2013). Our chapter has provided an overview of the possibilities and practices of queer role-play in three different contexts. As such, it has helped us understand the complexity of incorporating non-normative characters, situations, and affordances in gameplay. To sum up our findings, the emergence of queer play necessitates the affordances of the urtext of the game, each player's unique approach to play, and the core player group or online community in which the play is situated.

From a queer perspective, the affordances of the game's urtext are often subtle and open for interpretation. For instance, LGBTQ characters are not allowed in MMORPGs like *World of Warcraft*, but that has not stopped players from creating them—male blood elves, for example, are often read along the lines of male femininity and therefore interpreted to be "gay". As such they are vitally important for queer players (Sundén 2009; Super Timsy 2006). Similarly, the recognition of indirect queer possibilities can be detected in discussions on player forums: for instance, female night elves are rumored to be flirting with each other in the Dragonblight zone in *WoW* (emperium 2010).

Explicitly queer game mechanics remain uncommon in RPGs. They do exist, and a careful reader can tease them out sometimes in places where queerness is otherwise not mentioned (magic items that reassign gender, seduction mechanics). Yet even games that might include representations of queer characters often lack any specific mechanics for queer play. The mechanics found in *Monsterhearts* and some of the larps mentioned above are rare examples.

Yet, queering play may not need much encouragement, if the social context allows for it. In many play contexts, the players' practices of gender-bending and crossplay, or playing a character of a different sex, remain hidden, although they may be extremely widespread and are sometimes even encouraged by urtexts, such as the latest incarnation of *Dungeons & Dragons*. They can be read as an example of gender performativity taking part in articulations of non-normativity (Crowe and Watts 2014, 226). A connected practice is that of *masquerading*, where the person sitting at the keyboard and playing is performing a different gender than in offline contexts. Crossplay and masquerading, as well as tolerance of neuter characters, were an essential part of early 1990s digital role-playing experiences in places like Multi-User Dungeons. As these were text-based, the creation and maintenance of avatars, and their involvement in "tinysex" or "netsex" (Turkle 1995), were arguably easier than in more recent digital role-playing games. The introduction of voice chat had a significant impact on gender performances in this respect (Pearce and Artemesia 2009, 240–255). However, the early traditions of online game cultures readily acknowledged—even supported—the existence of these kinds of (cross-)gendered practices (Sundén 2003).

Another common way for players to manifest their approach to play and engage in queer performance is realized through irreprehensible-looking characters exhibiting odd behavior. MacCallum-Stewart (2008) describes a woman playing a male avatar in *WoW*: the avatar emotes actions such as /flirt, /kiss, and /hug near male characters, which obviously break the heteronormative code of conduct in public places. From a queer perspective, this can be regarded as an empowering act as well as playing with sexual norms. Queer play thus questions the assumptions about play and the normative uses of game characters and confuses appropriate and inappropriate role-play behavior: "Queer play is a symbolic act of rebellion, of disobedience, of deviance from dominating ways of inscribing and imagining 'the player'" (Sundén 2009, 7).

The immediate social context of play in multiplayer games remains an important factor in either encouraging or sanctioning queer play, as the examples of negotiating LGBTQ themes and bodies in Nordic larp show. Yet queer players can attempt to carve a space for themselves even in a potentially hostile environment that lack affordances for queer play. A player can adopt visual and behavioral cues that other queer players recognize, such as carefully curated character appearances. Even if a digital game service is hostile, it is possible to negotiate queer play on other sites, creating "safe harbors" for queer existence.

Ultimately, the issue at hand comes back to the question of role-play. Because the character is the primary means through which the player interacts with the game system (be it tabletop, MMORPG, or larp), a key question remains: what kind of an attitude exists toward the character the player adopts? If the game character is regarded merely as a cursor, it essentially consists of its visual representation and statistics. However, if a role-playing attitude is employed, the character is more in the mind of the player, it is (aiming to be) a coherent persona with an inner life.

Players with a cursor approach have fewer possibilities for queer gameplay, since only explicitly expressed queer content counts. In a role-playing attitude, a player can decide that their character is lesbian, and even if it is never stated out loud, it is still an important part of the character—for that player. The character as experienced by the player is not a written character sheet, statistics on a screen, or even the visible performance, but when role-play attitude is adopted, it also contains the motivations and secrets the player may never even disclose. The role-playing games, as experienced by a player, is a performance for a *first-person audience* (Montola 2012, 89–94), the player themself. While a first-person audience can be a fun, if solitary, experience, making that performance public and having others join brings with it not only recognition but becomes shared social play. My role-play is part of and understandable in relation to your role-play—and vice versa (Stenros 2015, 154–157).

Cues for queer play remain a controversial issue in numerous cultures of play. The publisher and designer, the creators of the urtext, signal if queer play is tolerated, encouraged, or expected. Certain game developers include queer cues in their games, like *Monsterhearts*, and queer players are becoming more visible especially online, having their own channels for organizing and negotiating queer play and for sharing their experiences. The urtext and local play culture can support queer play by providing cues for it, but in the absence of these queer plays emerges as transgression against the norm. While the issue of how and whether to include queer players or encourage queer play remains contested, queer play patterns proliferate. The gap between the game product and actual play is assuming more interesting and engaging forms as we speak—and the practices for navigating this gap are an interesting field for future research to map.

References

Ludography

Blizzard Entertainment. 2004. *World of Warcraft*.
Dansky, Richard. 1996. *Laws of the Night*. White Wolf.
Edman, Karin. 2016. Spin the Goddesses. In *#Feminism. A Nano-Game Anthology*, ed. Misha Bushyager, Lizzie Stark, and Anna Westerling. Stockholm: Fëa Livia.
Mcdaldno, Joe. 2012. *Monsterhearts*. Buried Without Ceremony.
Mearls, Mike, and Jeremy Crawford. 2014. *Dungeons & Dragons Player's Handbook*. 5th ed. Renton: Wizards of the Coast.

Nielsen, Elin, and Trine Lise Lindahl. 2013. Screwing the Crew: A Larp About Open Relationships, Monogamy and a Group of Old Friends. In *Larps from the Factory*, ed. Elin Nilsen, Lizzie Stark, and Trine Lise Lindahl. Copenhagen: Rollespilsakademiet.

Sheep, An, and Avery Alder Mcdaldno. n.d. *A Place to Fuck Each Other*. http://buriedwithoutceremony.com/aplacetofuckeachother/.

Bibliography

Adams, Megan Blythe. 2015. Renegade Sex: Compulsory Sexuality and Charmed Magic Circles in the *Mass Effect* Series. *Loading...* 9 (14). http://journals.sfu.ca/loading/index.php/loading/article/view/154/187.

Archer, Jesse. 2014. *Proudmoore: The Gay WoW Server*. Blog Post on Gaygamer.net, 1 May. http://gaygamer.net/2014/05/proudmoore-the-gay-wow-server/.

Björk, Staffan, and Jussi Holopainen. 2005. *Patterns in Game Design*. Hingham: Charles River Media.

Brown, Ashley M.L. 2013. *Sex Between Frames: An Exploration of Online and Tabletop Erotic Role Play*. Doctoral diss., University of Manchester.

———. 2015. *Sexuality in Role-Playing Games*. New York & London: Routledge.

Butler, Judith. 1999. *Gender Trouble: Feminism and the Subversion of Identity*. New York and London: Routledge.

Condis, Megan. 2015. No Homosexuals in *Star Wars*? BioWare, 'Gamer' Identity, and the Politics of Privilege in a Convergence Culture. *Convergence: The International Journal of Research into New Media Technologies* 21 (2): 198–212. https://doi.org/10.1177/1354856514527205.

Crowe, Nic, and Mike Watts. 2014. 'When I Click "Ok" I Become Sassy – I Become a Girl'. Young People and Gender Identity: Subverting the 'Body' in Massively Multi-Player Online Role-Playing Games. *International Journal of Adolescence and Youth* 19 (2): 217–231. https://doi.org/10.1080/02673843.2012.736868.

De Zwart, Melissa, and Sal Humphreys. 2012. Griefing, Massacres, Discrimination, and Art: The Limits of Overlapping Rule Sets in Online Games. *UC Irvine Law Review* 2: 507–536. http://heinonline.org/HOL/Page?handle=hein.journals/ucirvlre2&div=18&g_sent=1&collection=journals.

Doctorow, Cory. 2006. World of Warcraft: Don't Tell Anyone You're Queer. *Boing Boing*, 27 January. http://boingboing.net/2006/01/27/world-of-warcraft-do.html.

Edwards, Ron. 2001. *GNS and Other Matters of Role-Playing Theory*. www.indie-rpgs.com/articles/4/.

emperium. 2010. Forum Post on 10-03-2010, 11:40 AM. *Scrolls of Lore Forums > WarCraft Discussion > WarCraft Lore > Discussion: Any Canon Gay/Lesbian Characters in Warcraft Lore?* http://www.scrollsoflore.com/forums/showthread.php?t=8157.

Fox, Jesse, Jeremy N. Bailenson, and Liz Tricase. 2013. The Embodiment of Sexualized Virtual Selves: The Proteus Effect and Experiences of Self-Objectification via Avatars. *Computers in Human Behavior* 29: 930–938 http://www.media-alliance.org/downloads/fox-chb-sexualized-virtual-selves.pdf.

Gallagher, Rob. 2012. No Sex Please, We Are Finite State Machines: On the Melancholy Sexlessness of the Video Game. *Games & Culture* 7 (6): 399–418. https://doi.org/10.1177/1555412012466287.

Gerge, Tova. 2004. Temporary Utopias. The Political Reality of Fiction. In *Beyond Role and Play. Tools, Toys and Theory for Harnessing the Imagination*, ed. Markus Montola and Jaakko Stenros. Helsinki: Ropecon.

Gronemann, Casper, and Claus Raasted, eds. 2013. *The Book of Just a Little Lovin'. 2013 Denmark Run*. Copenhagen: Rollespilsakademiet.

Hardwick, Kevin. 1995. *Narrative and Style*. A Post in Usenet Group rec.games.frp. advocacy. https://groups.google.com/forum/?hl=en#!topic/rec.games.frp.advocacy/d4wBk52C4N4%5B651-675%5D.

Harviainen, J. Tuomas, Ashley M. L. Brown, and Jaakko Suominen. 2016. Three Waves of Awkwardness: A Meta-Analysis of Sex in Game Studies. *Games and Culture*, Online First.

Heliö, Satu. 2004. Role-Playing: A Narrative Experience and a Mindset. In *Beyond Role and Play: Tools, Toys and Theory for Harnessing the Imagination*, ed. Markus Montola and Jaakko Stenros. Vantaa: Ropecon.

Hitchens, Michael, and Anders Drachen. 2008. The Many Faces of Role-Playing Games. *International Journal of Role-Playing* 1 (1).

Ilmonen, Kaisa, and Tuula Juvonen. 2015. Queer Cultures as Sites of Becoming. *SQS* 9 (1–2): V–VIII.

Kelley, James. 2012. Gay Naming in Online Gaming. *Names: A Journal of Onomastics* 60 (4): 193–200.

Kornak, Jacek. 2015. What's in a Name? *SQS* 9 (1–2): 44–47.

Koski, Neko. 2016. Not a Real Man? – Trans* Politics in the Finnish Larp Scene. In *Larp Politics: Systems, Theory, and Gender in Action*, ed. Kaisa Kangas, Mika Loponen, and Jukka Särkijärvi. Helsinki: Ropecon.

Kreil, Jo. 2013. Mad About the Girl. In *Wyrd Con Companion Book 2013*, ed. Sarah Lynne Bowman and Aaron Vanek. https://dl.dropboxusercontent.com/u/1793415/WCCB13.pdf.

Krzywinska, Tanya. 2012. The Strange Case of the Misappearance of Sex in Videogames. In *Computer Games and New Media Cultures*, ed. J. Fromme and A. Unger, 143–160. London: Springer.

Laycock, Joseph P. 2015. *Dangerous Games. What the Moral Panic Over Role-Playing Games Says About Play, Religion, and Imagined Worlds*. Oakland: University of California Press.

MacCallum-Stewart, Esther. 2008. Real Boys Carry Girly Epics: Normalising Gender Bending in Online Games. *Eludamos* 2 (1): 27–40.

MacCallum-Stewart, Esther, and Justin Parsler. 2008. Role-Play vs. Gameplay: The Difficulties of Playing a Role in World of Warcraft. In *Digital Culture, Play, and Identity: A World of Warcraft Reader*, ed. H. Corneliussen and J.W. Rettberg, 225–246. Cambridge: MIT Press.

MacKnight, M. William. 2013. *Saving Prince Peach: A Study of "Gaymers" and Digital LGBT/Gaming Rhetorics*. Doctoral diss., University of Rhode Island.

Montola, Markus. 2008. The Invisible Rules of Role-Playing: A Structural Framework of Role-Playing Process. *International Journal of Role-Playing* 1 (1): 22–36.

———. 2012. *On the Edge of the Magic Circle: Understanding Role-Playing and Pervasive Games*. Doctoral diss., University of Tampere.

Montola, Markus, Jaakko Stenros, and Eleanor Saitta. 2015. The Art of Steering: Bringing the Player and the Character Back Together. In *The Knudepunkt 2015 Companion Book*, ed. Charles Bo Nielsen and Claus Raasted, 104–116. Copenhagen: Rollespilsakademiet.

Mortensen, Torill Elvira. 2003. *Pleasures of the Player: Flow and Control in Online Games*. Doctoral diss., University of Bergen.

Paisley, Erik Winther. 2016. Play the Gay Away: Confessions of a Queer Larper. In *Larp Politics: Systems, Theory, and Gender in Action*, ed. Kaisa Kangas, Mika Loponen, and Jukka Särkijärvi. Helsinki: Ropecon.

Pearce, Celia, and Artemesia. 2009. *Communities of Play: Emergent Cultures in Multiplayer Games and Virtual Worlds*. Cambridge: MIT Press.

Peterson, Jon. 2012. *Playing at the World: A History of Simulating Wars, People and Fantastic Adventures from Chess to Role-Playing Games*. San Diego: Unreason Press.

pixiestixy. 2011a. Azeroth's Beauty Contest: Top 10 Hottest WoW Characters (Part 1). Blog Post on *Lore Hound*, 14 April. http://lorehound.com/news/azeroths-beauty-contest-top-1 0-hottest-wow-characters-part-1/.

———. 2011b. Azeroth's Beauty Contest: Top 10 Hottest WoW Characters (Part 2). Blog Post on *Lore Hound*, 22 April. http://lorehound.com/news/azeroths-beauty-contest-top-1 0-hottest-wow-characters-part-2/.

Pohjola, Mike. 2004. Autonomous Identities: Immersion as a Tool for Exploring, Empowering and Emancipating Identities. In *Beyond Role and Play: Tools, Toys and Theory for Harnessing the Imagination*, ed. Markus Montola and Jaakko Stenros. Vantaa: Ropecon.

Pulos, Alexis. 2013. Confronting Heteronormativity in Online Games: A Critical Discourse Analysis of LGBTQ Sexuality in World of Warcraft. *Games & Culture* 8 (2): 77–97. https://doi.org/10.1177/1555412013478688.

Rakocky, Hannes. 2007. Play, Games, and the Development of Collective Intentionality. *New Directions for Child and Adolescent Development* 115: 53–66.

Schröder, Arne. 2008. 'We Don't Want It Changed, Do We?' Gender and Sexuality in Role Playing Games. *Eludamos. Journal for Computer Game Culture* 2 (2): 241–256.

Shaw, Adrienne. 2009. Putting the Gay in Games: Cultural Production and GLBT Content in Video Games. *Games and Culture* 4 (3): 228–253.

———. 2015a. *Gaming at the Edge: Sexuality and Gender at the Margins of Gamer Culture*. Minneapolis: University of Minnesota Press.

———. 2015b. Circles, Charmed and Magic: Queering Game Studies. *QED: A Journal in GLBTQ Worldmaking* 2 (2): 64–97.

Shaw, Adrienne, and Elizaveta Friesem. 2016. Where Is the Queerness in Games? Types of Lesbian, Gay, Bisexual, Transgender, and Queer Content in Digital Games. *International Journal of Communication* 10 (2016): 3877–3889.

Sherlock, Lee. 2013. What Happens in Goldshire Stays in Goldshire: Rhetorics of Queer Sexualities, Role-Playing, and Fandom in World of Warcraft. In *Rhetoric/Composition/Play Through Video Games: Reshaping Theory and Practice in Writing*, ed. Richard Colby, Matthew S.S. Johnson, and Rebekah Shultz Colby, 161–174. New York: Palgrave Macmillan.

Sihvonen, Tanja. 2011. *Players Unleashed! Modding The Sims and the Culture of Gaming*. Amsterdam: Amsterdam University Press.

Stark, Lizzie. 2012. Mad About the Techniques: Stealing Nordic Methods for Larp Design. In *Wyrd Con Companion Book 2012*, ed. Sarah Lynne Bowman and Aaron Vanek. https://dl.dropboxusercontent.com/u/1793415/WyrdCon%20Three%20CompanionBook.pdf.

Stenros, Jaakko. 2013. Amorous Bodies in Play: Sexuality in Nordic Live Action Role-Playing Games. In *Screw the System: Explorations of Spaces, Games and Politics Through Sexuality and Technology*, ed. Johannes Grenzfurthner, Guenther Friesinger, and Daniel Fabry. San Francisco: Re/Search and Monochrom.

———. 2015. *Playfulness, Play, and Games: A Constructionist Ludology Approach*. Doctoral diss., University of Tampere, Finland.

Stenros, Jaakko, and Markus Montola, eds. 2010. *Nordic Larp*. Stockholm: Fëa Livia.

Stenros, Jaakko, and Tanja Sihvonen. 2015. Out of the Dungeons: Representations of Queer Sexuality in RPG Source Books. *Analog Game Studies* II (V). http://analoggamestudies.org/2015/07/out-of-the-dungeons-representations-of-queer-sexuality-in-rpg-source-books/.

Stuart, Jamie L. 2008. *Performing Queer Female Identity on Screen: A Critical Analysis of Five Recent Films*. Jefferson, NC: McFarland.

Sundén, Jenny. 2003. *Material Virtualities*. New York: Peter Lang.

———. 2009. *Play as Transgression: An Ethnographic Approach to Queer Game Cultures*. Proceedings of DiGRA Conference. http://www.digra.org/wp-content/uploads/digital-library/09287.40551.pdf.

Super Timsy. 2006. *WoW Overwhelmed by Homophobes, Make Blood Elves Less "Feminine"!* Blog Post on Gaygamer.net, October 24. http://gaygamer.net/2006/10/wow_overwhelmed_by_homophobes.html.

Taylor, T.L. 2006. *Play Between Worlds: Exploring Online Game Culture*. Cambridge: MIT Press.

Turkle, Sherry. 1995. Tinysex and Gender Trouble. In *Life on the Screen: Identity in the Age of the Internet*. New York: Simon & Schuster paperbacks.

Williams, Dmitri, Tracy L.M. Kennedy, and Robert J. Moore. 2011. Behind the Avatar: The Patterns, Practices, and Functions of Role Playing in MMOs. *Games and Culture* 6 (2): 171–200.

Youngblood, Jordan. 2013. 'C'mon! Make Me a Man!': Persona 4, Digital Bodies, and Queer Potentiality. *Ada: A Journal of Gender, New Media, and Technology* 1 (2). http://adanewmedia.org/2013/06/issue2-youngblood/.

11

"Sexified" Male Characters: Video Game Erotic Modding for Pleasure and Power

Nathan Thompson

As someone who has identified as a console gamer for the majority of my life, I was relatively unfamiliar and unaware of the PC game-modding community. However, one day, while completing a previous research project on erotic role-playing in the MMORPG *World of Warcraft* or *WoW*, I came across a Tumblr blog titled "MMOBoys" that was hosting images of male Warcraft characters in the nude. Upon further investigation, it became clear that this blog was hosting much more than static images of naked Orcs and Night Elves. There were also a large number of videos of popular game characters engaging in male same-sex acts.[1] Unlike my previous work where virtual avatar bodies in *WoW* were required to remain in "G-rated mode" due to a lack of nudity and genitalia[2] (Thompson 2014), these characters from *Skyrim* and other games were engaging in explicit sexual activities that included oral sex, anal sex, mutual masturbation, and just about everything in-between. After some basic investigative work, it became clear that these videos were made possible through sex modifications or "mods" the blog's owner had downloaded and installed to use with his own copy of *Skyrim*. Using a variety of different mods, he was able to take characters from *Skyrim* as well as characters I knew from popular video games and turn them into erotic bodies in same-sex sexual positions and situations; the kinds of situations that counter a lot of the strictly heterosexual and heteronormative material one would typically see produced for mainstream video games.

N. Thompson (✉)
University of New Brunswick, Fredericton, NB, Canada

Intrigued by this intervention, I spent six months collecting data from the blog, other online sex modding sites, and interviewing the blog owner in order to get a better understanding of how this content was made and what its potential effects may be. I found that the erotic modding of *Skyrim* for same-sex interaction makes strange both game space, game characters, and mainstream pornography. The "making strange" of game space, play, and pornography is both Queer as a noun—in the sense that the content was made by a non-heterosexual person[3] but also queer as a verb[4] where traditional ideas and practices are troubled, resulting in greater discursive space for nonnormative forms of embodiment and experience (Spargo 1999, 40). There is a political and transgressive nature to the queering of normativity. In this case, gaming practices and the heterosexual and non-erotic play that often come with it are purposefully made strange in order to broaden possibilities for players who often feel marginalized or underrepresented. The blog and its content are no different. The blog's tagline states that the site contains "sexified male characters from various MMOs and some other games" and the owner explicitly stated in an interview that he started producing the content because of a lack of "male eye candy" in games for gay male and straight female players. Erotic modding provides an opportunity to challenge a medium that has traditionally offered very little in terms of content for Queer players, and the online presence of this particular blog offers a glimpse at one way video games and players interact to not only produce sexually meaningful practices and experiences but also counter and resist discourses found in gaming communities that are often heteronormative and homophobic (Thompson 2014; Pulos 2013; Kelley 2012; Shaw 2009; Schmeider 2009; Kafi 2008; Schröder 2008; Burrill 2008).

Background

I first made email contact with the owner of the blog in April of 2015. At that time, I told him I was interested in researching the content he produced and the relationship he had to his blog patrons. The blog owner responded enthusiastically and stated he would be happy to help in any way he was able. I then began to catalogue the blog content, including responses to the blog's content by viewers.[5] In addition, I asked the blog owner if he would be willing to participate in an interview. He agreed but stated he would prefer to answer the questions via text, as he wanted to remain anonymous, something he has done on his blog as well. All that is known from the blog is that he identifies as a gay male and, based on his interactions with his viewing audience, he loves creating modded gay sex content for his blog followers. He did, however, indicate that he was fine with the sharing of the blog name as well as any of the content posted on his site. The interview questions were forwarded to him at the end of April and he provided his answers in early May. We responded back and forth via email during the summer so that I could follow-up with any additional questions I had stemming from the initial interview. All of the questions were guided by my overarching research question: what does the production of the modded content found on MMOBoys mean for sexuality and gaming? While broad, I focused in on two main areas: (1) the modification of *Skyrim* for Queer sex and (2) the relationships between the modded products, the blog owner, and their viewing audience. The data was then analyzed using thematic analysis (Ryan and Bernard 2003) where a variety of techniques, such as noting of repetitive words, were used to discern themes from the interview transcript, the blog content, and the blog patron comments.

I have maintained contact with the blog owner and continue to update him on the progress of the publication. He has also informed me of certain changes that have occurred since my initial data collection that I have made note of throughout the chapter.

Connections to Fan Culture

The involvement of fans in the rearticulation of game narratives and characters for same-sex sexual purposes is not new. Slash fiction, for instance, is a strand of fan fiction in which same-sex characters (usually male) from television and film are reimagined as Queer subjects (Dhaenens et al. 2008, 335). Henry Jenkins (1992, 227) uses Star Trek slash fiction as an example to demonstrate what he calls "textual poaching," or the reclamation of media materials by fans for their own purposes. Jenkins suggests that there are political implications to textual poaching where media is not just reproduced but is transformed. Empirical investigations into slash fiction confirm that it *can* be political via the subversion of heteronormative practices in media and media genres such as television teen dramas (Barker 2002) and fantasy books (Tosenberger 2008). Game characters have also been the subjects of slash fiction. For instance, websites like "ArchiveofOurOwn.org" and "FanFiction.net" host numerous pieces of slash fiction involving popular game characters.

The use of game mods to produce erotic visual re-workings of popular game characters in non-heterosexual positions and acts could be seen as another form of slash fiction but with a slightly different trajectory. Both involve the re-working of character narrative, via textual or visual representation (or a mix of the two), by placing male same-sex characters in romantic and erotic relationships with one another. However, they deviate in their method of production. Evan Lauteria (2012, para. 23) describes modding as a form of fan production but with the added necessity of altering the code of the original commercial game product. In other words, it's not just about repurposing game narratives and characters into new homoerotic fiction hybrids, it's also about fundamentally re-working game code (Lauteria 2012, para. 27). More participation is needed by the fan in order to produce modded works of erotic same-sex sexuality and in order for the erotic fan work to be shared it must be remediated into photos and videos. In this sense, game modding for generating erotic content is more in line with fan-produced work that requires interaction directly with the original work, such as the use of video editing software to "cut" and "reedit" television and film (Dhaenens 2012).

Through their remediation of the modded game sexual content, the MMOBoys blog owner acts as a "bricoleur," where he is "repurposing and refashioning the old while using and making the new" for their own purposes and also to share with others (Deuze 2006, 71). In doing so, he queers normative notions of what kinds of sexualized identities and sex practices can appear in games. The *boundedness* of the video game as a coherent commercial product is destabilized through the act of modding in which the architecture of the game is ruptured while the "fixedness" of sexual identity is disrupted through a re-working of game characters as Queer sexual subjects.

Game Space

In order to make mods, the person doing the modification (or "modder") "must have knowledge of scripting languages, graphics programs, and software development kits especially designed for a given graphics engine associated with a game" (Postigo 2007, 302). In other words, the average game player does not have the ability to make their own mods. Instead, after a mod is made it is usually shared with others on a digital distribution platform such as Steam. Once the mod has been downloaded, the player needs to use mod management software (the most common being Nexus Mod Manager) to install and run the mod in their respective game. Mods vary widely and can do anything from making small changes in the appearance or physics of the game to completely altering the type of game you are playing (Postigo 2007, 301). For the purpose of this investigation, the mods being used by the blog owner made only small changes to character appearance, character animation, dialogue, and body physics. To run and install these mods, minimal knowledge would be needed on how to use mod management software and how to navigate the mod interfaces within the game. As a self-identified "non-modder," I took the time to install and use some of the mods used on MMOBoys and, while certainly requiring a few Internet searches and "how-to" guides, I was able to get them working just fine.

Skyrim, released in 2011, continues to be one of the most modded video games in the PC gaming community. Perhaps not surprisingly, a popular mod for the game is Skyrim SexLab, which provides the framework to allow characters (including the one you control as the player) to engage in erotic activities. It is a resource mod that other mods can draw from to use for erotic animations. Bethesda had no intentions of adding in-game explicit sexual content to *Skyrim*, even though they allow romantic partners and marriage, including the ability to sleep with your spouse in the same bed. However, with SexLab and other additional mods that modify the appearance and interaction of game characters, the player can modify the game beyond what was intended by the original game developer. Schleiner (2012, vi) refers to this as a "ludic mutation," where games are transformed by players who take back "the authorial reins of game-making from a risk-adverse commercial game industry." Wysoki, in their investigation of sexual modding, found that sex mods could be a space of resistance for players as the modders are not only generating sexual content that the game developer deems inappropriate but "for most, if not all games, modding content of a sexual nature is in clear violation somewhere in their EULAs, making the content perhaps not revolutionary, but rebellious" (Wysoki 2015, 208). Quite literally the sex modders are "breaking the rules" in order to produce the content for their ludic mutant.

In the case of Bethesda and *Skyrim*, it does not seem far stretched to believe the inclusion of explicit sexual content between same-sex characters, or any character for that matter, would be a risky move due to the mainstream industry taboo around adult content. However, by modders transforming *Skyrim* into a game that includes explicit sexual encounters, *Skyrim*, as Bethesda and players such as myself know it, is made strange. Unlike Bethesda, the modder I interviewed doesn't have to worry about a mainstream industry taboo and queers the game space of *Skyrim* through same-sex erotic modding and the production of sexually explicit photos and videos, all screen captured and recorded directly from his gaming experience. The inn in the small town of Riverwood is no longer just a quaint place to rest your eyes as you progress on your journey, or where you receive a miscellaneous quest from a barkeep; it has become a ludic mutation where the player can use a simple spell to initiate an orgy between patrons regardless of their gender or perceived sexual orientation.

For example, in the following screen capture (Fig. 11.1), two characters are engaging in sexual intercourse in the open and public area of one of *Skyrim*'s inns. Mods allow the characters to have sex pretty much anywhere and at any time. In this case, the gaming space of *Skyrim* is queered by making strange the inn as a place reserved for music, food, rest, and questing. However, not only has the open area of the inn become a place for public sex, the two people engaging in sex appear to be men. The world of *Skyrim* created by Bethesda is now a mutation where original settings and characters are combined with explicit homoerotic imagery via modding introduced by the blog owner wanting to participate and play in a game that allows explicit public sexual acts and same-sex sexuality: the inn and the game are made Queer.

The posting of this image onto the blog by its author also queers gaming space by turning the familiar inn into a set for a pornographic encounter, an artifact used for sexual and erotic pleasure by visitors to the blog, who may or may not be actual game players themselves. The setting and space of *Skyrim* becomes an erotic backdrop similar to many of the traditional pornographic backdrops of hotel rooms and couches found in conventional porn. Not only is *Skyrim* a place where players can fantasize about slaying dragons, they can now fantasize about engaging in sexual intercourse with game characters in old Medieval and Nordic style inns, homes, and castles. The scenery created by Bethesda takes on a different shape and form within the imagination of the players and those viewing the explicit image, regardless of the original artists' intentions.

Fig. 11.1 Two male characters engaging in sexual intercourse in the main dining area of an Inn. Posted to MMOBoys on February 1, 2014

Game Characters

Of course, it is not only game play or the game space that is queered via the introduction of same-sex erotic mods into *Skyrim* but also its characters. As mentioned earlier, the playable character is able to marry a number of non-player characters (NPCs) in *Skyrim* but you are unable to engage in any sort of erotic or sexual activity with them. Many players, having found themselves attracted to or otherwise sexually aroused by NPCs,[6] have turned to the creation of fan fiction in order to further those relationship narratives into ones that include eroticism and explicit sexual practices. For instance, the blog owner uses many of the original *Skyrim* characters in their photographs and videos. While the author may not find those particular NPCs attractive or desirable, their blog visitors certainly do.[7]

One example of the queering of game characters occurs when the player's protagonist is engaging in sexual intercourse with an NPC named Amren, a former Redguard soldier found in the town of Whiterun (Fig. 11.2). In the original game, Amren is married to a woman named Saffir and they have a daughter named Braith. Amren presents the player with a quest to retrieve a stolen sword, and he increases the player's offensive and defensive skills upon completion. The game writers also present Amren as a man who loves his wife and daughter via dialogue lines such as "[s]ometimes I miss the soldier's life, but when I hold my daughter in my arms, I know I've made the right choice" and "[m]y wife's a good woman. She can be a little hard-headed sometimes,

Fig. 11.2 NPC Amren having sex with the player's protagonist in Whiterun's market square. Posted to MMOBoys on February 1, 2013

but I love her just the same." However, with the help of mods, Amren is now penetrating the game player's male protagonist in the middle of the street in Whiterun along with a number of onlookers. Amren could be seen as cheating on his wife, participating in lewd public sexual behavior, and, in the least, participating in sexual acts outside a heterosexual norm.

No longer the strictly heterosexual ex-solider happily married and with a daughter, Amren becomes the sexual partner of the male protagonist, even if just for a short time. Of course, and perhaps not without some irony, Amren's NPC family are not aware of his sexual encounter and turn a blind eye, even if they happen to walk by during the explicit display of public sex. But while the game characters do not change their relationships or dialogue with one another, regardless of random public sexual encounters, those viewing the picture on the blog or those who participate in sex with Amren in the game via the mod may change how they understand his narrative. Perhaps like the ludic mutation mentioned previously in relation to game play, this kind of character modification could be considered a form of narrative mutation. Is he now the closeted ex-soldier living a bearded life? Or perhaps, the sex is part of a "unique erotic domain" (Ward 2015, 27) akin to fraternities and bathhouses, where heterosexual men can engage in sex without attachment to queerness or gay identification? If that is the case, the modded sex scene queers the understanding that sex between two men automatically renders the participants as gay. By generating new narratives where straight men engage in sexual encounters without attachments to a gay identity, there is potential to subvert restrictive masculinized norms around attraction, eroticism, and closeness.

One of the most important facets of modding is its use as a creative and artistic outlet (Sotamaa 2010, 243). Provided the modder has the coding abilities and/or the knowledge needed to use a particular mod, elements from one game can be imported and incorporated into another, thus resulting in possibilities for even more creative and mutated game-play elements. While *Skyrim* and its characters make up a large part of the pornography found on the blog, the blog owner uses another mod that allows them to import a number of different avatar skins into *Skyrim*—thus allowing for a variety of non-*Skyrim* characters to engage in same-sex erotic play as well. For instance, the blog owner produces a video series where characters such as Spiderman, Link (from the *Zelda* series), and Commander Shepherd (from the *Mass Effect* series) participate in sexual activity with other characters either from *Skyrim* or from other games. Video stills are posted that link to a pornographic website where the videos are hosted, thus officially making the jump from fan sex modding on a niche blog to pornography viewable by just about anyone. For example, in Fig. 11.3, Superman is seen penetrating Geralt from *The Witcher*

Fig. 11.3 Superman and Geralt from *The Witcher* performing in one of the pornographic videos. Posted to MMOBoys and Xvideos on September 4, 2014

series in what appears to be Vlindrel Hall in the *Skyrim* city of Markarth. The video has over 65,000 views and has an approval rating of 100 percent.[8] Another video depicts James Vega from *Mass Effect 3* engaging in an explicit scene with Dante from the *DmC: Devil May Cry*[9] in some undefined *Skyrim* location. The video is a newer one but already has almost ten thousand views and an approval rating of five stars.[10]

Not only are *Skyrim* characters such as Amren made strange through this process of modding for the purpose of explicit same-sex sexual content but characters imported from other games are too. Many of the characters mentioned such as Geralt and James Vega are explicitly heterosexual based on background narratives from their games and yet are seen here engaging in same-sex sexual acts. Others are more youthful characters that are rarely, if ever, sexualized, such as Link. However, based on the number of video views, comments, and the popularity of the blog, there is an audience. As mentioned earlier, the blog creator stated that part of their motivation in generating the content was because "there was very little male eye candy in games" thus probably mirroring the sentiments of many of the blog visitors. But they also stated that part of their motivation was to occasionally get a rise out of "insecure heterosexual dudes" by putting a penis on and in hypermasculine heterosexual characters. In this way, the queering of game narrative via sex modding can be a pleasurable experience for those wanting to see the sexualization of male characters engaging in homoerotic encounters, while it can also be a political move to challenge mainstream gaming's heteronormativity.

Traveling Pornography

One way to investigate the potential impact of male same-sex modding is by looking at how many people have downloaded the mods and how many people are viewing the user-generated content. As I stated earlier, in order to mod a game for sexual purposes one needs to download a mod management program and then install the appropriate mods needed to generate the same-sex erotic content. The most popular male nude mod for *Skyrim* is called Better Males and has almost two and a half million unique downloads from the Nexus site since its first iteration in December of 2011. While that mod allows the user to view male characters in the nude, it does not allow them to engage in sexual acts. In order to do that, the user must download and install the Skyrim SexLab mod talked about earlier in this chapter. The Sexlab mod includes the animations necessary to allow the modder to participate in sexual activities between characters in the game and has been downloaded almost two million times.

At this point the player has the ability to engage male characters in same-sex erotic activities in the game. However, the blog owner suggests a few other popular mods in order to further enhance the sexual experience. For example, Schlongs of Skyrim is the most popular mod for controlling erections and editing penis size and shape, and it has been downloaded over 700,000 times since December of 2013. A popular add-on to the Schlongs of Skyrim mod is called SexLab Cumshot (downloaded over 150,000 times), which adds visual options for male ejaculation.

When analyzing the forum posts associated with each mod, it becomes quickly apparent that those participating in the discussion are not there to harass or "troll" but to report bugs and to encourage the mod creator and thank them for their work. It seems the sex modding community I investigated is mostly a friendly one, in which like-minded gamers come together to create a new gaming experience in which their male characters are "sexified." While still somewhat underground and unfamiliar to mainstream gamers, erotic modding for male eroticism and/or Queer sex is growing and is providing new possibilities for game players to experience games in ways that challenge both their tendency to replicate hegemonic heterosexual norms and their lack of explicit sexual interactions. As these mods are downloaded and installed with increasing frequency, and as more mods emerge, the possibilities for erotic game-play proliferate. The increased use of these mods also has the potential to encourage game developers to produce games with characters and narratives that take seriously non-heterosexual identities and male eroticism.

In other words, perhaps the growing popularity of male-only erotic sex mods will encourage mainstream game developers to "sexify" their male characters so that modders do not have to.

In addition to the mod downloads, the pornographic videos created by the blog owner are usually hosted on the popular pornographic websites Xtube and Xvideos.[11] The blog owner's Xtube channel hosts 155 different sex-modded male erotic pornographic videos and in total, the videos have amassed almost three million views. Viewers of the videos sometimes leave comments that indicate the content is new to them and that they find it exciting and pleasurable. On one video a commenter writes, "If I knew this was possible in *Skyrim* I would've played it a long time ago. Hot!" and another writes, "this is incredible, I want more plz." Others more explicitly reference the fact that the videos are made possible by mods and express a desire to go out and mod their own games. One viewer writes, "What sex mod do you use?," another writes "what mod is it exactly?," while another writes, "fucking hot, wish I had the mods for this kinda thing." The hosting of these videos on pornographic sites where anyone can discover them demonstrates that same-sex modding "travels" outside those in the sex modding community and into the mainstream through pornographic sites where, based on ratings and comments, both gamers and non-gamers enjoy them and become curious about their application and implementation.

The inclusion of human virtual bodies in the videos posted to mainstream pornographic sites also troubles the notion that pleasure and eroticism need to come from human actors. While the avatars used in the blog pictures and videos already mentioned *appear* human-like through 3D graphical representation, they are not. However, with the push to introduce more virtual reality (VR) hardware and as graphical representations become more and more lifelike in their appearance, the space between reality and fantasy begins to blur even more, perhaps best demonstrated in the now infamous Oculus Rift commercial parody video (Gildin 2013). The owner of the blog stated that they feel we "are moving into an age of more involved online sexual interactions" and that "there is a huge demand for sexual fantasy [that] regular passive porn" cannot provide. Other researchers have come to similar conclusions and the introduction of avatar-body and virtual pornography is not new. For instance, Robert Brookey and Kristopher Cannon's (2009) work looked at sex practices in *Second Life* and they found that many players enjoyed viewing sexually explicit content similar to what you find when modding *Skyrim* with SexLab. However, they also found that sex in *Second Life* tended to be heteronormative and any non-heterosexual sex was relegated to private and confined areas. Unlike *Second Life*, the pornographic Queer material produced via

Skyrim modding and hosted on well-known pornography websites is easily accessed and not confined to a special "strange" or "abnormal" category. One could easily come across the videos or even the blog without ever intending to do so, thus augmenting their ability to queer normative understandings of pornography and gaming through their public presence.

Queer but Not Queer Enough

Lauteria, in their work on Queer modding, concluded that it was one way "to resist the powerful forces of sexual and gender normativity in gamified global capitalism" (Lauteria 2012, para. 30). While I have confirmed that to be the case with regard to Skyrim, I also found that Queer modding could perpetuate problematic ideas of race and bodies often embedded in what Lisa Duggan refers to as homonormativity or "a politics that does not contest dominant heteronormative assumptions and institutions but upholds and maintains them" (Duggan 2002, 179). This came as no surprise as I came to similar conclusions in my previous work examining a male-dominated role-playing community in *WoW* (Thompson 2014). I found that the role-playing community pushed normative gender and sexual boundaries, resulting in the emergence of queer gaming space. However, I also found that the community actively made racist jokes and used racist language. In other words, just because something is made "queer" does not mean it is automatically intersectional and destabilizing of other identity markers such as race.

For instance, while many of the characters used in the videos produced on MMOBoys involve various humanoid races found in *Skyrim* such as the Khajiit (cat-like) and the Argonian (reptile-like) very few human characters were anything other than white. Part of this is due to the fact that many of the male skins imported are protagonists from AAA games such as Geralt from *The Witcher* or Nathan Drake from *Uncharted*.[12] However, all of the user-generated *Skyrim* characters could be constructed as nonwhite but almost never are. The issue of a lack of racial diversity in video games is well documented (Burgess et al. 2011; Nakamura 2010; Williams et al. 2009; Everett and Watkins 2008), and, in particular, character generators have been critiqued by nonwhite gamers for their lack of racialized options such as hairstyles (Velazquez 2016; Narcisse 2015). Racism has also been well documented within the gay male community (Mowlabocus 2016; Davidson 2014; Kulick 2013). Not only are most of the human avatar bodies used in the modded erotic material white, they also tend to replicate other desirable physical features commonplace in mainstream gay male culture. That is, bodies based on a disavowal of fatness (Whitesel 2014) and the propping up of hegemonically masculine characteristics such as muscularity (Lanzieri and Hildebrandt 2011), able-bodiedness (McRuer 2006), and large penis size (Drummond and Filiault 2007).

Even though the modded content generated by the blog user *does* contest and challenge a traditionally heterosexual video game environment through the production of erotic male same-sex interactions, it also reinforces a white hegemonically masculine gay norm where only certain kinds of bodies are seen as legitimate objects of desire.

Conclusion

In this chapter I explored a few ways *Skyrim* modding for the purpose of same-sex sexual content queers game space, play, characters, and pornography. Using a popular blog as an example, I demonstrated how one modder's user-generated content both produces sexually meaningful material for their viewing audience and challenges an often heteronormative and homophobic gaming world. While little can be deduced in terms of the effects such material may have on games, gamers, or those that happen to come across the pornography on a popular website, the mere existence and popularity of the mods, the blog, and its content demonstrate that there is impact. The blog and its author demonstrate that Queer people are claiming gaming spaces and purposefully forging queer game play and content in an industry that has often left them feeling excluded and neglected. The ludic and narrative mutations that emerge from the blog owner's sex modding of *Skyrim* are quite literally Queer games made by Queer people while still maintaining the integrity of the original "parent" game.[13] Gamers and non-gamers alike then view the pornographic videos recorded in the game, where traditionally heteronormative and hypermasculine male game characters are turned into sexual and erotic objects. At the same time, the content produced by the blog owner was found to replicate homonormative ideals of hegemonic masculinity that include whiteness, able-bodiedness, and muscularity. So while erotic modding, and modding in general, opens up possibilities for player-generated game play and new gaming experiences, we need to pay close attention to whom those possibilities are for and what they reproduce.

Notes

1. All characters appeared to be cisgender men, but recently the blog owner has started creating content with explicitly trans male characters.
2. There are nude skins available for *WoW*, but they are notoriously buggy and only available for female avatars.
3. In this case the content was made by someone who is non-heterosexual but that does not have to be the case. For instance, slash fiction involving male-male relationships began as a practice by mostly heterosexual women. For more see Alexis Lothian, Kristina Busse, and Robin Anne Reid, ""Yearning Void and Infinite Potential": Online Slash Fandom as Queer Female Space," *English Language Notes* 45 (2007).
4. Throughout the chapter I use Queer (uppercase "Q") as an umbrella term for non-heterosexual people and queer (lowercase "q") as a verb.
5. On Tumblr, users cannot leave comments. All feedback from viewers was retrieved from comments left under the videos that were hosted on Xtube and Xvideos.
6. Based on conversations in online forums and article posts, a large number of these NPCs tend to be companions, or NPCs that can quest alongside the protagonist and with whom the protagonist can build longer and more meaningful relationships. For instance, a quick Internet search on the companion "Lydia" will yield a plethora of sites and posts dedicated to erotic content.
7. The blog acquires roughly 1300 new followers a month and their videos have received almost three million views.
8. Approval rating based on the number of approval votes a video receives.
9. Both Vega and Redfield are popular characters as they appear in a number of videos and pictures.
10. The video is hosted on Xtube and its rating system is based on a possible five out of five stars instead of a percentage of approval votes.
11. During the process of writing, the blog owner's Xvideos account was deleted.
12. For an excellent overview of a lack of protagonist diversity in popular contemporary games, see this speech by Manveer Heir (BioWare game designer) delivered at the 2014 Game Developers Conference: http://www.gdcvault.com/play/1020420/Misogyny-Racism-and-Homophobia-Where.
13. For a good discussion on divisions between mod types and the impact these divisions have on the integrity of the original game, see Tanja Sihvonen, *Players Unleashed! Modding The Sims and the Culture of Gaming* (Amsterdam: Amsterdam University Press, 2011).

Bibliography

Barker, Meg. 2002. Slashing the Slayer: A Thematic Analysis of Homo-Erotic Buffy Fan Fiction. In *Blood, Text and Fears*, 19–20. Norwich: University of East Anglia.

Brookey, Robert, and Kristopher Cannon. 2009. Sex Lives in Second Life. *Critical Studies in Media Communication* 26 (2): 145–164.

Burgess, Melinda, Karen E. Dill, S. Paul Stermer, Stephen R. Burgess, and Brian P. Brown. 2011. Playing with Prejudice: The Prevalence and Consequences of Racial Stereotypes in Video Games. *Media Psychology* 14 (3): 289–311.

Burrill, Derek. 2008. *Die Tryin': Videogames, Masculinity, Culture*. New York: Peter Lang Publishing.

Davidson, Judy. 2014. Racism Against the Abnormal? The Twentieth Century Gay Games, Biopower and the Emergence of Homonational Sport. *Leisure Studies* 33 (4): 357–378.

Deuze, Mark. 2006. Participation, Remediation, Bricolage: Considering Principal Components of a Digital Culture. *The Information Society* 22 (2): 63–75.

Dhaenens, Frederik. 2012. Queer Cuttings on YouTube: Re-Editing Soap Operas as a Form of Fan-Produced Queer Resistance. *European Journal of Cultural Studies* 15 (4): 442–456.

Dhaenens, Frederik, Sofie Van Bauwel, and Daniel Biltereyst. 2008. Slashing the Fiction of Queer Theory: Slash Fiction, Queer Reading, and Transgressing the Boundaries of Screen Studies, Representations, and Audiences. *Journal of Communication Inquiry* 32 (4): 335–347.

Drummond, Murray, and Shaun Filiault. 2007. The Long and the Short of It: Gay Men's Perceptions of Penis Size. *Gay and Lesbian Issues and Psychology Review* 3 (2): 121–129.

Duggan, Lisa. 2002. The New Homonormativity: The Sexual Politics of Neoliberalism. In *Materializing Democracy: Towards a Revitalized Cultural Politics*, ed. Russ Castronovo and Dana D. Nelson, 175–194. Durham, NC: Duke University Press.

Everett, Anna, and S. Craig Watkins. 2008. The Power of Play: The Portrayal and Performance of Race in Video Games. In *The Ecology of Games: Connecting Youth, Games, and Learning*, 141–166. Cambridge, MA: The MIT Press.

Gildin, Tyler. 2013. Oculus Rift Gets the Hilarious Sexual Parody Nobody Asked For. *Elite Daily*, October 4. Accessed October 15, 2015. http://elitedaily.com/humor/oculus-rift-gets-the-hilarious-sexual-parody-nobody-asked-for-nsfw/.

Jenkins, Henry. 1992. *Textual Poachers: Television Fans and Participatory Culture*. New York, NY: Routledge.

Kafi, Yasmin. 2008. Gender Play in a Tween Gaming Club. In *Beyond Barbie & Mortal Kombat*, ed. Yasmin Kafai, Carrie Heeter, Jill Denner, and Jennifer Sun, 111–124. Cambridge, MA: The MIT Press.

Kelley, James. 2012. Gay Naming in Online Gaming. *Names: A Journal of Onomastics* 60 (4): 193–200.

Kulick, Alex. 2013. *How Gay Stayed White: Millennial White Gay Men and the Production of and Resistance to Racism, Sexism, and Heterosexism*. Honours thesis, University of Michigan.

Lanzieri, Nicholas, and Tom Hildebrandt. 2011. Using Hegemonic Masculinity to Explain Gay Male Attraction to Muscular and Athletic Men. *Journal of Homosexuality* 58 (2): 275–293.

Lauteria, Evan W. 2012. Ga(y)mer Theory: Queer Modding as Resistance. *Reconstruction: Studies in Contemporary Culture* 12 (2): 7.

Lothian, Alexis, Kristina Busse, and Robin Anne Reid. 2007. 'Yearning Void and Infinite Potential': Online Slash Fandom as Queer Female Space. *English Language Notes* 45 (2): 103–111.

McRuer, Robert. 2006. Compulsory Able-Bodiedness and Queer/Disabled Existence. In *The Disability Studies Reader*, ed. Lennard Davis, 301–308. New York: Routledege.

Mowlabocus, Sharif. 2016. *Gaydar Culture: Gay Men, Technology and Embodiment in the Digital Age*. New York: Routledge.

Nakamura, Lisa. 2010. Race and Identity in Digital Media. In *Mass Media and Society*, ed. James Curran, 336–347. New York: Bloomsbury.

Narcisse, Evan. 2015. The Natural: The Trouble Portraying Blackness in Video Games. *Kotaku*, October 14. Accessed on June 10, 2016. http://kotaku.com/the-natural-the-trouble-portraying-blackness-in-video-1736504384.

Postigo, Hector. 2007. Of Mods and Modders: Chasing Down the Value of Fan-Based Digital Game Modifications. *Games and Culture* 2 (4): 300–313.

Pulos, Alexis. 2013. Confronting Heteronormativity in Online Games: A Critical Discourse Analysis of LGBTQ Sexuality in World of Warcraft. *Games and Culture* 8 (2): 77–97.

Ryan, Gery W., and H. Russell Bernard. 2003. Techniques to Identify Themes. *Field Methods* 15 (1): 85–109.

Schleiner, Anne-Marie. 2012. *Ludic Mutation: The Player's Power to Change the Game*. PhD diss., Amsterdam School for Cultural Analysis.

Schmeider, Christian. 2009. World of Maskcraft vs. World of Queercraft? Communication, Sex and Gender in the Online RPG World of Warcraft. *Journal of Gaming and Virtual Worlds* 1 (1): 5–20.

Schröder, Arne. 2008. 'We Don't Want It Changed, Do We?': Gender and Sexuality in Role Playing Games. *Eludamos: Journal for Computer Game Culture* 2 (2): 241–256.

Shaw, Adrienne. 2009. Putting the Gay in Games: Cultural Production and LGBTQ Content in Video Games. *Games and Culture* 4: 228–253.

Sihvonen, Tanja. 2011. *Players Unleashed! Modding the Sims and the Culture of Gaming*. Amsterdam: Amsterdam University Press.

Sotamaa, Olli. 2010. When the Game Is Not Enough: Motivations and Practices Among Computer Game Modding Culture. *Games and Culture* 5 (3): 239–255.

Spargo, Tamsin. 1999. *Postmodern Encounters: Foucault and Queer Theory*. New York, NY: Totem Book.

Thompson, Nathan. 2014. Queer/ing Game Space: Sexual Play in World of Warcraft. *Media Fields Journal* 8. http://mediafieldsjournal.squarespace.com/queering-game-space/.

Tosenberger, Catherine. 2008. Homosexuality at the Online Hogwarts: Harry Potter Slash Fanfiction. *Children's Literature* 36 (1): 185–207.

Velazquez, Ashley. 2016. I Am My Hair: Racial Diversity in Video Games. *Not Your Mama's Gamer*, February 10. Accessed on June 10, 2016. http://www.nymgamer.com/?p=12913.

Ward, Jane. 2015. *Not Gay: Sex Between Straight White Men*. New York: NYU Press.

Whitesel, Jason. 2014. *Fat Gay Men: Girth, Mirth, and the Politics of Stigma*. New York: NYU Press.

Williams, Dmitri, Nicole Martins, Mia Consalvo, and James D. Ivory. 2009. The Virtual Census: Representations of Gender, Race and Age in Video Games. *New Media & Society* 11 (5): 815–834.

Wysoki, Matthew. 2015. It's Not Just the Coffee That's Hot: Modding Sexual Content in Video Games. In *Rated M for Mature*, ed. Matthew Wysoki and Evan Lauteria, 194–209. New York, NY: Bloomsbury Academic.

12

Let's Come Out! On Gender and Sexuality, Encouraging Dialogue, and Acceptance

Maresa Bertolo, Ilaria Mariani, and Clara Gargano

The effectiveness of persuasive games and games for social change (G4SC henceforth) is as known as it is debated. However, when a game explicitly intends to problematise and question matters of social concern—communitarian or individual—designers must push themselves beyond the promotion of mere entertainment, crafting artefacts able to create meaningful experiences of interaction, between representation and simulation (Frasca 2003; Bogost 2007), interpretation and comprehension (Sicart 2011). Approaching this issue bearing in mind the design theory of wicked problems (Rittel and Webber 1974; Sicart 2010), designers should depict and stage ill-defined problems that require ethical reflection and moral skills. In the following we focus on how a board game challenges and reproduces deeply rooted ideologies about gender and sexual issues, rather than examining or mapping how gender and sexuality are depicted or expressed in games and discussed in the literature on the topic of games. We dig into how biases and prejudice have been expressed within a game aimed to activate sense-making and critical reflection.

Taking a step in this direction, we asked ourselves: *How can games about gender and sexual non-heteronormativity have a positive impact on our views and attitudes? And what can we do to challenge years of misleading portrayals and beliefs?*

M. Bertolo (✉) • I. Mariani • C. Gargano
Politecnico di Milano, Milan, Italy

© The Author(s) 2018
T. Harper et al. (eds.), *Queerness in Play*, Palgrave Games in Context,
https://doi.org/10.1007/978-3-319-90542-6_12

Stepping into the Closet

In a society that culturally judges and exerts negative prejudice against non-binary and non-heteronormative orientations, representations of gender and sexuality in games have the power to create a space of dialogue and exchange. The article presents the board game *Let's Come Out* (*LCO* henceforth) and the ludic enquiry about its effectiveness in dealing with the common belief that sexual relations should occur between people who belong to the two distinct and complementary male and female genders.

Lesbian, gay, bisexual, and transgender (LGBT) characters have been present in video games since the 1980s (Kanter 2012). However, if heterosexuality is portrayed as normalised, homosexuality has been frequently ridiculed or made subject to additional censorship. Acknowledging the significant role served by sexual orientation and gender identity in some video games, a significant number of recurring stereotypes, clichés, tropes, and archetypes about LGBT sexuality are still present. In parallel, the research on this topic is generally conducted on representation, focusing on gender and race (Huntemann and Media Education Foundation 2002; Leonard 2006; Shaw 2009; 2010), as well as on violence and aggressive behaviour (Glaubke and Children Now 2002; Dietz 1998). On the other hand, tackling the issues of LGBT discrimination, and arguing the consequent prejudice of being considered diverse, we investigate a game designed to creatively distrust the idea of "normality" by overtly unveiling historical and cultural facts that are not generally known, as well as exposing established prejudices.

Conceived and designed by Clara Gargano with Ilaria Mariani, *LCO* sprang from a context (Italy) where civil unions between people of the same sex became legal just in February 2016, several rights are not acknowledged to LGBT people, and the idea of male and female as "the only family" is still deeply rooted in the common sense. In order to move beyond simply studying games to offer insight and analysis into how race and racialised tropes are depicted, this game suggests a discussion about some larger implications in terms of bias. For example, who plays with the lesbian in-game orientation won't be allowed to step on any dress icon, as the dress is seen as a symbol of the stereotypical ideal of woman and femininity, an ideal that does not fit the common biased description of lesbian. This mechanic slows down the player's run to win and forces her to follow a certain path. This limit becomes particularly significant considering that players have to protect and keep hidden their in-game sexual identity until the end, or they lose. In doing so *LCO* reflects a real-life dynamic. By embedding similar mechanics that pressure non-heteronormative in-game behaviours into the gameplay, the game relies on roles that are representations of stereo-typed and usually inaccurate ideas and knowledge culturally rooted in certain communities and social groups. Game mechanics, as explained below, include informing players about the many individuals who left a mark in our history or culture, regardless of their sexual orientation. In this process, social factors, misbeliefs, and opinions frequently mistaken for facts are questioned in effort to open the discussion on rhetorical/verbal/psychological violence, bullying, stereotypical and prejudicial treatment of gay people on a procedural and semantic level.

Players are challenged to reveal their in-game secrets, showing how coming out is a difficult process for anyone. They are pushed outside their comfort zone, having them take a step into each other's shoes. The game is designed to be a stage wherein players can experience other roles (Goffman 1974), even very far from their usual ones, facing the awkwardness that comes from freely insulting sexual minorities just because "that's a game" (Bateson 1956). This mechanic is meant to stress and betray the irrationality of the most wide-spread opinions that then emerge as overused or senseless.

As designers, we took the meaningful stance of using offences, insults, and hate speech to enlighten the lack of sense—and hence validity—of most of the stereotypes and prejudices. The choice of in-game legitimising categorisa-tion, stressing the discourse on genders and related clichés, can appear coun-terproductive, but it allows the exposure of the absurdity and gravity of certain assertions and beliefs (as the aforementioned example in which the in-game lesbian orientation is built to stress the inconsistency of the prejudices). Players are asked to trespass their sexual identities and knowledges, and they are given the opportunity to experience outside of their closet. As researchers we need to enquire and assess the effectiveness of this approach and how the game and its meaning are perceived by players.

Problematising the fact that games convey meanings, we refer to Bogost (2007) and Sicart (2011) as two diverse approaches and perspectives on designing games with potential social results. In reference to the reasoning about games as systems potentially able to trigger and shape player's ethics, resulting in possible moral, political, or cultural impact, there are indeed two main positions. On the one side, Bogost's procedural rhetoric (2007) provides the idea that the meaning is transferred via rules and game structure; on the other Sicart (2011) questions such an operational view, advancing a critical review on the limits and validity of Bogost's perspective, claiming the player's central role as an active subject in the process of meaning- and sense-making from experience. Through games' rhetoric (Bogost 2007; Swain 2010) and the social experience they engender (Sicart 2011), games can create a *safe*

(Crawford 1984), or, better, a *safer environment*, wherein communication is facilitated and encouraged (Kaufman and Flanagan 2015). This allows players to encounter delicate issues and deal with them within the protected space of the game, where *real* fear and pain are absent (Laurel 1993). As in Bowman (2010) and Weiner (in Blatner 2007), games allow to safely experiment and explore possibilities, namely, other choices, being at least partially insulated from real-life consequences like being judged or even punished. Player's awareness of moving within an established safer mental, physical, and emotional space enables and entitles the exploration of the self, as well as of the relationships between the self and others. By tracing a more or less visible magic circle that separates what is play from what is reality, each game structures an ideal and to a certain extent *protected scenario* wherein players can put themselves to the test. In the game space *LCO* creates, dialogue is not simply facilitated but approached and stimulated. The gameplay itself engenders reasons and excuses to bring up conversations and test each other's knowledge on gender issues and mostly on sexuality subjects. In doing so the game fills the social gap of silence, insecurity, fear, and misunderstanding that often characterises the topic and its surroundings. Encouraging openness to debate and exchange of opinions or concerns, the game makes cultural biases explicit and gives players an abstracted, relatively consequence-free space in which to explore the implications of those biases. From adults and young, to parents and children, men, women, and in-betweens: everybody is as welcomed and prompted to enter the closet and explore its darkest and little-known corners. It is an unreal, reduced (Goffman 1974), but equally meaningful situation wherein players can experience the anxiety of being outed, as well as the difficulties of being prepared to come out. Albeit we recognise that games cannot solve any situation, we acknowledge that through their mechanics (Bogost 2007; Swain 2010) and the interpretation of the experience they suggest (Sicart 2011), G4SCs can abstract and mirror complex matters of social concern. They give the game designer the opportunity to communicate her point of view and players the chance to confront ethical messages and reasonings (Swain 2010). They can explore either subtle and manifest issues of civic, political, social matter enabling a first-hand experience of some of its elements. This allows players to embrace diverse perspectives and as a consequence to analyse or understand the covered issues, with the awareness of being in a safe space. An increasing variety of games are grounded in a set of patterns and procedures able to capture and reproduce determined situations, tapping into the full range of the human experiences to pick and enhance in turn specific dynamics, showing how certain systems or processes work (Bogost 2007, 29). By playing games built on such logic and rhetoric, players are led to initiate a dialectic and critical reasoning intended for enquiring into the real nature of some processes—as existing frames of mind related to sexual orientation that underpin negative stereotypes and biases— acquiring a gameplay-driven knowledge (Mariani 2016). Their elevated interactivity empowers games to actively engage players as parts of the experience rather than outsiders and passive observers. In consequence, recalling Flanagan and Nissenbaum's reasoning (2014), since each game embeds meanings, it becomes as clear that each game can be considered to be a collector of values emerging through the interaction between the game and the player—meaningful examples are the games developed in the Tiltfactor lab and analysed accordingly to this specific perspective (Kaufman et al. 2015). Thereby the designer must *conscientiously* (Flanagan and Nissenbaum 2014) and consciously craft the game as a repository embedding persuasive messages. As such, it can represent a perspective and even assume the shape of a potential social commentary, especially when sensitive topics of social, cultural, or ethical matter are addressed and challenged.

Since the preliminary research (Mieli and Jordà 1979; Cantarella 1988; Butler 2004) that preceded the development of the project, it has clearly emerged how silence (and negligence) is always the main obstacle to the recognition and acceptance of different realities. Silence generates lack of knowledge, which leads to discrimination and injustice. Gender non-binarity and sexual non-heteronormativity for too long have been considered alterations of the norm and therefore kept quiet by institutions, media, families, and by the stakeholders themselves, who fear that revealing such a *dark secret* could influence/damage/change people's lives. In an effort to bring our contribution to the LGBT struggle for equality, with the specific aim of shaking the public opinion that still holds on to an antiquated perspective on the subject, and in an effort to push the research forward, we chose to take a stance towards explicitness. Backing up from the stealth approach we often use (Kaufman and Flanagan 2015), *LCO* chooses a simple but direct language, giving players a taste of their own medicine: it is very clear from the name to the aim what your challenge is. The explicit approach is often considered to be a limit to the persuasive impact and the optimal outcome of the game: it is seen as a potential source of hostility towards the topic (Kaufman and Flanagan 2015), resulting in the player refusing to open up and to leave room for reflection or change. However, we account the straight approach as a compelling strategy because we consider it necessary to openly discuss an often-concealed argument, avoiding roundabout expression or euphemisms. Any previous thoughts and beliefs regarding the topic affect the gameplay and the player's possibility to proceed/win, but would not impact the game persuasive potential.

Misbeliefs and lack of knowledge are counterproductive: as we will shortly see, they prevent players to advance, but they are the core of the game, being as expected as necessary to unveil the final message.

LCO's mission is to affect attitudes and positions in order to improve mutual coexistence and comprehension. This game is part of a broader research that follows a through-design approach (Frayling 1993) counting on case studies as key elements for the investigation and verification of research hypotheses on G4SCs. As such each game goes through an iterative cycle of conceiving, prototyping, and evaluating (Laurel 2003; Mariani 2016). In particular, to understand the effectiveness and the impact that each game brings to the player's attitudes, we conduct an enquiry that is qualitative and to a lesser extent quantitative. The data collection process involved a sample of 22 persons in 8 game sessions.

Foreplay: Exposing Sexual Bias Through Mechanics

LCO is a game about bias and clichés, knowledge, and discovery. Through its mechanics, it intends to provide players with means to recognise and have a better understanding of sexual stereotypes and (sex- and gender-based) discrimination. The game is inspired by today's (Italian) social context and people's tendency to be affected—often even troubled—by the discovery of someone's non-heteronormativity. It consists of two phases. During phase 1, players find out which in-game sexuality they have been assigned, keeping it secret. In phase 2, they have a simplified experience of how prejudices can affect their life on the path of self-acceptance and self-realisation. Players advance in the game influenced and hampered by stereotypes related to their newly discovered orientation, namely, the in-game sexuality. They have to recognise and accept the limitations imposed by the clichés characterising their in-game sexuality. Through this process, they bump into the specificities, features, and curiosities of each orientation, understanding how the in-game difficulties are actually metaphors for real-life difficulties. Consequently, they are enabled to make sense of the entire game, as well as of its curious and apparently contradictory gameplay.

To support the research, and verify the need for an intervention aimed to raise awareness about the issues of inclusion and lack of equal rights for the LGBT community, we have reached out to AGEDO (National Association of Parents and Friends of Homosexuals), the Italian equivalent of the American

PFLAG (Parents, Families, and Friends of Lesbians and Gays). They helped define the topics to put at play and the most suitable type of ludic artefact to reach a very diverse audience. AGEDO demonstrated a vivid interest in *LCO* and confirmed its enthusiasm participating in various playtests and in the subsequent data collection. The collaboration with AGEDO is still ongoing.

The game material (Fig. 12.1) is composed of Question Cards, Insult Cards, (sexual) Orientation Cards, Definition Cards, a set of Cheat Sheets with (sexual) categories on the front and revelations on the back, and a triangular-shaped board.

The gameplay consists of two phases. In phase 1 each player chooses her token and places it on one of the pyramid tips. Then everyone moves aiming to be the first to reach the centre of the board. Insult Cards and Question Cards are shuffled together and placed on the table in a single deck. Players take turns in drawing a card from this deck and consult with each other to give a collective response. In case of a correct answer, all players can move one step ahead; otherwise no movement is allowed. The game proceeds this way until one player gets to the centre of the board and unlocks the Orientation Cards for everyone. At this point all players discover their in-game sexual orientation. Depending on it, they are instructed on which icons they are

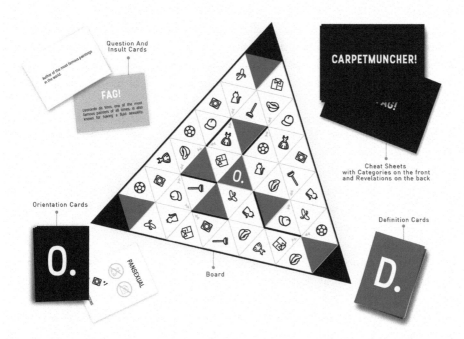

Fig. 12.1 *Let's Come Out* and its elements

forbidden to step on and which others provide extra movements instead. The cards also dictate the number of definitions each player needs to obtain to come out. The one who comes out first wins the game. Definition Cards can only be drawn when stepping on the pink boxes.

In phase 2 players compete against each other. The first to answer correctly to the Question or the Insult can move ahead—paying attention to the icons on the boxes, which define whether the player can step that way or follow a different path. If the answer is wrong the player loses her chance, while the opponents can still try to guess. However, if the player who gives the wrong answer is in possession of at least one Definition Card, she has to put it face up on the table as penalty. This will give the opponents the opportunity to make a guess at her Orientation prematurely, outing and eliminating her from the game. Once a player has collected all the definitions required, she can head to one of the pyramid tips to come out and win. Once the game is over, players can turn the Revelation Cards around and investigate the relation between orientations and icons, revealing their connections, the biases on their ground, and how they affect the movements on the board.

Players discover that each step has been dictated by stereotypes related to the player's newly discovered in-game sexuality, stated on Orientation Cards. The limitations imposed by the game rules are symbolic representations of how that orientation is usually seen and judged. Insult Cards challenge the player to use some words and reflect on how their cruelty can encourage unjustified discrimination and inequity, harming the way of living of another person (Fergusson et al. 1999; Ryan et al. 2009). Then, Definition Cards reflect the self-identification process that precedes coming out and leads to acceptance.

Six categories are vetted here: *heterosexual, homosexual, lesbian, bisexual, asexual,* and *pansexual.* The features of each sexual orientation and some of its protagonists are unveiled during the gameplay. The point is that it doesn't matter what your identity is, within this game everyone will be targeted at some point. This game simulates dynamics of hate speech, highlighting the ease with which one can become hurtful and drawing attention to how simple it is to become or make someone vulnerable.

In fact, the game puts all the players in the same condition. Not taking any sexuality for granted, it asks them to perform the same activity: strive to come out. All orientations at play have a chance at winning, and everybody can incur in the same risks and anxiety of being "outed" before being ready to "come out" on their own. Effectively even in-game heterosexuals are brought to experience a reduced and abstract practice that in contemporary society is ordinarily considered *unnecessary*: having to come out.

Counting on a compelling interplay between subjective opinions and socio-cultural positions, the game exposes personal thoughts and beliefs. It creates situations wherein a constructive exchange of ideas can take place, triggered by the game mechanics and dynamics. As a consequence, general reflections and individual awareness are raised on a topic that has often assumed the features of a social issue or a wicked problem (Rittel and Webber 1974; Sicart 2010).

The game board, the orientations assigned to players, and the resulting possibilities to move/act are designed to experientially communicate how things (Bogost 2007, 29) and biases work, providing both a fertile source of individual reasonings and a situation of collective commentary. This point underpins potential awkward identifications: when players draw a sexual Orientation, it can coincide with their real one, or not. Recalling Gee's relevant analysis of the term (2003), the player is asked to identify with (1) a player with a real-world identity, (2) a member of a group with a virtual identity, and (3) the in-game character, as a projective identity. This simultaneous plurality of identifications, the licence to experiment with alternative identities, and their potential overlapping with the player's real gender or sexual identity can cause an important self- and meta-reflection on the identity construction itself. Identity is also crucial to LGBT communities, particularly in those situations when a person is addressed only as a carrier of non-heteronormativity instead of being recognised in her entirety and complexity as an individual; therefore, the theme acquires a further meaning. This being said, Orientation Cards act as identity-makers that ask players to perform in-game roles very different or very similar to their own. In this duality of meanings, through the identification process triggered by the game mechanics and their procedural rhetoric (Bogost 2007), the dialogue between reality and fiction overlaps, creating a liminal space for discussion and growth (Turner 1982). In this space, the transgression of social and cultural norms is enabled, "allow[ing] for empathic experience of the pleasures of exploration and adventure which are absent in the real world" (Kennedy 2002, np).

Discrimination and prejudices of society are embedded and mirrored in *LCO* mechanics and symbolically represented by movements and icons. To grasp this meaning, players are asked to unveil the actual interplay between the game elements. Using processes and mechanics persuasively (Bogost 2007), and acknowledging that the real message is intertwined with how players comprehend and receive the meanings of the game (Sicart 2011; Mariani 2016), we observed how players reacted to the game, its gameplay, and its contents. Albeit *LCO* and its mechanics were crafted to transfer specific values, in order to verify their effectiveness, as well as if players are able to correctly transpose and understand them, a specific enquiry was required.

Mixed Methods and Complementary Approaches

The research methodology of this study is grounded on the approach framed as "design as research" (Laurel 2003), where design acts as a means of knowledge construction to build results through reflective insights on the creative process. To understand how effective *LCO* is in covering and transferring its message, the play(er) experience has been thoroughly observed, assessed, and enquired. We employed a qualitative and quantitative approach and a set of concurring mixed methods (Mariani 2016), posing specific attention on how subjects interpreted the game, its elements, and the experience itself.

The sessions were:

- Preceded with sociological forced-choice questions to profile players
- Observed conducting qualitative rapid ethnographies
- Followed by questionnaires
- Concluded with semi-structured interviews and focus groups

To gather data through questionnaires, we relied on a format composed of 35 items, framed as visual analogue scale (VAS) questions. Using such tool, we asked 22 players to state their level of agreement (100) or disagreement (0) on a continuous scale (negative items have been inverted to uniform the values), where numbers around 50 are a statement of neutral position. The cohort of players involved was composed of LGBTQ-identified individuals as well as heterosexual. Accordingly to the aim of our investigation, we considered it not relevant to explicitly ask our players to state their gender and sexual identities. We aimed at understanding how they received the game and the consequent discourses activated, independently of their specific sexual orientation or gender; the fact itself of not exposing their identities allowed to enhance the idea that the game is a safe environment of exploration, free of judgements and prejudices.

Rainbow Results

Approaching games as procedural systems (Bogost 2007), and in parallel recognising and stressing Sicart's emphasis on play as an interpretative (2011), appropriative, creative, and expressive action (2014), we acknowledge that the meaning of a game is partially situated in its rules. Concurring with the author, we recognise on the one hand that games are sense-making systems that lay their foundations in the creation of meaning activated by players and on the other that play is appropriative because it initiates a space where people *take over* their ordinary activities, being empowered to shape the world (Sicart 2014). *LCO* includes and encourages such dynamics challenging appropriation and fostering the creation of critical reflections.

This paragraph outlines how players experienced and perceived this game both as a systemic, social system and as a commentary of non-heteronormative sexual identities as a contemporary social issue. *LCO* is characterised by a background contrast between the seriousness of the issue addressed and the fun and cheerfulness it elicits. The following reasonings built on the gathered data (in part presented in Fig. 12.2) show that players enjoyed the game, gleaning relevant meaning out of the experience. An average of 85.2 reveals that players largely agreed in stating the game was fun, and 87.1 also says it was a source of satisfaction. We observed how unexpected disclosures or intuitions caused the sought reaction and opened a further channel of interpretation, giving the player new information to transpose in-game facts outside the magic circle. In particular, through a re-attribution of sense, the game mechanics and elements are reviewed, and complementary meanings are assigned, aiming at making the ground fertile for openness and receptiveness towards the topic.

As players we are asked to overtly insult well-known and less-known sexual identities; we are pushed to explore the borders of our knowledge and biases on the topic and look into the abyss of the cultural, rudest denigrations. In order to urge the debate and win, the game motivates and even justifies foul play, rudeness, malice, and cruelties. In the spur of the moment, we are solicited to abandon the tracks of political correctness and moral boundaries, giving voice to things we do not believe to begin with. Willingly walking in the shoes of perpetrators, players try their best (or worst) to be a nuisance to others and undermine their game, as someone said during a match: "I'll stay right here and I'll obstruct the lane." Statements like "We are more or less at the same point here. Well, except for me cause I'm ahead!" resulted in brief moments of frustration associated with exclamations as "You are such an ugly person" or "So cruel you are" and "Don't do anything, you've already done enough!"

Sharpening the wit and evaluating the broader situation, some players gained a better understanding of the issues addressed, as well as of their historical and contemporary traits. To answer the questions posed by cards, they relied on their former knowledge, but often answers were far beyond it. Those who reasoned about circumstances or historical periods to locate some of the facts stated in the cards managed to narrow the range of possible solutions: they focused on the more plausible categories fitting for the time or context.

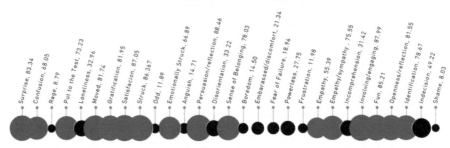

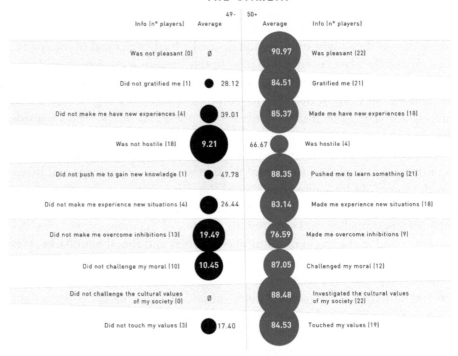

Fig. 12.2 Player feelings. Above: the feelings players felt. Magenta is used when the average is above the neutral threshold of 50, black when it is lower. Below: the area of the circles is directly proportioned to the amount of people who expressed that view; it consists indeed of the amount of players who situated themselves below (left and black) or above (right and magenta) the threshold of 50. This amount is also declared at the end of the sentences among brackets. Into the circles, the average in stating "I agree" or "I disagree." For example, 22 players stated the game was pleasant, and the average of their levels of agreement is 90.97

For example, referring to a question about the first American female astronaut, who travelled in space in 1983, the players argued that she could not possibly be married because she would not have been allowed to leave her home, "Leaving her husband on Earth," waiting for her.

Reflecting on the game-based experience and its connection to the real life is a crucial step in terms of potential long-lasting knowledge. It allows to find meaning in what has been done. According to Nicholson (2015, 15), it gives the player the opportunity "to step back and think about their game-based experiences. This opportunity for reflection creates the situation where a learner can connect what happened in the game to elements in his or her own life." Although not every player immediately puzzled out the real point of using hate speech against each other as a form of awareness acquisition, nobody backed down from insulting someone else, though they often felt the need to justify their assumptions. Once the embedded meaning is identified, it tends to take a leading role, emphasising troublesome truths that become matters of collective discussion. *LCO* players agreed in stating that additional considerations and self-reflection (averages of agreement are, respectively, 88.5 and 81.5) had been activated as a consequence of the experience, attesting how the in-game message can stimulate reflection and open up dialogue and critical debate.

The effectiveness of the game to induct critical reasonings, and of the player in establishing and translating their implications, as an agent who contributes in conveying meaning, highly relies on the qualitative enquiry conducted after the game sessions. Interviews and focus groups are sources of significant clarifications and corroborations. For example, the desire to unfold the reasonings behind the mechanics starts to take on the shape of a need. Encouraging the exposition of the rhetorics and processes on the ground of discrimination and of the game mechanics themselves, the game exhorts players to feed common discussions on hatred and extend the conversations about diversity and opportunities beyond the game. Especially the Cheat Sheets (Fig. 12.1) activate serious reasoning. On their back are written explanations (revelations) that help decode the game's two levels of abstraction: procedural and semantic.

Players stated they did not feel frustration (11.98), neither fear of failing (18.94) or embarrassment (21.34), confirming that the game had been perceived as a safe environment where they felt at their ease in speaking about such a critical issue. Notwithstanding, it happened that some players showed evident unease: for example, heightened colour betrayed their embarrassment while impelled to unmask someone else's orientation. Moreover, especially when plain labelling and categorising, some players clearly manifested defensive body language, including crossed arms and legs. Even in phase 1 when players had to state to which of the five categories a certain character belonged to, many felt the need to justify their accusations in front of others: "I do not want to be sexist, but … it has to be a boy"; someone else clearly affirmed "stating a category makes me feel uncomfortable."

This condition is further corroborated by players' high agreement on asserting that the game provoked identification (78.67): those who played felt the existence of a striking link between their in-game attitudes and the way people in reality act. It is noteworthy to notice the prominent accordance with declaring that the game investigated the cultural values of our society (88.48), as well as their own values (84.53). In general players admitted to have learnt something (88.35), for example, the fact that in Italy women usually earn 30% less than men, which provoked spread unpleasantness. In particular, it turned out that it is not in the information per se but in the amount of other elements that goes in the same direction that an overt societal attitude towards discrimination emerges. An awareness that thwarts existent behaviours and trends. This fact is bound to having made new experiences (85.37), where the experience of diversity and transgression from the ordinary is not just allowed but encouraged, letting players explore the limits of personal knowledge about the information portrayed. Sometimes this reasoning also extends to a societal perspective, seeking to acquire further awareness. The semantic/informative level of the game communicates facts by means of culturally relevant occurrences, often unveiling the untold, leading players to consistently agree on stating that the game provoked surprise (83.34) and also sympathy (75.55). Relevant examples are the reactions to the question regarding the incursions conducted by the Inquisition of the Catholic Church in the twelfth century: players are asked which was considered to be a "symptom" of female homosexuality. In discovering that it relied on the erectile part of the female genitals and that was revealed by actually measuring the size of the clitoris (Cantarella 1988), most players were astonished; a common reaction was "I mean… Does it mean that everybody takes a look?"

In parallel to the enquiry on the game experience, we vetted the pleasantness of the game as an artefact with specific features. Figure 12.3 synthesises some results. In particular, it emerges as significant that social values are perceived as embedded by a large amount of players (89.20 of agreement), and the tone of voice is considered coherent and consistent with the topic (82.62). This result is meaningful and not obvious considering the irreverence of the game and the sensitive and complex topic it addresses.

In addition, the high levels of immersion in the "magic circle" world that the game creates (86.36) invited players to speak freely and with enthusiasm. It is not a coincidence that a player used the phrase "I would go with fag. Let's

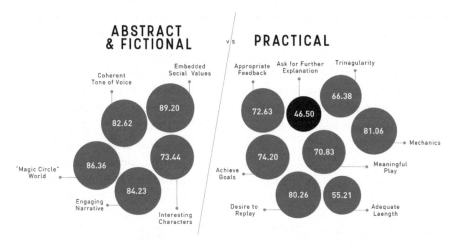

ABSTRACT & FICTIONAL   v/s   **PRACTICAL**

Fig. 12.3 Player positions. We asked our players to state their position according to some abstract and practical aspects of the game. The area of each circle shows the average (also expressed in their centre) of how players situated themselves on the continuous scale: magenta identifies averages under the threshold of 50 stating "I disagree with the given statement," and black identifies the average above it asserting "I agree." In particular, players confirmed they did not feel the need to ask for further explanation, reinforcing the fact that the game and its gameplay are clear and easily comprehensible

go fagging!" when convincing his mates to declare that who painted the most known portrait in the world was gay, supposing it was Leonardo da Vinci. Then there is the example of a player who grasped the orientation of another player and disqualifies her saying triumphantly "You are bisexual! You have my same card. I could tell from your movements." Her urge to *out* the opponent was so intense that she did not realise that in doing so she was outing herself too. As a matter of fact, speaking of movement and mechanics, players showed to have quickly seized the meaning of the barriers, as well as of the icons.

Players spent part of their post-game time exploring the topic together, deepening the reasonings on the sexual orientations and categories presented (73.44 of agreement in stating characters were interesting). They were also curious to discover which icons distinguished different orientations. This process articulated interesting debates on the logics beyond their movements. It became clear that orientations prevent players from walking certain paths—like it often happens in real life, for example, the possibility to get married or adopt a child. Players agreed in saying that the limits imposed by the icons impeded them to accomplish their objectives. During the interviews, they affirmed they did not have enough possibilities as they wished, highlighting the coherence with the reality of facts. Indeed, who held the heterosexual orientation was almost completely barrier-free and allowed to rapidly advance (obviously running the risk to be discovered and outed as *hetero*!). The limits of the Orientation Cards have been matter-of-factly designed to reflect the societal stereotypes bounded to the sexual orientation. Notwithstanding all these limits, deprivations of freedom, and hate speeches, the game was not perceived as hostile (19.7 of agreement, therefore a strong disagreement); furthermore, the interest and will to play again (80.26) demonstrate how the game was capable of covering LGBT discrimination in a fascinating way.

After the Closet: Disclosing Meanings

LCO presents a possible way to expose and deal with gender non-binarity and sexual non-heteronormativity issues, creating understanding and awareness not only through the game rules and mechanics but through interaction and interpretation. The latter are also on the ground of the game ethical contribution, which does not lie on the seriousness of its subject nor on the mechanics used to expose it. It depends on the game ability to interact with players activating meaning and sense through play and players' interpretation. In this sense, the game interacts with players, and players interact with the game. As a consequence, players are encouraged to make sense of the issues addressed.

LCO creates a *forcedly democratic* environment, where everyone—independently of their sexual identity—is provided with the same chances. Everyone can advance, but they have to cope with the limits on their movements. This mechanic, metaphorically mirroring and reducing the repercussions of existing bias, turned out to be successful in establishing a *fundamental equity* among players. On the one hand, this condition balanced the gameplay, providing each player with the possibility of winning, and on the other hand, this condition also activated a significant rumination about its contemporary impracticality.

Moreover, asking everybody to take action by means of offensive behaviour, the player's ethics are challenged in order to unveil the frivolousness and nonsensicality of the principles on which discrimination is based. In doing so *LCO* (1) creates a situation that unconsciously leads players to act according to stereotypes and clichés and (2) allows to dispel and release the negative meaning associated with the offensive words included as categories. Considering the aim of the game, using insults can be argued to be a dissonance and a counterproductive way of dealing with such a controversial topic.

But here is where the main insight of our analysis emerges: the fundamental role played by using such an approach that directly challenges players to face the bare issue, with no mediation. Aware of operating within the game as a safer space distinguished from the real life, players felt that being mean(er) to each other was *legitimated* by that context. They freed themselves from inhibitions and social constrictions, bringing to the surface all those misleading messages and deeply rooted inequities that are distinctive of a specific frame of reference (Bateson 1972; Goffman 1974), namely, the one that is grounded on a patriarchal structure that—almost exclusively—favours binarity and heteronormativity. Nevertheless, this approach also encourages players to connect the meaning of the in-game actions to their real, non-fictional essence. *LCO* succeeds in creating the ideal circumstance where players feel free to constructively speak and exchange opinions on discrimination, a topic usually hidden or not plainly discussed. Our observation confirms that the game repeatedly created a safe space that encouraged discovery, failure, dialogue about cultural, historical, social facts. A space where breakdowns and inconsistencies between the ideal and the reality make the conflict even more engaging. Especially phase 1 focuses on making players stumble on a collection of information about orientation of historical and well-known people that are meant to make them question former thoughts and realise that (1) non-heteronormative orientations are much more widespread than people might think; (2) that anyone can bring an important contribution to the cultural, political, scientific, and any panorama regardless of gender or sexual orientation; and that (3) it doesn't (and shouldn't!) have any impact on personal skills and possibilities. Phase 2 echoes Bateson's concept (1956) that being aware that "this is a game" allows to explore other perspectives, encouraging players to challenge their own positions. The enquiry presented above shows that the experience provoked is significant since it highlighted the meaningful sense on the ground of the mechanics, and in doing so, it succeeded in including and conveying important messages that positively impacted on players' attitudes and views. To challenge years of misleading portrayals and beliefs, *LCO* doesn't focus on educating or providing mere information about the topic but rather on raising awareness on the issue and its surroundings. It is intended to unveil that biases against non-heteronormativity and preconceived notions of LGBT behaviour are groundless clichés and stereotypes.

Comparing designer's expectations with facts, it emerged that the game is effective. Players took actual advantage of the spaces of openness and receptiveness that games encourage through immersion and projection (Gee 2003), suspension of disbeliefs, and liminality (Turner 1982); this game does more than just send a clear message in favour of non-heteronormativity. Acknowledging that the game space is to a certain extent different and distant from the one of the real life, we consider *LCO*'s contribution to the matter significant and substantial. It allows indeed players to make an abstracted, partially insulated from reality, first-hand, gameful experience of the consequences brought by prejudice. The game mechanics ask players to physically move only within the limits imposed by their category of belonging, limits that are simplifications and metaphors of spread discriminations. As a consequence, players are encouraged to critically as well as safely explore the biased interplay between subjective opinions and socio-cultural positions in a relatively consequence-free space, the one of the game.

Bibliography

Bateson, Gregory. 1956. The Message 'This Is Play'. *Group Processes* 2: 145–241.
———. 1972. *Steps to an Ecology of Mind*. New York: Ballantine Books.
Blatner, Adam. 2007. *Interactive and Improvisational Drama: Varieties of Applied Theatre and Performance*. New York/Lincoln/Shanghai: iUniverse.
Bogost, Ian. 2007. *Persuasive Games: The Expressive Power of Videogames*. Cambridge: MIT Press.
Bowman, Sarah Lynn. 2010. *The Functions of Role-Playing Games: How Participants Create Community, Solve Problems and Explore Identity*. Jefferson/North Carolina/London: McFarland.
Butler, Catherine A. 2004. An Awareness-Raising Tool Addressing Lesbian and Gay Lives. *Clinical Psychology* 36: 15–17.
Cantarella, Eva. 1988. *Secondo natura: La bisessualità nel mondo antico*. Roma: Riuniti.
Crawford, Chris. 1984. *The Art of Computer Game Design*. New York: Osborne/McGraw-Hill.
Dietz, Tracy L. 1998. An Examination of Violence and Gender Role Portrayals in Video Games. *Sex Roles* 38: 425–442.
Fergusson, David M., John L. Horwood, and Annette L. Beautrais. 1999. Is Sexual Orientation Related to Mental Health Problems and Suicidality in Young People? *Archives of General Psychiatry* 56 (10): 876–880.
Flanagan, Mary, and Helen Nissenbaum. 2014. *Values at Play in Digital Games*. Cambridge: MIT Press.
Frasca, Gonzalo. 2003. Simulation Versus Narrative. In *The Video Game Theory Reader*, ed. Mark Wolf and Bernard Perron, 221–235. New York: Routledge.
Frayling, Christopher. 1993. *Research in Art and Design*. London: Royal College of Art London.
Gee, James Paul. 2003. *What Video Games Have to Teach Us About Literacy and Learning*. New York: Palgrave Macmillan.

Glaubke, Christina R., and Children Now. 2002. *Fair Play?: Violence, Gender and Race in Video Games*. Oakland: Children Now.

Goffman, Erving. 1974. *Frame Analysis*. Cambridge: Harvard University Press.

Huntemann, Nina, and Media Education Foundation. 2002. *Game Over: Gender, Race & Violence in Video Games*. Northampton: Media Education Foundation.

Kanter, A. 2012. *An Analysis on the Influence of Fictional Gay Television Characters on the GLBT Community*. PhD diss., American University.

Kaufman, Geoff, and Mary Flanagan. 2015. A Psychologically 'Embedded' Approach to Designing Games for Prosocial Causes. *Cyberpsychology* 9 (3): Article 5.

Kaufman, Geoff, Mary Flanagan, and Max Seidman. 2015. Creating Stealth Game Interventions for Attitude and Behavior Change: An 'Embedded Design' Model. *Proceedings of the Digital Games Research Association (DiGRA) Conference* 12: 1–12.

Kennedy, Helen W. 2002. Lara Croft: Feminist Icon or Cyberbimbo? On the Limits of Textual Analysis. *Game Studies: International Journal of Computer Games Research* 2 (2).

Laurel, Brenda. 1993. *Computers as Theatre: A Dramatic Theory of Interactive Experience*. Boston: Addison-Wesley.

———. 2003. *Design Research*. Cambridge: MIT Press.

Leonard, David J. 2006. Not a Hater, Just Keepin' It Real. *Games and Culture* 1: 83–88.

Mariani, Ilaria. 2016. *Meaningful Negative Experiences Within Games for Social Change*. PhD diss., Politecnico di Milano.

Mieli, Mario, and Joaquim Jordà. 1979. *Elementos de crítica Homosexual*. Barcelona: Anagrama.

Nicholson, Scott. 2015. A Recipe for Meaningful Gamification. In *Gamification in Education and Business*, 1–20. New York: Springer.

Rittel, Horst W.J., and Melvin M. Webber. 1974. Wicked Problems. *Man-Made Futures* 26 (1): 272–280.

Ryan, Caitlin, et al. 2009. Family Rejection as a Predictor of Negative Health Outcomes in White and Latino Lesbian, Gay, and Bisexual Young Adults. *Pediatrics* 123 (1): 346–352.

Shaw, Adrienne. 2009. Putting the Gay in Games Cultural Production and GLBT Content in Video Games. *Games and Culture* 4 (3): 228–253.

———. 2010. *Identity, Identification, and Media Representation in Video Game Play: An Audience Reception Study*. PhD diss., University of Pennsylvania.

Sicart, Miguel. 2010. Wicked Games: On the Design of Ethical Gameplay. *DESIRE '10 Proceedings*: 101–111.

———. 2011. Against Procedurality. *Game Studies* 11 (3).

———. 2014. *Play Matters*. Cambridge: MIT Press.

Swain, Chris. 2010. The Mechanic Is the Message: How to Communicate Values. In *Ethics and Game Design: Teaching Values Through Play*, ed. Karen Schrier, 217–235. Hershey: IGI Global.

Turner, Victor. 1982. *From Ritual to Theatre*. New York: Paj Publications.

Part IV

No Fear of a Queer Planet: Gaming and Social Futures

13

Outside the Lanes: Supporting a Non-normative *League of Legends* Community

Nicholas Taylor and Randall Hammond

E-sports—professional, spectator-driven gaming—is an emergent media industry comprised of players, leagues, sponsors, tournaments, and viewing platforms, collectively engaged in transforming gaming into a professionalized, spectator sport (Taylor 2012b). Long struggling for economic viability in North America, e-sports have recently exploded. The finals of the 2015 World Championship for *League of Legends* (commonly referred to as *League*, one of the most successful e-sports titles) attracted 14 million concurrent spectators (Kollar 2015). Sports media giant ESPN has expanded its e-sports offerings, in reaction to positive numbers for viewership of world championships in another highly popular competitive game, *Defense of the Ancients 2* (more commonly referred to as *Dota 2*).

As these stories suggest, the North American e-sports industry has gained a degree of stability it has not had in the past, due in part to the rise of live-streaming platforms and the global popularity of games like *League* and *Dota 2*. In an effort to continue expanding the North American audience base for e-sports, a number of organizations—notably, Riot Games (publisher of *League*) and Blizzard Entertainment (publisher of numerous e-sports titles, including *Starcraft 2*, *Overwatch*, and *Hearthstone*)—have begun making concerted efforts to form collegiate e-sports associations. In fact, a number of American colleges now offer scholarships for top *League* players (Mueller 2015), highlighting a concerted effort on the part of many universities, student popula-

N. Taylor (✉) • R. Hammond
North Carolina State University, Raleigh, NC, USA

© The Author(s) 2018
T. Harper et al. (eds.), *Queerness in Play*, Palgrave Games in Context,
https://doi.org/10.1007/978-3-319-90542-6_13

tions, and e-sports associations to transform campus-based gaming into a legitimate (and lucrative) component of the e-sports industry. At the forefront of these efforts are University League of Legends (uLoL, run by Riot), TeSPA (run by Blizzard and formerly known as The eSports Association), and Collegiate StarLeague (CSL), associations which provide college-based gaming teams with a league-based infrastructure, centrally run tournaments, and dedicated viewing platforms. uLoL offers incentives for university-based *League* teams to self-organize; if they recruit a faculty sponsor, obtain recognition as an official student club, and then register with Riot, the company will in turn give them promotional items and logistical support for matches against other collegiate teams. The ethnographic study we report on here follows one such *League* club, based at North Carolina State University.

A *League* of Their Own

In the fall of 2014, we received an email from an undergraduate student, inviting Taylor to become faculty advisor for his newly formed campus *League* club. The student explained that he had arranged a leadership structure with his friends; they had a secretary, a treasurer, a communications director, and a president (himself). He noted that they needed a faculty member to make them a registered student organization—a prerequisite for status as an official *League* college club—and that after googling "NCSU faculty" and "e-sports," he had identified Taylor as a potential supervisor. Both of us were suprised by the diversity represented by the president and club officers: the president identifies as queer, and each of the officers is a woman of color. This is fairly remarkable given *League*'s reputation as supporting a predominantly white, overwhelmingly male player base (Ratan et al. 2015).

As they explained to us in this meeting, the president and his officers wanted their club to explicitly enact principles and practices of inclusivity; they stated that they were far less concerned with fielding a competitive *League* team than with providing *League* enthusiasts with a safe, welcoming place to play. This runs contrary to the narrative enacted by the industry in its push to form a more robust collegiate e-sports scene—namely, cultivating opportunities to identify and professionalize new competitive gaming talent. We enthusiastically agreed to sponsor the group, with Taylor signing on as faculty supervisor and providing the group space for weekly meetings; every Monday night from fall 2014 to spring 2016, the campus-based research studio co-directed by Taylor became the club's meeting and play space.

Our chapter documents efforts by this group's leadership to construct and maintain a "safe space" in which student players of all skill levels and backgrounds could have the chance to play the game and participate more broadly in *League* fandom without the gender-, skill-, and sexuality-based toxicity that often characterizes online *League* play (Kou and Nardi 2013). What we see operationalized in these attempts is an enactment of inclusivity that acknowledges, and works against, the persistent intersections of skill- and gender-based *exclusions* so characteristic of competitive gaming (Harper 2013; Taylor, Jenson and de Castell 2008; Witkowski 2013; Voorhees 2014). That is, we see the club leadership's deliberate de-emphasis on competition and progression, and its elevation of other forms of participation with the game, as central to their attempts to make a more welcoming space for non-normative gaming bodies.

Methodology: Almost at PAR

Our study is inspired by the interventionist approach to studying gameplay practiced by feminist ethnographers of gender and games (Carr 2007; Jenson and de Castell 2008), in which researchers help create opportunities for female players to develop competencies and preferences with gaming experiences to which they do not conventionally have easy or unfettered access.

We characterize our work with this club as an ethnography informed by participatory action research (PAR). As with some ethnographic traditions (namely feminist, post-colonial, and queer), PAR represents a commitment to understanding social arrangements from the point of view of those at the margins; it does so by both documenting marginalized communities and working with them in active support of their goals (Kindon et al. 2007). Its aim is to leverage the institutional power and privilege of academic research to directly serve the needs of underprivileged groups. While we supported this community through providing them with official faculty support and offering a technology-rich space on campus to meet and play, club leaders did not express interest in collaborating with us in "the planning, implementation, and dissemination of the research process"—the conventional criteria for PAR (Macintyre 2008). For this reason, we view our work as hewing more to traditions of feminist ethnographic research than to PAR (Fisher and Harvey 2013).

Our research is driven by the following question: how did this club's leadership articulate and enact inclusivity, particularly with regard to a game most often characterized by instances of hostility and antagonism between players?

At the outset, we explicitly asked the club leaders if we could sit in on their weekly meetings, to which they consented. Here, we draw from Hammond's field notes from weekly meetings between October 2014 and May 2015, held in the club's meeting space. For each meeting, Hammond took up a spot along one wall and, with his laptop, noted interactions between club members, spatial arrangements of participants and technologies, and instances in which problematic behavior was regulated. The number of participants varied between 7 and 19, contingent on weather and work and school commitments. Initially, Hammond remained relatively aloof from club members, avoiding sustained interaction. Over time, both in order to establish greater rapport with the group and to gain additional insights by playing with club members, Hammond took on a more active role in the club. Hammond also conducted semi-structured interviews with five members over this same period, each approximately 50 minutes long. The interviews included questions on gaming background, experience with *League* specifically, and their experiences with the club. Three of these interviews were conducted with club leadership.

In addressing our research question, we hope to contribute to ongoing discussions about the fraught relationship between player subjectivity and inclusion in (or exclusion from) gaming cultures, particularly around competitive play and e-sports. These discussions concern who can(not) embody the subject positions (and attendant rewards) associated with highly competent gameplay. At the same time, we hope our case study sheds light on the complex, tenuous, and volatile nature of "safe spaces" as a way to engage marginalized individuals and groups in video game culture. This is particularly important given, on one hand, the gaming industry's increased but uneven attention to issues of inclusivity and, on the other, the urgency and (im)possibility of safe spaces following recent, horrific acts of violence against LGBTQ communities.

Making Spaces Safer: An Overview

According to one history, "safe spaces" can be traced to two distinct but overlapping political projects in North American cities during the 1950s and 1960s: the development of locales, most often bars, in which gays and lesbians could be out, and the intensification of a women's movement that honed strategies such as consciousness-raising workshops to create a shared sense of community and place (Kenney 2001, 22–24). While the former project enacted temporary respite from the geographic and material enactments of homophobia (such as anti-sodomy laws and often virulently homophobic police), the latter drew more on discursive constructions of safety—envisioned as both a respite from and intervention into patriarchal modes of communication and relation (Kenney, 24). The term has transformed over the last few decades. On the one hand, it has become associated with primarily university-based attempts to create solidarity among conventionally threatened groups (Fox and Ore 2010). On the other hand, as Hanhardt notes, notions of safety in relation to the gay rights movement are morphing as the movement itself grows more mainstream and its historic spaces became gentrified; under these emergent socio-economic conditions, safety shifts from "protection from state-sanctioned violence" to "protection from the racialized poor" (Hanhardt 2013, 14).

For these reasons, Fox and Ore (2010) and Halberstam (2014), among others, raise concerns that contemporary safe spaces rely on essentialized notions of sexual identities and an erasure of intersecting forms of oppression such as race and ability that prevents more inclusive forms of coalition building. They also insist on the term "safer spaces" to signal that the project of safety is never complete; no space is, or can be, wholly safe. In a slightly different vein, Weems (2010) and Mayo (2010) urge for a less static and place-based and more historicized, relational, and dynamic understanding of safe spaces. Weems, in particular, builds on Puar's queer re-tooling of Deleuze and Guattari's notion of "assemblage" (2007) to consider how spaces, objects, bodies, and affects collectively constitute "networks of contact and control" that make particular social relations—including safety—(im)possible (Weems 2010, 559–560).

These various accounts of "safe space" offer rich theoretical grounds for our consideration of the NCSU *League* club's attempts to make an inclusive and welcoming environment for students to participate in what is often regarded (including by these students themselves) as a game characterized by toxic, unsafe interactions. Like the scholars we mention above, club leaders sought, and often conflated, shared space and a shared commitment to respectful and inclusive communication; they puzzled over what constituted appropriate uses of humor and provocation, and they acknowledged the vulnerability of the boundaries, both material and discursive, protecting their space. Following the club leaders, our own understanding of space is *not* informed by a priori distinctions between virtual and physical environments. The club's guidelines for conduct applied to both in-game and co-situated behaviors and were informed equally by the institutional rules of the university, the code of conduct for

League play, and the physical layout of the studio in which they met. Likewise, the affects that circulated through this "network of contact and control" moved fluidly between virtual and physical bodies. Internal tensions between club members, for example, might materialize as exclusions from teams during rounds of *League*, which in turn reproduced those same tensions. Safety and risk, pleasure and anxiety, inclusivity and marginalization—in keeping with contemporary discussions around safer spaces, we see these embodied states as outcomes of relations between heterogeneous actors, together constituting the tenuous assemblage of this campus competitive gaming club.

Before offering our observations of this club, we outline existing academic literature that draws connections between various contexts of digital gameplay and the (non-)normative practices, dispositions, and subject positions with which they are associated.

Subjectivity and Safety in Play Spaces

Our aim in this literature review is to show how a persistent conflation of gaming expertise with heteronormative masculinity, particularly in North America, operates to produce *un*safe play environments for (predominantly) women and LGBTQ players.

Virtually Safe?

Early enthusiasm for online environments as spaces in which conventionally marginalized subjectivities could find acceptance, community, and safety quickly gave way to the recognition that virtual spaces can be just as permeated with gender-, sex-, ability-, and race-based bigotry and violence (see, e.g. Stone 1991). Particularly relevant for our look at this *League* club are the forms of toxicity associated with large-scale, commercial, and fantasy-themed online games, such as *World of Warcraft* (WoW) and *EverQuest*. Scholars have documented these games' binary portrayals of gender (Taylor 2006), limited and often stereotypical depictions of queerness (Harper 2011; Pulos 2013), origins in the masculinized and heteronormative domains of computing (Wajcman 2010) and tabletop role-playing (Trammell Forthcoming), relative anonymity and lack of consequences for online harassment (Phillips 2015), and, in some cases, a paternalistic, ambivalent, and/or dismissive attitude toward marginalized (and particularly queer) players themselves (Collister 2014).

At the same time, ethnographies of online play communities demonstrate how these games can, with proper care and support, be used to cultivate safer spaces for LGBTQ players, despite these barriers. Not surprisingly given its (now waning) popularity and its contentious relationship with LGBTQ players (Chang 2015), WoW is the focus of many such studies. Stabile (2014) points out that binary gender representation is often of lesser importance to LGBTQ players than playing the game with supportive peers and allies; the sexual dimorphism hardwired into the design of playable WoW characters does not prevent players from "doing gender" in non-normative ways. Similarly, Sundén (2009) and Sherlock (2011) both explore how participants in their respective ethnographies of WoW guilds found room for modes of in-game interaction and communication that are "transgressive" to the discursive ideal of the straight, cis-male gamer.

Subjectivity in Physical Gaming Contexts: On the Safe Handling of Meatspace

These ethnographies offer rich examples of how LGBTQ players construct safer spaces within online gaming environments that are often rife with misogyny homophobia. Given that the *League* club at NCSU coalesced within a shared physical space for play—in no small part, out of a desire to play with and against other club members and thereby mitigate against the game's online toxicity—we turn now to a brief consideration of subjectivity and safety in physical play contexts. We focus on spaces meant to showcase expert and/or competitive play. Works by Kocurek (2015) and Alloway and Gilbert (1998) both note the ways early video game arcades became discursively and materially associated with cultures of boyhood, while ethnographic scholarship on the gendered interactions at gaming cafes and large-scale LAN parties (Taylor et al. 2014; Taylor and Witkowski 2010), dormitories (Lin 2008), and e-sports tournaments (Witkowski 2013) shows how play in public and semi-public places continues to be a privilege accorded primarily to straight, cis-male bodies.

It should be noted that while there are numerous examples of attempts to set up safe gaming contexts for LGBTQ-friendly gamers—whether in the form of Barcade nights, LGBTQ LAN parties, game jams, and so on—these have yet not been documented in academic research.

Re-tooling Expertise

This conflation between gaming competency and straight, cis-male subjectivity is explicitly targeted via feminist interventionist research with gaming communities. These studies begin with the realization that particular gaming genres—paradigmatically, the first-person shooter (FPS), real-time strategy (RTS), and, increasingly, multiplayer online battle arena (MOBA) genres—are conventionally masculinized. At the same time, these scholars actively resist the notion that preferences for these games (or the ability to play them competently) are reflective of differences rooted in innate sex-based differences. Indeed, such claims naturalize, and thereby dismiss, the culturally rooted, gender-based inequalities that characterize access to and enjoyment of intensive digital play. Instead, Carr (2007) and Jenson and de Castell (2008) demonstrate how the dispositions and behaviors we often associate with boys and men's gameplay—competitive, often highly instrumental, frequently involving trash-talking—are a reflection of expertise, not gender.

While these studies address the need to re-think *gender* in relation to particular game genres and experiences, we hope to direct their insights toward disrupting the conflation between *heteronormativity* and competitive gaming. We do so, in particular, by illuminating the NCSU *League* club leadership's attempts to re-purpose the uLoL infrastructure for cultivating professional competitive gameplay toward, instead, creating a safer space for bodies, practices, and pleasures that are conventionally at the margins of competitive gaming and e-sports cultures.

Observations: Playing Safe

Weekly meetings for the *League* club typically involved some administrative and logistical discussion, led by the club's officers (maintenance of the studio, membership dues, upcoming events), followed by fairly unorganized rounds of play, with teams organized interpersonally rather than via *League*'s own team-finding algorithms. In what follows, we identify a small number of themes most salient to our understanding of (1) how this club developed and practiced inclusivity and (2) how individual members related their involvement in *League* to their own embodied subjectivities and gaming experiences. These themes are as follows: "(un)safe words," "re-orienting play," and "gaming the culture."

(Un)Safe Words

One of the tensions we observed at an early stage in our fieldwork was around what constitutes acceptable speech in this community and what sorts of utterances are accepted within an ostensibly safe space. Language use is, of course, a key site in which identities are contested and performed, as has been documented in studies of queer youth communities (Andrews 2003; Vaccaro 2012) and digital gaming communities, whether of predominantly heteronormative (Taylor 2012a), queer-identifying (Sundén 2009), or marginalized players (Gray 2012; Kennedy 2007). During one of the first meetings, Hammond noted that one player used the word "faggot"—a term that for those accustomed to heteronormative player communities may seem unremarkable. It was uttered two more times during that session, before the club president requested a stop to it. In fact, this response was common in the room—some players yelled out, "Woah! Woah! Who dropped the 'F' bomb?" In this instance, the club's leadership patiently and calmly addressed the use of a problematic term, with very little apparent or immediate backlash from other members (the term was not used again in club meetings), establishing a precedent for how this term and other, similarly problematic ones could and should be policed by club members.

In an ethnography of a WoW guild comprised of "female, LGBT, and other minority members," Collister (2014) notes that the guild's mechanisms for regulating hateful and problematic speech were modeled after Blizzard's code of conduct but were refined to include more precise guidelines and more direct consequences. *League* has experimented with reporting mechanisms similar to the one Blizzard uses for WoW, which is no surprise, as *League* has a reputation as a toxicity. In early 2011, a "Tribunal" system was introduced to allow players to police each other, with Kou and Nardi (2013) regarding it as a productive, if somewhat limited, instance of an online community-given tools to regulate their own behavior. As of the time of this writing, however, the Tribunal system has been under maintenance for over two years. There has been very little in terms of updates or indications that the system will return soon. Instead, there is a proprietary automated system operating now. Jeffrey Lin, who left Riot in May this year, was the primary architect and designer of the most recent policing structures in *League*. Those structures were automated, were informed by "machine learning" processes, and according to Lin had a 92 percent reform rate—recidivism in negative language shrank drastically (Parkin 2015). This tracking also accounts for contextualized harassment, according to Lin; ribbing or sarcastic but positive banter is analyzed as well and accounted for in this language policing structure.

As with the WoW guild Collister studied, the NCSU *League* club could turn to the game publisher's code of conduct for guidance in regulating acceptable language and behavior but still had to determine to what sorts of utterances were permissible in their specific group. The club leadership did seem open to—in fact, encouraging of—sexualized language that is less explicitly homophobic. In another early meeting, one of the club's founders, a woman of color, referred to Fiddlesticks—a champion she was playing against—as "Fiddledicks" in a moment of frustration during a match. This outburst was received enthusiastically by other participants, who used the term "Fiddledicks" throughout the rest of the meeting.[1] We think this indicates the club's approach to monitoring and policing potentially hurtful language and the use of (un)safe words: they refused to tolerate explicitly homophobic (and misogynist and racist) slurs but made room for (indeed, in some instances gleefully engaged in) forms of sexualized, but less overtly homophobic or misogynistic terms that circulate in the *League* community.

Re-orienting Play

While the club leadership, and the president in particular, sought to make weekly meetings safe in terms of acceptable discourse, they also attempted to generate an atmosphere in which participants of any level of competence and experience could feel welcome. Other e-sports associations at NCSU, including a club devoted to fielding a competitive campus-based *League* team, have an explicit focus on skilling up. Unlike these clubs, and many other officially designated *League* clubs at other universities involved in the uLoL network, the community we studied was deliberately *not* oriented toward high-level competitive play. At several times during the first months of the club, the president and other leaders floated the idea of more formalized coaching or mentor/mentee collaborations, but this was never taken up by club members. Similarly, the club did not undertake many of the competitive gaming practices associated with deliberate competence building, such as watching and analyzing match replays, holding tryouts and scrimmages against other teams in the region, and generally practicing; instead, most meetings consisted of watching trailers, discussing new champions, and engaging in local matches between participants. One interviewee (a white male) said of the group, "I think it's a lot more fun-oriented, versus competition oriented." A four-year veteran of *League*, he had much more experience with the game than most other participants. In fact, this member had originally joined the more competitive *League* organization on campus but, after the two groups met during one of our weekly meetings, decided that he preferred the relaxed atmosphere of this *League* club.

We think it is important here to acknowledge the productive ambivalence embedded in the uLoL infrastructure. On the one hand, it provides an apparatus for campus-based gaming communities to professionalize players, an apparatus that is bolstered by efforts on the part of a number of universities to recruit top talent via scholarships and dedicated gaming facilities (Kollar 2016). At the same time, connecting official club status to university-based rules for student organizations, rather than to aims or outcomes related to inter-college competition, effectively uncouples competitiveness from legitimacy. Clubs can be at once officially recognized by Riot and wrapped into the uLoL network, while also wholly unconcerned with fielding a competitive team. As we discuss below, this uncoupling of legitimacy from professionalization at the college level may have significant implications for competitive gaming—possibly destabilizing the deep-rooted association between competitive play and straight male subjectivity.

Gaming the Culture

In the absence of an overt emphasis on improving members' technical proficiencies with the game, members were free to pursue less instrumental and more culturally expressive forms of engagement with the game. One participant, one of the three women of color who formed the club's leadership together with the president, stated that her goal with the club is "to get closer to people" and "to make long-lasting friendships." She added that she also wanted the club to be a place where women could talk more openly about their concerns with *League*'s handling of diversity, including character design for female champions.

This participant also told us that she and a number of friends became involved in *League* first through cosplay (costume play); she began playing because of her friends' interests in cosplaying as *League* champions. Likewise, the club's president used Halloween as an opportunity to cosplay as Ahri, one of the most well-known female *League* champions, showing pictures of himself in costume at the opening of the following meeting. As he did so, he related an anecdote about wearing the costume to a campus cafeteria and overhearing one student ask "Is … that a dude?" to which another replied, "I don't know!" For this player, cosplay is a legitimate mode of engaging with the game, as well as a compelling site for subversive gender performance. Scholarly writing about cosplay, and "crossplay" in particular, is ambivalent as to whether and how these practices constitute forms of resistance to heteronormative gender practices (Leng 2013; Ng 2011). That said, cosplay is generally regarded as an acceptable way for women to become involved in gaming and other fandom communities. Its presence in this club, however temporary, signals attempts on the part of the club's leadership to de-center instrumental *League* play, associated with the masculinized world of e-sports, and to engage other forms of participation with the game.

Trailers and promotional videos were another set of artifacts around which club members organized. Several meetings involved repetitive viewings of new promotional videos released by Riot. During viewings, all other activities ceased, and members watched and re-watched short, professionally produced animations featuring *League* characters and environs. These instances generated moments of intense affect and pleasure, as participants collectively responded to moments in the videos, commented on their favorite (or most hated) characters, and so on. While video is integral to most competitive gaming communities (Taylor 2016), what makes the viewing practices of this club notable is that they are organized less around discourses of improvement and training often associated with e-sports spectatorship and more around participation in the narrative world of *League*—less power gaming, more fandom.

Taken together, the club's emphasis on textual and material artifacts as a mode of engaging with *League* effectively re-positions the game (at least for club members) as a means for cultural expression more closely related to the aesthetic practices of geek culture than to the hyper-competitive practices of e-sports communities. Of course, this set up its own forms of exclusions, as players concerned more with training for competition than with participating in *League* fandom often did not stay for more than one or two meetings.

Discussion

Previous research on identity and gaming expertise, particularly from interventionist approaches, shows how expertise is contingent on both material considerations (unfettered access to games, gaming technologies, and leisure time) and discursive conditions (forms of misogyny, racism, homophobia, and ableism promoted by gaming texts, paratexts, and tools, as well as by other players). The conventional material and discursive terrains of digital play often favor straight, predominantly white cis-men and boys—normative associations that are too often naturalized by researchers who see things like preference and ability as culturally, if not biologically, predetermined. E-sports, as both an industry and a set of practices that valorize highly skilled play (often through overtures to the masculinized world of professional sports), serves to further entrench and intensify these deep-rooted connections between expertise and heteronormative masculinity. This makes competitive gaming—at any level, from casual to pro—a deeply masculinized domain that can be difficult for anyone who is not a straight, cisgender male to participate in for any length of time, much less achieve some degree of success.

At the time of writing, there are promising signs of change at the professional level, including collaboration between the Electronic Sports League (ESL) and Intel; the initiative, called "AnyKey," involves T. L. Taylor, a pioneering researcher of gender, games, and e-sports, and is committed to "supporting diverse participation in esports ... we hope to foster welcoming spaces and positive opportunities for competitive players of all kinds" (http://www.anykey.org/about/). The effectiveness of this initiative for creating "welcoming spaces" for historically marginalized individuals to engage in competitive gaming has yet to be determined, but several of its features—strong research presence, involvement from both corporate stakeholders and e-sports organizations, and outreach to grassroots organizations—seem promising.

Based on our ethnographic study of this *League* club, we also think it is possible that one route toward creating safer spaces for marginalized groups to participate in competitive gaming communities may be to diversify the range of activities the space offers. As we learned, practices such as cosplay and viewing parties—normally regarded as peripheral to e-sports—were key sites through which club members whose embodied subjectivities normally mark them as outsiders to competitive gaming could engage with *League*. One example, from outside a university context, is Stockholm Esport (http://www.sthlmesport.se/index.php/om-sthlm-e-sport/), which explicitly foregrounds inclusivity and builds community through gaming-themed charity events, pub crawls, panel discussions, and viewing parties. In other words, it is an e-sports community that strives for inclusivity through de-centering competitive play.

We also think it is worth re-emphasizing the implications of Riot's decision to base membership in the uLoL network on official student organization status, independent of any commitment or ability to field a competitive campus *League* team. This meant that the *League* club we worked with was able to obtain coveted promotional items (like *League*-themed lanyards and posters), gain formal recognition from Riot, and attract a core group of members, all the while approaching *League* as a site of cultural expression and fandom rather than an e-sport. Tethering uLoL club status to university criteria for establishing student organizations not only has implications for governance and the policing of harassment (i.e. applying any university rules for anti-harassment, including Title IX,[2] to uLoL clubs), but it also opens up the *possibility* that clubs may be aligned with other, potentially inclusive and/or activist groups on campus. Put differently, uLoL's organizational requirements allow for (without arguably explicitly promoting) less normative understandings and enactments of what an official competitive gaming organization can become.

Many of Riot's recent activities, including their visible sponsorship of the second GaymerX conference (Sarkar 2014) and their implementation of player governance systems targeting (among other things) homophobic language, suggest they are committed, at least ostensibly, to promoting diversity. That their support takes not only monetary but institutional and regulatory forms is promising, as it suggests a more than superficial concern with making the game safer for non-normative expressions and subjectivities.

Conclusion

By way of conclusion, we wish to acknowledge the difficulties in both maintaining and reporting on this safe space carved out within the masculinized and frequently toxic culture of *League*. The first difficulty is methodological and points to the importance of considering *addressivity* in qualitative research with marginalized players and player communities. Hammond encountered courteous but persistent resistance to his requests for interviews with the women who formed the club's leadership, and only one of these women agreed to an interview after Hammond had spent considerable time coming to club meetings and, importantly, playing and discussing *League* with the group, thereby demonstrating his interest in the game. We think that Hammond's presence as white, slightly older, cisgender male created barriers to establishing a smoother and more easygoing rapport with many participants. On the one hand, his intersectional privilege and the institutional authority he represented (as colleague to the club's supervisor) ensured he encountered no outright challenges to his presence; on the other hand, these embodied forms of authority meant that Hammond was unable to gain the full trust of some members, even after earnest and sustained participation in the week-to-week activities of the club. It may be that despite his best efforts, his presence formed a kind of institutional and patriarchal authority that complicated the intended safety of the space, even though Hammond eventually became a welcome fixture in the weekly meetings.

The second difficulty is both theoretical and practical and relates to the politics of labor in a space like this. Entering into its third semester, the club's first president (the young man who first established contact with Taylor) removed himself from the club for reasons that have not been divulged to us. The club treasurer, the young woman who described her reasons for being involved with the club in terms of wanting to deepen friendships and wanting to discuss problematic gender representations in the game, now serves as club president. This means that in a club committed to inclusivity, women occupy all the administrative roles and carry out the work of maintaining the club, while the male members of the group show up, chat, hang out, and play. Even in a safe space meant to provide alternate points of entry into an often unsafe player community, the affective labor required to maintain the space remains the exclusive responsibility of women. At a theoretical level, we wonder if redressing this imbalance might begin with a more explicit theorization of *temporality* (Halberstam 2005; Sharma 2014) in queer and non-normative communities: what might it mean to think about this club not just in terms of a safe space but as a safe *time*—a time *for* subjects who normally do the work of making time for others to play? While a broader theorization of gameplay, inclusivity, and (queer) temporalities is beyond the scope of this chapter, such an attention may at the minimum entail engaging (paid) research assistants as co-administrators as well as observers. This might allow club members, particularly those who occupy both leadership positions in the club and, more broadly, who embody the more precarious subject positions in competitive gaming communities, to pay more attention to the important work of inclusive play.

Notes

1. It should be noted that "Fiddledicks" is a fairly common nickname for the character among the broader *League* player community.
2. Established as US federal law in 1970, Title IX stipulates that any school receiving federal funding must provide equal resources for males and females.

Bibliography

Alloway, Nola, and Pam Gilbert. 1998. Video Game Culture: Playing with Masculinity, Violence and Pleasure. In *Wired-Up: Young People and the Electronic Media*, ed. Sue Howard, 95–114. London: University College London Press.

Andrews, Peter J. 2003. Isolation or Inclusion: Creating Safe Spaces for Lesbian and Gay Youth. *Families in Society* 84 (3): 331–337.

Carr, Diane. 2007. Contexts, Pleasures, and Preferences: Girls Playing Computer Games. In *Worlds in Play: International Perspectives on Digital Games Research*, ed. Suzanne de Castell and Jennifer Jenson, 313–322. New York: Peter Lang.

Chang, Edmund Y. 2015. Love Is in the Air: Queer (Im)Possibility and Straightwashing in FrontierVille and World of Warcraft. *QED: A Journal in GLTBQ Worldmaking* 2 (2): 6–31.

Collister, Lauren B. 2014. Surveillance and Community: Language Policing and Empowerment in a *World of Warcraft* Guild. *Surveillance & Society* 12 (3): 337–348.

Fisher, Stephanie, and Alison Harvey. 2013. Intervention for Inclusivity: Gender Politics and Indie Game Development. *Loading... The Journal of the Canadian Game Studies Association* 7 (11): 25–40.

Fox, Catherine O., and Tracy E. Ore. 2010. (Un)Covering Normalized Gender and Race Subjectivities in LGBT "Safe Spaces". *Feminist Studies* 36 (3): 629–649.

Gray, Kishonna L. 2012. Intersecting Oppressions and Online Communities. *Information, Communication & Society* 15 (3): 411–428.

Halberstam, Jack. 2005. *In a Queer Time and Place: Transgender Bodies, Subcultural Lives*. New York: NYU Press.

———. 2014. You Are Triggering Me! The Neo-Liberal Rhetoric of Harm, Danger and Trauma. *Bullybloggers*, July 5. https://bullybloggers.wordpress.com/2014/07/05/you-are-triggering-me-the-neo-liberal-rhetoric-of-harm-danger-and-trauma/.

Hanhardt, Christina B. 2013. *Safe Space*. Durham, NC: Duke University Press.

Harper, Todd. 2011. *Gay-for-Play: Addressing the Challenge of Relevant Gay Game Content*. Presentation at the Annual Meeting of the Association of Internet Researchers, Seattle, WA, October 10–13.

———. 2013. *The Culture of Digital Fighting Games: Performance and Practice*. New York: Routledge.

Jenson, Jennifer, and Suzanne de Castell. 2008. Theorizing Gender and Digital Gameplay: Oversights, Accidents and Surprises. *Eludamos. Journal for Computer Game Culture* 2 (1): 15–25.

Kennedy, Tracy. 2007. *Women's Online Gaming Communities: Don't Hate the Game, Hate the Players*. Presentation at the Annual Meeting of the American Sociology Association, New York, NY, August 11–14.

Kenney, Moira R. 2001. *Mapping Gay LA: The Intersection of Place and Politics*. Philadelphia, PA: Temple University Press.

Kindon, Sara L., Rachel Pain, and Mike Kesby. 2007. *Participatory Action Research Approaches and Methods: Connecting People, Participation and Place*. New York: Routledge.

Kocurek, Carly A. 2015. *Coin-Operated Americans: Rebooting Boyhood at the Video Game Arcade*. Minneapolis, MN: University of Minnesota Press.

Kollar, Philip. 2015. *League of Legends* 2015 World Championship Broke a Bunch of Records. *Polygon*, December 10. http://www.polygon.com/2015/12/10/9886500/league-of-legends-2015-world-championship-records-viewership-numbers.

———. 2016. University of California, Irvine Announces a *League of Legends* Scholarship. *Polygon*, March 30. http://www.polygon.com/2016/3/30/11330776/league-of-legends-university-california-irvine-esports-scholarship-riot.

Kou, You, and Bonnie Nardi. 2013. Regulating Anti-Social Behavior on the Internet: The Example of League of Legends. *iConference Proceedings*, pp. 616–622.

Leng, Rachel. 2013. Gender, Sexuality, and Cosplay: A Case Study of Male-to-Female Crossplay. *The Phoenix Papers: First Edition*, pp. 89–110.

Lin, Holin. 2008. Body, Space and Gendered Gaming Experiences: A Cultural Geography of Homes, Cybercafés and Dormitories. In *Beyond Barbie and Mortal Kombat: New Perspectives on Gender and Computer Games*, ed. Yasmin B. Kafai, Carrie Heeter, Jill Denner, and Jennifery Y. Sun, 54–67. Cambridge, MA: The MIT Press.

Macintyre, Alice. 2008. *Participatory Action Research*. Thousand Oaks, CA: Sage.

Mayo, Cris. 2010. Incongruity and Provisional Safety: Thinking Through Humor. *Studies in Philosophy and Education* 29 (6): 509–521.

Mueller, Saira. 2015. At Least Five Colleges Now Have *League of Legends*, Esports Scholarship Program. *Daily Dot*, November 6. http://www.dailydot.com/esports/league-of-legends-college-scholarships.

Ng, Joel. 2011. Queer Simulation: The Practice, Performance and Pleasure of Cosplay. *Continuum: Journal of Media & Cultural Studies* 25 (4): 583–593.

Parkin, Simon. 2015. A Video Game Algorithm to Solve Online Abuse. *MIT Technology Review*. https://www.technologyreview.com/s/541151/a-video-game-algorithm-to-solve-online-abuse/.

Phillips, Whitney. 2015. *This Is Why We Can't Have Nice Things: Mapping the Relationship Between Online Trolling and Mainstream Culture*. Cambridge, MA: The MIT Press.

Puar, Jasbir K. 2007. *Terrorist Assemblages: Homonationalism in Queer Times*. Durham: Duke University Press.

Pulos, Alex. 2013. Confronting Heteronormativity in Online Games: A Critical Discourse Analysis of LGBTQ Sexuality in *World of Warcraft*. *Games and Culture* 8 (2): 77–97.

Ratan, Robby, Nicholas Taylor, Jameson Hogan, Tracy Kennedy, and Dmitri Williams. 2015. Stand by Your Man: An Examination of Gender Disparity in League of Legends. *Games and Culture* 10 (5): 438–462.

Sarkar, Samit. 2014. GaymerX Rebranded as GX: Everyone Games, Organizers Launch $80K Kickstarter. *Polygon*, August 26. http://www.polygon.com/2014/8/26/6069549/gaymerx-gx-everyone-games-gx3-kickstarter.

Sharma, Sarah. 2014. *In the Meantime: Temporality and Cultural Politics*. Durham, NC: Duke University Press.

Sherlock, Lee. 2011. What Happens in Goldshire Stays in Goldshire: Rhetorics of Queer Sexualities, Governance and Fandom in *World of Warcraft*. In *Rhetoric/Composition/Play Through Video Games: Reshaping Theory and Practice of Writing Through Video Games*, ed. Richard Colby, Matthew S.S. Johnson, and Rebecca Shultz Colby, 161–174. New York, NY: Palgrave Macmillan.

Stabile, Carol. 2014. 'I Will Own You': Accountability in Massively Multiplayer Online Games. *Television & New Media* 15 (1): 43–57.

Stone, Allucquere R. 1991. Will the Real Body Please Stand Up?: Boundary Stories About Virtual Cultures. In *Cyberspace: First Steps*, ed. Michael Benedikt, 81–118. Cambridge, MA: The MIT Press.

Sundén, Jenny. 2009. Play as Transgression: An Ethnographic Approach to Queer Game Cultures. In *Breaking New Ground: Innovation in Games, Play, Practice and Theory*. Proceedings of Digital Games Research Association, West London.

Taylor, T.L. 2006. *Play Between Worlds: Exploring Online Game Culture*. Cambridge, MA: The MIT Press.

Taylor, Nicholas. 2012a. "A Silent Team Is a Dead Team": Communicative Norms in Competitive FPS Play. In *Guns, Grenades, and Grunts: First-Person Shooter Games*, ed. Gerald Voorhees, Joshua Call, and Katie Whitlock, 251–275. New York: Continuum.

Taylor, T.L. 2012b. *Raising the Stakes: E-Sports and the Professionalization of Computer Gaming*. Cambridge, MA: The MIT Press.

Taylor, Nicholas. 2016. Play to the Camera: Video Ethnography, Spectatorship and E-Sports. *Convergence* 22 (2): 115–130.

Taylor, T.L., and Emma Witkowski. 2010. *This Is How We Play It*. Proceedings of the Fifth International Conference on the Foundations of Digital Games.

Taylor, Nicholas, Jen Jenson, and Suzanne de Castell. 2009. Cheerleaders/Booth Babes/Halo Hoes: Pro-Gaming, Gender and Jobs for the Boys. *Digital Creativity* 20 (4): 239–252.

Taylor, Nicholas, Jennifer Jenson, Suzanne De Castell, and Barry Dilouya. 2014. Public Displays of Play: Studying Online Games in Physical Settings. *Journal of Computer-Mediated Communication* 19 (4): 763–779.

Trammell, Aaron. Forthcoming. Militarism and Masculinity in *Dungeons & Dragons*. In *Mediated Masculinities in Play*, ed. Nicholas Taylor and Gerald Voorhees. New York: Palgrave Macmillan.

Vaccaro, Annemarie. 2012. Campus Microclimates for LGBT Faculty, Staff, and Students: An Exploration of the Intersections of Social Identity and Campus Roles. *Journal of Student Affairs Research and Practice* 49 (4): 429–446.

Voorhees, Gerald. 2014. Neoliberal Masculinity: The Government of Play and Masculinity in E-Sports. In *Playing to Win: Sports, Video Games, and the Culture of Play*, ed. Robert Alan Brookey and Thomas P. Oates. Bloomington, IN: Indiana University Press.

Wajcman, Judy. 2010. Feminist Theories of Technology. *Cambridge Journal of Economics* 34 (1): 143–152.

Weems, Lisa. 2010. From "Home" to "Camp": Theorizing the Space of Safety. *Studies in Philosophy and Education* 29 (6): 557–568.

Witkowski, Emma. 2013. Eventful Masculinities: Negotiations of Hegemonic Sporting Masculinities at LANs. In *Sports Videogames*, ed. Mia Consalvo, Konstantin Mitgutsch, and Abe Stein, 217–235. New York: Routledge.

14

The Abject Scapegoat: Boundary Erosion and Maintenance in *League of Legends*

Elyse Janish

At the end of the summer half (Summer Split) of the 2015 North American *League of Legends* Championship Series (NA LCS), Team Renegades qualified to play in the 2016 season as one of the ten professional North American teams. Among their numbers was Remilia, also known as Remi and Maria Creveling, the first woman to ever qualify to the professional level of *League of Legends* (hereon *League*) competitive play, anywhere in the world (Eberhard 2015; LeJacq 2015). She played in only six professional games before quitting during the 2016 Spring Split (Conditt 2015; Boatman 2016). Although team rosters often change due to players being traded or retiring during the off-season, players rarely leave their teams during the season and even more rarely quit the LCS while still playing at the top-tier level.

In the period between Remilia's entrance to and exit from the professional *League* scene, everyone seemed to have an opinion about her. This alone is not unusual; many professional players are the subjects of discussion on forums, in videos and comments, in chatrooms, or in articles. However, unlike discussion about male players, which typically centers on their skill and prowess, the majority of their discussion about Remilia focused on her gender and how she (does not) fit in to the gaming community (a group I will define momentarily).

More specifically, the community most often focused on naming Remilia as a transgender woman and then debating what exactly her presence means for *League*, e-sports, and gamers more generally. This debate is particularly

E. Janish (✉)
University of Colorado, Boulder, CO, USA

© The Author(s) 2018
T. Harper et al. (eds.), *Queerness in Play*, Palgrave Games in Context,
https://doi.org/10.1007/978-3-319-90542-6_14

243

relevant to the North American *League of Legends* e-sports community, which, alongside other professional gaming communities, has been wracked with anxiety over defining and legitimizing itself for quite some time (Taylor 2012). The North American *League* community (hereon "the community"), by which I mean the players, fans, journalists, and analysts involved with the NA LCS tournament, fixated on what they deemed her in-betweenness; for many of the community members, she was neither female nor male, athlete nor geek. To them, she was not properly an e-sports player, yet neither was she properly outside of e-sports. What to do with such a person, and how to understand her place in their community? Where are the borders that for so long have helped maintain masculine privilege in e-sports, when Remilia's presence seems to throw those to the wind—at least as understood by many community members?

Indeed, Remilia's presence highlights the erosion of many boundaries that are important to the community, such as between male and female, gamer and athlete (a particularly unstable boundary across platforms and games), human and technology. To cope with this and to shore up those boundaries, community members discursively construct Remilia as abject (Kristeva 1982; Caslav Covino 2004; Lorek-Jezińska 2014). This chapter asks us to critically examine the negative impact of abjectification, especially in relation to the transgender body. People construct the abject body discursively and socially, making the *Other* out of *I* through the shared sense of being at once attracted to and yet disgusted by another human. This process allows the *League* community to conceptualize her as an abnormal spectacle that reifies cismasculine norms, rather than a person or player of significance. By abjectifying Remilia, they have discursively constructed a scapegoat, a straw-person silhouette of the real person into which they pour their anxieties about the blurring of boundaries. In so doing, they circumvent the underlying fear of boundary erosion, while simultaneously rebuilding those boundaries which effectively maintain cisgender masculine privilege in e-sports.

To examine the discursive construction of Remilia as an abject body and the crux of the gaming community's anxiety about boundaries in flux, I engage with transgender studies, queer theory, and theories of the abject. I situate these literatures within e-sports specifically, suggesting that boundaries have been in flux for some time and that those fluctuations are related to both queerness and abjection. From there, the analysis moves to the discourse surrounding Remilia, demonstrating how the community abjectifies her and discussing how abjectification is a crucial tool for maintaining cisgender, heteronormative, masculine privilege that exists within e-sports generally and specifically within the North American *League* scene.

Before moving into this work, however, I am compelled to confess a driving anxiety of my own with this project. Remilia has overtly stated her wish to not be held up on a pedestal as a champion for LGBTQ gamers and has explicitly asked people not to discuss her personal life. I believe that making claims about the discourse surrounding Remilia is possible without making claims about Remilia herself. Those claims moreover illuminate structures of cisgender, heterosexual, and masculine privilege in gaming which continue to marginalize women and queer players. As such, I do my best to discuss the talk about Remilia, while making no claims about her identity or person. It bears pointing out that many, even most, NA LCS community members are *not* making the kinds of comments that abjectify Remilia. Many men strive to make gaming more hospitable for women and LGBTQ people. Nevertheless, the sheer number of comments on YouTube videos and during NA LCS games of the tenor later discussed is daunting and suggests more than just a "few bad eggs."

Method

In order to analyze the discourse surrounding Remilia within the community, I began by searching all of the sites online that typically house discourse about the NA LCS. I collected data in a variety of ways in each context, including field notes, screenshots, and preserving text when possible. This began with Twitch.TV, the host service for all LCS tournaments, on which I watched all of the games in which Remilia played professionally—which totaled just six, at the beginning of the 2016 Spring Split. I also spent time immersed in the individual channels of several high-profile *League* players, both men and women. During these streams, I took screenshots and field notes of overtly gendered comments.

Beyond Twitch comments, I collected mentions of Remilia and women in e-sports from other notable internet arenas, such as gamer and geek publication websites (i.e., *Kotaku* and *Polygon*), online publications of mainstream newspapers and magazines, *Reddit* and other forum-based sites, and YouTube. Among these, it is notable that I excluded the forums hosted by Riot Games due to their policy of removing any and all discussions of Remilia. I chose YouTube as a primary site of data collection because Riot Games publishes all of the NA LCS games on YouTube, and many community members use it as a place to publish their own video analyses of players and teams. Altogether, the exact count of comments used is difficult to come by, since among the data collected are video clips and screenshots, as well as qualitative field notes designed to capture trends and patterns rather than exact quotes. However, those comments which can be counted totaled 87, complemented by 3 YouTube videos and 13 news articles.

Having collected this data, I followed the methodology of critical discourse analysis to come to an understanding of how the talk about Remilia reproduces and resubstantiates hegemonic power. Discourse analysis is based in the assumption that language and words constitute the many power structures that make up society and which benefit certain groups while oppressing others. The methodology, developed explicitly by Fairclough (1995), draws on work of Michel Foucault, in that critical discourse analysts seek to undercover the ways in which those structures are created and deployed, while keeping an eye toward resistance and subversion in the interest of dismantling hegemonic forces.

Framework: The Abject, Queer Theory, Transgender Studies, and Gaming

In the midst of a community focused on digital gaming, in which most (read: cisgender male) players are examined for how well or poorly they perform in-game, Remilia's corporeal presence kicked the metaphoric anthill. For the *League* community, her liminal body transgresses "the borders between categories guarded by cultural and social prohibitions and taboos" (Lorek-Jezińska 2014, p. 24). Abjection is caused by "what disturbs identity, system, order. What does not respect borders, positions, rules. The in-between, the ambiguous, the composite" (Kristeva 1982, p. 4). The abject body moves across boundaries and threatens the people who sit firmly on one side or the other of the boundary and who are thus legible to the community. The "self, or 'I,' depends on the abject to constitute its border, to be that which lies outside beyond the set" (Harold and Deluca 2005, p. 279). The abject refuses to conform, however, setting it apart from being simply the Other to the "I" of the community members. Unlike the Other, the abject points to the "border of [our] condition as a living being" (Kristeva 1982, p. 3), or our inevitable death. The ongoing presence of an abject body, which by nature refuses to conform, transforms the "I" and forces the self to adjust and adapt or else completely lose hold on that which separates it from the abject and thereby die (Harold and Deluca 2005, p. 280).

Critics have used the abject as an explanatory mechanism for discursive manifestations of cultural anxiety (see Gronnvoll and McCauliff 2013), and as such the concept is a useful framework for looking at the anxiety over diversification within the NA LCS community. *League* and other e-sports have always been plagued with toxic masculinity that strives to choke out queer and feminist challenges (see Gera 2014; Warr 2014; Campbell 2015). Thus, when the abject body erodes the boundaries that permit misogynist and anti-queer culture, it points not to the "inevitable death" of community *members* but rather to the inevitable end to what has traditionally been a safe haven for toxic masculinity.

Abjection was originally theorized as the physiological excess of body fluids that ooze beyond the boundary of the skin or fat and waste which exceed what is necessary to sustain life. Queer theorists have long pointed to the connection between queerness and excess (see Halberstam 1993). Given dominant binary understandings of gender and sexuality—man and woman, female and male, heterosexual and homosexual—anything that does not fit within this framework is by definition excessive. Queer excess, as with the oozing bodily fluids, refuses to stay contained and thereby threatens to expose the inherent instability and weakness of cultural boundaries regarding sex and gender.

Butler (1993) makes explicit this connection between queer excess and the abject. She argues that the performance of gender always has the potential to delineate the boundaries between that which is normal and acceptable and that which is abject and rejected. In fact, Butler contends that "the threat of the collapse of the masculine into the abjected feminine threatens to dissolve the heterosexual axis of desire; it carries the fear of occupying a site of homosexual abjection" (p. 206). In other words, the performance of hegemonic masculinity must always include a rejection of the feminine out of fear of finding oneself doubly abject: feminine and queer. Bodies that bend and play with gender performance, such as transgender bodies, always trouble the boundaries of gender and focus attention on gender's inherently performative and unstable nature.

In both popular culture and everyday life, this troubling of gender boundaries is often met with violent and objectifying responses. In Scott and Kirkpatrick (2015), trans activists discuss the reality that "trans women are hated and attacked more than trans men" (p. 164). This is supported by many studies on violence against transgender people (rampant among both MTF and FTM populations; see Stotzer 2009), which find that transgender women are often the most vulnerable within the larger category, especially to sexual abuse (Lombardi et al. 2002; Nadal et al. 2012).

Beyond sexual and physical violence, transgender people are also particularly prone to microaggressions. Chang and Chung (2015) laid out the terrain of microaggressions specifically experienced by transgender people, which become essential for understanding the abjectification of Remilia. Of the 12 themes of microaggressions identified by Chang and Chung, several stand out as particularly relevant to the harassment of Remilia: "(1) use of transphobic and/or incorrectly gendered terminology... (3) exoticization... (4) discomfort/disapproval of transgender experience... (5) endorsement of gender-normative and binary cultures of behavior... (7) assumption of sexual pathology or abnormality... (10) denial of bodily privacy (e.g., others feel entitled to make comments and objectify the bodies of transgender persons)" (p. 222).

Transgender studies scholars have also theorized about the conditions of possibility for transphobic violence. Namaste (2000) suggests that such "aggression can be linked to commonsense assumptions of what constitutes 'public' space, and how people should interact therein" (p. 141). She goes on to argue that the violence "can be interpreted in terms of a defense of the 'public' as that domain belongs to men—heterosexual men, to be more precise ... [transgender people] pose a fundamental challenge to public space and how it is defined and secured through gender" (p. 142). Considering the ways in which video gaming culture, like the public sphere, has also been a clearly masculine domain, we can extend Namaste's claim into gaming culture and work from the premise that transgender people within gaming communities fundamentally challenge cismasculine hegemony.

There has been little work on transgender identities and bodies within queer gaming studies. Kennedy (2002) briefly considers the potential of men playing as female avatars to be understood as transgendering. She suggests that by playing as a woman, the men could possibly experience their own selves within a female body. However, the author acknowledges that this transgendering has little effect. Beyond this, few studies take explicit interest in transgender identities of gamers or game characters. Within e-sports scholarship regarding gender more generally, more attention is paid to the gender and sexuality disparity in players and fans. T. L. Taylor focuses on gaming communities (2006) and e-sports (2012) and incorporates an in-depth discussion of the masculinist culture that often repels women and queer players, while Shaw (2014) considers the larger relationship between identifying as queer, gaming, and representation. Ratan et al. (2015) provide a succinct and thorough breakdown of how digital play is definitively gendered, where cismasculine people are privileged and others face discrimination and harassment. All of these studies are important and informative for understanding how gaming relates to gender identity, while also focusing primarily on cisgender people.

The very presence of a woman in e-sports can threaten the masculine-centric bonds formed between male players (Magnet 2006; Vanderhoef 2013). Games are homosocial spaces, which often result in overtly violent performances of misogyny and heteronormativity to offset the threat of same-sex attraction that comes from homosociality (Sedgwick 1985; Martino 2000;

Taylor 2011). Thus, if demands that gaming practices be more inclusive were successful, misogyny and homophobia would no longer be accepted, removing the first line of defense for these men to reassure themselves and each other that *I'm not gay*.

E-Sports as a Site of Excess and Boundary Fluctuation

Much literature on video games acknowledges that digital games occupy a liminal space in many senses. T. L. Taylor (2012) argues that "[pro gaming] warrants our consideration because it ... leads us into the heart of questions about the nature and status of play in computer games, the possibilities for (and limitations of) new forms of sport in the this digital age, and the challenges faced by gaming subcultures as they (often ambivalently) find themselves sliding into the mainstream" (loc. 88). She highlights several important boundaries in flux: those that define what counts as video games and gamers, those that define the difference between the physical (traditional sports) and the cyber (e-sports), and those that bound the mainstream, which has often been rejected by video game players as Other to gaming and geek identities. Games break down boundaries and yet often do not necessarily reform them and therefore potentially expose the ways that these boundaries are not based in some objective truth.

E-sports further complicate boundaries by adding athletics to the mix. If these video games are sports, then the players are athletes. But what, then, is an athlete, when the players do not run, dribble, skate, or swim but instead sit, click, push buttons, and manipulate a computer mouse or console controller? These physical acts still tax the body, asserts Taylor (2012), though in a very different way than the actions of traditional sports. Witkowski (2012) agrees, going on to suggest that to understand e-sports we have to confront the materiality of digital play, exposing the slippery boundary between physical and non-physical. Moreover, e-sport is a site of emergence, where the collision between geek and jock masculinity has produced a new yet familiar sports environment. *League* community members are especially interested in protecting the budding popularity of e-sports (Apstein 2015).

In addition, sports cannot be separated from sex and gender, as Miller (2001) contends. Contemporary sports culture subjects both the male and female athletic body to commodification and sexualization, though Miller notes a significantly greater burden on female athletes to appeal to the heterosexual male gaze. Sports have always been an institution in which patriarchy reigns; institutionalized sports are "bodily practices that are defined by physical power, aggression, and violence... It is a site of domination and privilege,

[…and] still, by and large, a space that is actively constructed by and for men" (Messner 2002, p. XVIII). The fact that feminine pronouns have traditionally been used to degrade male athletes further links discursive practices in sports to the assumption that women are the athletically inferior sex (McDonagh and Pappano 2008, p. 40). Although female athletes at large suffer due to this, lesbians (Travers 2006) and MTF transgender athletes (McDonagh and Pappano 2008) have faced unique and elevated discrimination. Altogether, sports do not just reflect gender and sexuality disparities, they actively contribute to the constitution and perpetuation of such disparities.

These characteristics of sports have transferred, in part or whole, to the culture of e-sports in North America. N. Taylor et al. (2009) describe the way male game players discursively relegate women in e-sports to inferior status, such as supporting male players or seeking male attention for pleasure or advertising. There is no space within the boundaries of "cyber athlete" for women; they may be within the physical space of e-sports tournaments, but the definition of top-tier athlete summarily excludes them from being considered professional players. A woman who excels at sports or e-sports is in excess to good womanhood and is therefore prone to abjectification.

All of these areas identified are sites in which socially constructed boundaries are eroding away as people play with and challenge their often problematic power dynamics and histories. Sometimes this erosion is even beneficial to the gaming community, giving it a uniqueness and offsetting it from other mainstream forms of entertainment. But boundary erosion induces anxiety and moral panics, especially among those who benefit most from the boundaries remaining firmly in place. That is why the abject is terrifying; it makes unavoidable that which people know but ignore—that these boundaries were never firm or fixed in the first place, which in turn imply that the ultimate border between life and death is also just a breath away from disappearing.

Constructing the Abject: Accounts of Remilia Within the *League* Community

In the midst of these unstable dynamics of e-sports culture, Remilia rose from the Challenger Series to the Championship Series and became the first woman worldwide to ever play in the LCS. Immediately there was hubbub among the community about the first female player, and just as quickly, there was extensive debate over whether or not Remilia could hold that title. Her gender identity became the crux of her Otherness; her in-betweenness made her too masculine to be treated like a woman in gaming but too feminine to be treated like a man. So, she was treated as abject.

In comments on videos and articles about her, people made it very clear that they found Remilia to be unintelligible, monstrous. Those who did so constructed monstrosity from their perception of her body, with comments focusing on things that didn't seem "right" about her. Her shoulders and assumed genitalia were the topic of many comments, such as "those shoulders, though," "IT HAS A PENIS," and "BOOOBS" pointed to the excess of her body, that she has *too much* body to be intelligible as female but also the wrong appearance to be intelligible as male, making her something altogether different: monstrous, abject.

These elements of unintelligibility and monstrosity are wrapped up in her perceived border crossing. Comments about her gender include dehumanizing tactics, such as referring to her as "it" or a "thing." By dehumanizing Remilia, the commenters suggest that she belongs in neither binary category of male or female. She has transgressed the binary and is now in excess to it, and as a result, the commenters do not recognize her as fully human. However, their discursive punishment does not make the transgression go away. She still played *League*, for a time, and this persistent visibility made cisgender community members feel the need to constantly rearticulate the identity of the *League* community as a place that is cisnormative and masculine through harassing and abjectifying behavior.

The transgression of crossing the boundary between male and female is made even more appalling to these spectators because it subverts the sexualized gaze that men are accustomed to applying to women in sports and video games. She is a woman who cannot be safely sexualized by heterosexual men. This, more than anything, makes her ambiguous and non-conforming to the community. Either she is a woman, and therefore the mandatory object of sexual desire and ridicule as an inferior player, or a man, and therefore a desirable and worthy companion for play but decidedly *not* an object of sexual desire. One commenter asks, "Am i the only one around here who wants a real girl in lcs just for fapps [masturbation]?," thus affirming in one short sentence that Remilia is not a "real" girl and that a "real" girl in the LCS would be welcome insofar as heterosexual men could masturbate to her image. Comments like this abound. The people making them at once turn toward her and away from her; they see her as female and also reject her as female by acknowledging that she *should* have sex appeal, then distancing themselves from the possibility of being attracted to her for fear of bringing homosexual desire into the community.

A quality of the abject is that it is deceptive, seeking to undermine the status quo. The commenters find that Remilia's "transgression" makes her deceptive, challenging norms by hiding and lying. In comments and in chat, people sometimes say that they find her attractive or "fuckable," but other community members consistently reply to such comments with phrases like "he's a dude" and "Remi is a man." These vigilant chat heroes are always prepared to swoop in and make sure that Remilia's feminine appearance does not deceive their fellow cisgender, heterosexual men into mistakenly wanting to "fap that." As one commenter put it, "bieng [sic] homosexual i think is more acceptable at least we know your [sic] a guy." These comments seek to correct the "lie" of Remilia's appearance—a "lie" that is only relevant under the conditions of heterosexual male gaze, the objectification of all women, and homophobia. The idea that a transwoman is deceptive hinges on the fact that these men feel their own masculinity and heterosexuality threatened by desiring a transgender body. They insist she is off-limits to their desire, which in effect challenges their right to sexually desire that which they please.

Another commenter on a video about her prowess as a *League* player says, "He [Remilia] and you may believe he's a cute girl but in the end he still has a dick and probably won't get laid unless its some desperate beta who takes anything he gets." This commenter denies that Remilia is a "cute girl" despite the fact that the video never asserts that Remilia is cute or attractive, only that she is a girl. This commenter found Remilia's attractiveness relevant regardless of the video content, suggesting the only framework in which to understand women in e-sports is sexual appeal. She fails to pass as a woman, making her immediately devoid of all sexual power and appeal. The commenter states that men who desire transwomen are "betas" and therefore unable to get the attention of a "real" woman and would have to settle for Remilia. Remilia the person is completely erased; instead, this commenter uses a straw-person version of her to promote violent masculinity at the expense of women, transgender folk, and gay men.

In contrast to how people talking about her construct her, Remilia herself does not meet the criteria of Kristeva's abject person. The few things she has posted online herself are sometimes angry or insulting in tone, yet she is very direct in tone—even combative—rather than deceptive. Yet the men who talk about her nevertheless accuse her of being deceitful. She prefers to remain private and keep her personal life out of the public sphere, but her very presence in the public arena of the NA LCS was constructed as an affront to women and men alike. The community constructed an abject body out of their perception of the actual person in question.

Reacting to the Abject: Transmisogyny as a Tool of Boundary Maintenance

Remilia's perceived transgression, a border crossing between male and female, pointed to the erosion of traditional gender norms and to the long-felt anxiety over the so-called death of the gamer. Gamer identity is so tightly wrapped up in masculinity that when masculinity begins to erode, gamer identity begins to erode. In conjunction with louder and louder demands for inclusive game design and community, and the changing face of gaming due to the rise of e-sports, gamer identity has never been more in flux. What was once a boys' club of games made for and by men—a counterculture safe haven for masculine geeks and nerds and a breeding ground for rampant sexism and misogyny—is becoming mainstream, jock, feminine, and gender diverse. This diversification may even have been one of the catalysts for the professionalization of hardcore gaming, as "real" gamers wanted a resort for traditional but controversial gaming practices (Taylor 2009). For those who wish to keep gaming as a stronghold of misogynist, homophobic masculinity, it becomes imperative to police the boundaries of male and female and many other boundaries besides.

Most prevalent in the current study is a constant, clinical insistence that one's gender aligns with one's genitalia at birth, end of story, and that any other gender/sex configuration is pathological. Many of these commenters reference physiology and biology as evidence, even displaying knowledge of hormone therapy and other treatments a transgender person might choose to undergo. Such evidence is invoked to demonstrate that there is something unnatural at work in the transgender body. People also located the pathology of transgender folk in their mental health, arguing that they must be confused, depressed, misguided, spoiled, and weak. This argument tends to include the assertion that being transgender is not a "real" thing but rather invented by people who want attention or are mentally ill. Such comments affirm that there is in fact a solid boundary between male and female, and those who cross it do so because they are sick or selfish, thus denying the queer possibilities of gender and sexuality beyond the binary.

Having established Remilia's true gender and pathology to their own satisfaction, the community also goes to great length to discuss what this means for *League* (see for example FPS Diesel 2015; Verticalex 2015). One resounding theme is that there is yet to be a woman in the LCS. Some people simply assert that this accolade remains unclaimed, but others use this claim as further evidence that women are inferior game players or are constitutionally unlikely to succeed in a high-stress environment. The discussion about the implications for *League* is strikingly absent of any notion of consent: this is done *despite* Remilia's overtly stated request that people not discuss her personal life. Her presence within the community as a professional player simultaneously constitutes her as an outsider—the community acknowledges her presence but now must decide what to do about that presence via discourse in which her voice is excluded.

This discourse works to reinforce the boundary around "good" and "bad" game player identity. Men are constructed as superior game players, as has been believed for a long time within the gaming community. It separates women out as unnecessary and even harmful to gaming, since they cannot compete with the big dogs or handle the intensity of the competition (read: harassment). Moreover, the *League* community is invested in the success of *League* as an e-sport, not just a gaming tournament (Taylor 2012), and to have a female athlete competing among the men could suggest it is not a real sport. After all, traditional sports are almost always divided by sex and thereby reproduce and naturalize the male/female binary, (re)constituting the female body as inferior to the male—weaker, less dedicated, slower. If a woman could compete with the men, then perhaps this is not a sport at all. This is exactly what linking video gaming to sport does; it naturalizes arguments about the inherent superiority of hegemonic-masculine men as athletes, or in this case cyber athletes, and therefore justifies discrimination against female, transgender, and/or queer players.

Thankfully the comments described here are among the worst, both in quality and in medium. YouTube comments are known for being horrendously unmoderated and full of inflammatory arguments representing the worst of online communities. What makes them more than cherry-picked examples, however, is their sheer number, and the correlation to the spamming of similar comments in the live chat that runs alongside the audio/visual stream of LCS matches on the host service Twitch.

If YouTube comments have the reputation for being hateful and immature, Twitch chat is often worse. Hundreds of thousands of viewers tune in for NA LCS games each weekend during the season, and all of them could potentially use the chat function simultaneously (though many opt to not contribute to chat). Chat flies by at an alarming pace, mostly short comments filled with memes that others copy and paste in order to spam. What results is that only certain ideas gain visibility by being copied and pasted by sometimes hundreds of users within the same span of seconds. Only those comments deemed funniest or most relevant get picked up and amplified by enough people and for a long enough period to really be noticed by a more casual viewer.

When Remilia or Team Renegades was on screen while she was still play-ing, chat was full of abusive jokes and memes about her body. The safety-in-numbers and mostly anonymous nature of Twitch chat results in a particularly enticing platform for those who might not otherwise voice transphobic com-mentary, revealing widespread prejudice. For most, it seems a joke to spam comments like "Remi-chan, wrong hole!" and "THEY THINK IM A GRILL, BUT I HAVE A P3NISS. WHO AM I? NONE OF YOUR BUSINESS." In the context of transmisogyny and sexualized aggression toward MTF trans-gender people, however, these "jokes" are quite sinister, and not just because they treat rape with levity. They reflect a collective mentality, a group sanc-tioning of treating Remilia's body and identity as an object of ridicule for the pleasure of the community. These types of comments reaffirm cisgender, mas-culine dominance at the expense of women and transgender folk.

Conclusion

The *League* community has a lot of work to do to define and legitimize itself to the world. E-sports defy many cultural boundaries, but the response to this blurring of boundaries has been fraught with hyper-rigid, even violent attempts to build them right back up. The entry of Remilia threw this strife into sharp relief, highlighting the many ways in which e-sports erode socially constructed boundaries around gender, sex, sexuality, athleticism, and geeki-ness. The community reacted by constructing Remilia as abject, not simply Other. They obsessed over Remilia's gender and identity and then promptly rejected that gender identity which they themselves decided for her. This is where we draw the line in the sand, they said. This is the boundary we will hold, no matter what: that between man and woman, also known as good gamer and bad social justice warrior, also known as competitive athlete and wannabe newb. This afforded them the tools not only to reject her as a legiti-mate player and thereby avoid acknowledging that women and queer folk are competitive and valuable members of the *League* community but also to firmly rebuild and defend the boundaries that keep cisgender, heterosexual, and masculine men in a position of power.

This analysis shows that a community can abjectify a body, as opposed to understanding abjection as an inherent quality of a body. This distinction underscores the discursive and social nature of abjection, which should aid in the decoupling of abjection from psychoanalysis and further extend the term's usefulness within other methodologies. We should be committed to knowing not just what *effects* abjection has on a society but also the *how* and *why* of the process that results in a body being understood as abject. In this case, understanding the process gives us a more nuanced understanding of transphobia within e-sports and the ways that abjectification is related to transphobia more largely. For example, fans and other community members of the NA LCS used tactics of transphobia as tactics of abjectification, wherein they connected Remilia's gender to their own anxiety over boundary erosions. Knowing that transphobic tactics easily can be coopted to abjectify a body gives us further tools for understanding transphobia itself. Perhaps this even points us to the possibility that transphobia and abjectification cannot truly be fully separated, that to understand transphobia demands us to consider abjection and its discursive construction.

In addition, the analysis here offers a straightforward mapping of one of the toxic areas of e-sports culture. Few studies or journalistic pieces ask game players to confront or address transphobia, including those that reported on Remilia's status as the first woman in the LCS. Indeed, most journalistic coverage of Remilia and the harassment she faced shied away from any kind of explicit reproach of the transphobic comments, usually instead referencing vague, gender-based harassment. To collapse transphobia, and moreover transmisogyny, into gender-based harassment overlooks the fact that across the board, transgender people are more likely to experience hate-motivated violence than almost any other group of marginalized people (Stotzer 2009; Weber 2016). The harassment against Remilia cannot only be classified as misogyny. People invested in dismantling the power structures that protect cismasculine hegemony, especially in games spaces but also more generally, must be committed to recognizing and stopping transphobia and transmisogyny. To do so, we must begin by recognizing the differences in discursive violence against transgender people from that against cisgender women and cisgender queer people.

A good place to start is to stop making excuses for harassment in gaming-related contexts. Many people ignore or excuse the harassment that occurs in Twitch chat and YouTube comments, writing it off as simply a bunch of young boys getting a thrill from using crude language forbidden by authority figures in more monitored contexts. This is not a sufficient defense. For one, these boys are learning this language somewhere, and it resonates enough that they desire repeating it among their peers. In addition, Twitch and YouTube are also places where boys and others *learn* what is acceptable behavior within the *League* community, so the messages on such sites are not only the product of misogyny and transphobia but also the means of perpetuating the production of such. Moreover, the anonymous hordes of chat contributors spamming these rape-centered, anti-woman, anti-LGBTQ memes reward each other for such hateful language and contribute to a sense of "I'm not the only one." Finally, if it's really just a batch of bad apples, where is the purported majority of good apples? For every one message that tries to address the hate speech in chat, hundreds chime in to call that person oversensitive, a buzzkill, a feminist, or social justice warrior (the worst insults among gamers, it seems).

League of Legends is a young-enough e-sport, however, that perhaps this misguided direction could be adjusted to be a more inclusive space. If *League* is still striving to define itself, both internally and to the world at large, and given that gender does not actually impact skill, then *League* stands at a crucial crossroads wherein the community could do much for inclusivity in e-sports and gaming. The owners of *League of Legends* at Riot Games, players, fans, and journalists all have a role to play in actively combatting the blatant transphobia and gender-based harassment leveled against Remilia during her brief stint in the NA LCS. Her entry and exit may have been occasion for transphobic abjectification, but it can also be an opportunity for active and purposeful inclusivity.

Bibliography

Apstein, Stephanie. 2015. E-Sports Nation: How Competitive Gaming Became a Flourishing Spot. *Sports Illustrated*, October 29. http://www.si.com/more-sports/2015/10/29/esports-competitive-video-gaming.

Boatman, Brandon. 2016. Remilia Has Left Renegades. *HardcoreGamer*, February 2. http://www.hardcoregamer.com/2016/02/02/remilia-has-left-renegades/190696/.

Butler, Judith. 1993. *Bodies That Matter: On the Discursive Limits of "Sex"*. New York: Routledge.

Campbell, Colin. 2015. Smite, Sexism and the Soul of Esports. *Polygon*, November 3. http://www.polygon.com/features/2015/11/3/9660094/smite-sexism-and-the-soul-of-esports.

Caslav Covino, Deborah. 2004. *Amending the Abject Body: Aesthetic Makeovers in Medicine and Culture*. Albany: SUNY Press.

Chang, Tiffany K., and Y. Barry Chung. 2015. Transgender Microaggressions: Complexity of the Heterogeneity of Transgender Identities. *Journal of LGBT Issues in Counseling* 9: 217–234. https://doi.org/10.1080/15538605.2015.1068146.

Conditt, Jessica. 2015. League of Legends' First Pro Female Player Weighs Her Options. *Engadget*, August 13. http://www.engadget.com/2015/08/13/league-of-legends-female-pro-player/.

Eberhard, J.T. 2015. Professional *League of Legends* to Get Its First Female and Transgender Player. *Patheos*, August 15. http://www.patheos.com/blogs/wwjtd/2015/08/professional-league-of-legends-to-get-its-first-female-and-transgender-player/.

Fairclough, Norman. 1995. *Critical Discourse Analysis*. London: Pearson Education Limited.

FPS Diesel. 2015. *LCS Has Its First Female?/Riot Silencing the Controversy?* YouTube Video, August 16. https://www.youtube.com/watch?v=pacBVDJxDlQ.

Gera, Emily. 2014. Where Are the Women in eSports? *Polygon*, May 27. http://www.polygon.com/2014/5/27/5723446/women-in-esports-professional-gaming-riot-games-blizzard-starcraft-lol.

Gronnvoll, Marita, and Kristen McCauliff. 2013. Bodies That Shatter: A Rhetoric of Exteriors, the Abject, and Female Suicide Bombers in the 'War on Terrorism'. *Rhetoric Society Quarterly* 43: 335–354. https://doi.org/10.1080/02773945.2013.819989.

Halberstam, Judith. 1993. Imagined Violence/Queer Violence: Representation, Rage, and Resistance. *Social Text* 37: 187–201.

Harold, Christine, and Kevin Michael DeLuca. 2005. Behold the Corpse: Violent Images and the Case of Emmett Till. *Rhetoric & Public Affairs* 8: 263–286.

Kennedy, Helen W. 2002. Lara Croft: Feminist Icon or Cyberbimbo? On the Limits of Textual Analysis. *The International Journal of Computer Game Research* 2 (2). http://www.gamestudies.org/0202/kennedy/.

Kristeva, Julia. 1982. *Powers of Horror: An Essay on Abjection*. Trans. Leon S. Roudiez. New York: Columbia University Press.

LeJacq, Yannick. 2015. The *League of Legends* Championship Series Has Its First Woman Player. *Kotaku*, August 14. http://kotaku.com/the-league-of-legends-championship-series-has-its-first-1724136651.

Lombardi, Emilia L., Riki Anne Wilchins, Dana Priesing, and Diana Malouf. 2002. Gender Violence. *Journal of Homosexuality* 42: 89–101. https://doi.org/10.1300/J082v42n01_05.

Lorek-Jezińska, Edyta. 2014. The Body, Desire, and the Abject: The Corpse and Cannibalism Is *Monty Python's Flying Circus* Sketches. In *Nobody Expects the Spanish Inquisition: Cultural Contexts in Monty Python*, ed. Tomasz Dobrogoszcz, 23–34. London: Rowman & Littlefield.

Magnet, Shoshana. 2006. Playing at Colonization: Interpreting Imaginary Landscapes in the Video Game *Tropico*. *Journal of Communication Inquiry* 30: 142–162. https://doi.org/10.1177/0196859905285320.

Martino, Wayne. 2000. Policing Masculinities: Investigating the Role of Homophobia and Heteronormativity in the Lives of Adolescent School Boys. *Journal of Men's Studies* 8: 213–236.

McDonagh, Eileen, and Laura Pappano. 2008. *Playing with the Boys: Why Separate Is Not Equal in Sports*. New York: Oxford University Press.

Messner, Michael A. 2002. *Taking the Field: Women, Men, and Sports*. Minneapolis: University of Minnesota Press.

Miller, T. 2001. *Sportsex*. Philadelphia: Temple University Press.

Nadal, Kevin L., Avy Skolnik, and Yinglee Wong. 2012. Interpersonal and Systemic Microaggressions Toward Transgender People: Implications for Counseling. *Journal of LGBT Issues in Counseling* 6: 55–82. https://doi.org/10.1080/1553860 5.2012.648583.

Namaste, Viviane K. 2000. *Invisible Lives: The Erasure of Transsexual and Transgendered People*. Chicago: University of Chicago Press.

Ratan, Rabindra A., Nicholas Taylor, Jameson Hogan, Tracy Kennedy, and Dmitri Williams. 2015. Stand by Your Man: An Examination of Gender Disparity in *League of Legends*. *Games and Culture* 10: 438–462. https://doi.org/10.1177/1555412014567228.

Scott, Suzanne, and Ellen Kirkpatrick. 2015. Trans Representations and Superhero Comics: A Conversation with Mey Rude, J. Skyler, and Rachel Stevens. *Cinema Journal* 55: 160–168. https://doi.org/10.1353/cj.2015.0060.

Sedgwick, Eve Kosofsky. 1985. *Between Men: English Literature and Male Homosocial Desire*. New York: Columbia University Press.

Shaw, Adrienne. 2014. *Gaming at the Edge: Sexuality and Gender at the Margins of Gamer Culture*. Minneapolis: University of Minnesota Press.

Stotzer, Rebecca L. 2009. Violence Against Transgender People: A Review of United States Data. *Aggression and Violent Behavior* 14 (3): 170–179.

Taylor, Nicholas. 2009. *Power Play: Digital Gaming Goes Pro*. PhD diss., York University.

———. 2011. Play Globally, Act Locally: The Standardization of Pro *Halo 3* Gaming. *International Journal of Gender, Science and Technology* 3: 228–242.

Taylor, Nicholas, Jen Jenson, and Suzanne de Castell. 2009. Cheerleaders/Booth Babes/Halo Hoes: Pro-Gaming, Gender and Jobs for the Boys. *Digital Creativity* 20: 239–252. https://doi.org/10.1080/14626260903290323.

Taylor, T.L. 2006. *Play Between Worlds: Exploring Online Game Culture*. Cambridge: MIT Press.

Taylor, T.L. 2012. *Raising the Stakes: E-Sports and the Professionalization of Computer Gaming*. Cambridge: MIT Press.

Travers, Ann. 2006. Queering Sport: Lesbian Softball Leagues and the Transgender Challenge. *International Review for the Sociology of Sport* 4: 431–446. https://doi.org/10.1177/1012690207078070.

Vanderhoef, John. 2013. Casual Threats: The Feminization of Casual Video Games. *Ada: A Journal of Gender, New Media, and Technology* (2). https://doi.org/10.7264/N3V40S4D.

Verticalex. 2015. *Remilia the LCS Girl*. YouTube Video, August 13. https://www.youtube.com/watch?v=gdeXFdcCgbI.

Warr, Philippa. 2014. Esports for All? How to Get More Women into Pro Gaming. *The Guardian*, July 31. https://www.theguardian.com/technology/2014/jul/31/esports-how-to-get-more-women-into-pro-gaming.

Weber, Shannon. 2016. 'Womanhood Does Not Reside in Documentation': Queer and Feminist Student Activism for Transgender Women's Inclusion at Women's Colleges. *Journal of Lesbian Studies* 20: 29–45. https://doi.org/10.1080/1089416 0.2015.1076238.

Witkowski, Emma. 2012. On the Digital Playing Field: How We 'Do Sport' With Networked Computer Games. *Games and Culture* 7: 349–374. https://doi. org/10.1177/1555412012454222.

15

Out on Proudmoore: Climate Issues on an MMO

Carol A. Stabile and Laura Strait

Introduction

The short history of online communities is filled with instances of deception and egregious cases of online harassment. Sherry Turkle (1997) tells the apocryphal story, repeated in the annals of what were then described as virtual communities, of a man masquerading as a woman. Allucquére Rosanne Stone tells a similar tale in her chapter on a "cross-dressing psychiatrist" (1995). Julian Dibbell (1998) devotes a chapter of *My Tiny Life* to how a "rape in cyberspace" impacted the members of one early online community. In the near 20 years since this first wave of research was published, scholars, artists, and activists have documented the toxic dimensions of gaming and hostile game climates in particular, in games ranging from *Halo* to the *Call of Duty* franchise to *League of Legends* (*LoL*).[1]

More recently, programmer Zoe Quinn, Yahoo CEO Ellen Pao, video game critic Anita Sarkeesian, and scholar and activist Melissa Click all received death threats and experienced other forms of violence after coordinated online campaigns against them. Documenting these instances remains a critical project for feminist media studies since women, queer people, and people of color continue to encounter intensely hostile climates both online and in real life (IRL) (Nakamura 2002, 2009; Nelson 2011; Consalvo 2012; Cross 2014; Daniels 2009; Higgin 2009; Kolko et al. 2013; Marwick and Boyd 2014;

C. A. Stabile (✉) • L. Strait
University of Oregon, Eugene, OR, USA

© The Author(s) 2018
T. Harper et al. (eds.), *Queerness in Play*, Palgrave Games in Context,
https://doi.org/10.1007/978-3-319-90542-6_15

Nelson et al. 2001). At the same time, pooling information about how feminist, anti-racist, queer players and their allies are working to carve out spaces for work and play can help communities create strategies to intervene in, and hopefully transform, such hostile climates. The interactive context of online gaming offers examples of resistance to oppressive practices and harassment, as well as interventions into the reproduction of hostile climates, from which scholars and activists can learn (Phillips 2012).

The following analysis turns to one such example: the struggle over online climate and culture on *World of Warcraft* (*WoW*) server Proudmoore. Our project seeks to balance a critique of the relations of inequality that exist in online spaces with our desire to encourage, as writer, artist, and educator Walidah Imarisha (2015) puts it, "organizers and movement builders to be able to claim the vast space of possibility, to be birthing visionary stories" (p. 3). Encouraging people to use "their everyday realities and experiences of changing the world," Imarisha continues, allows us to "form the foundation for the fantastic and … build a future where the fantastic liberates the mundane." Through its focus on the agency people exercise within the constraints of online spaces, utilizing some of the affordances that online spaces uniquely provide, this chapter documents how a specific play culture was transformed and how the fantastic effectively transformed the mundane.

Defining Online Harassment

In what follows, we use the term sexual harassment to describe behaviors that create unwelcome and hostile online climates. We find it useful to borrow the US Equal Employment Opportunity Commission's (EEOC) definition, understanding online sexual harassment to include unwelcome sexual advances, requests for sexual favors, and additional verbal or physical harassment of a sexual nature. According to the EEOC, harassment does not have to be sexual in nature but can also include offensive remarks about a person's sex. Defining these acts as sexual harassment allows us to theorize the impact of them on the broader environments in which they take place (importantly for our purposes, play cultures). Sexual harassers' behaviors, that is, do not just affect one person: they have the potential to transform cultures for the worse for all involved.

Of course, harassment in online environments is mediated: a player does not experience harassment in physically vulnerable ways, although they do in ways that can be psychologically and emotionally harmful. For example, players' affective investments in characters, communities, and virtual worlds are often deep and sustaining, particularly for groups of people whose everyday lives are often characterized by powerlessness. T.L. Taylor describes how precarious groups can have powerful experiences of virtual geographies, free of the precarity through which they must navigate embodied spaces (2009). In online games, harassment is often severe enough to cause players to stop playing a particular game. Online harassment thus deprives them of experiences in fantastic realms that can provide spaces outside everyday realities of harassment and gender-based and racially motivated violence.

Harassment in online games can take different forms. Some of the harassment takes the shape of visual acts. Unlike early text-based MUDs (multi-user dungeons), today's massively multiplayer online games (MMOs) depict avatars as physical entities that can be embodied and controlled by the player with a mouse or touchpad. In some online games, tea-bagging (squatting and dipping one's crotch over the head of another player's corpse, using the command "/crouch") is used to humiliate targeted players. In crowded cities on *World of Warcraft* (*WoW*), players '/flirt,' '/kiss,' and/or '/follow' "female" characters (also known as toons), for example, virtually enacting forms of street harassment and stalking. In games like *Halo*, the *Call of Duty* franchise, and *Left 4 Dead*, players retaliate against women, people of color, and players perceived as queer by killing teammates thought to occupy these categories. For example, Lisa Nakamura (2009) documents racially motivated harassment toward Chinese gold farmers on *WoW*.

While these forms of discrimination are visible markers of toxic MMO gaming culture, much harassment in online games occurs via text-based communication channels in a chat log box located at the bottom of the player's screen. In *WoW*, these communication channels have multiplied since the game's launch and include trade chat, guild chat, and group chat. The channel with the most traffic is generally trade chat, a channel through which players in a particular geographical region on a given server can send public messages to all players in their region. Over time, particular regions' trade channels have become well known for rampant sexism and routine performances of aggressive masculinity, especially those regions where the game's two factions (Horde and Alliance) routinely cross paths. Guild chat is more limited in its reach, because only members of a particular guild (an in-game social group) can view the messages. Another channel, group chat, is temporally contingent and accessible only to members of groups formed for specific, time-limited purposes (e.g. quests or dungeons). Players can also "whisper" or send direct messages to individual players, whether the sender is known to the message's recipient or not. On *WoW* and other platforms, these forms of what is effectively instant messaging provide multiple avenues for harassment of other players.

The interactive dimensions of online games make experiences of sexual and racial harassment more analogous to the EEOC's definition of harassment than other traditional media. Where media like film and television represent sexist practices, unlike online games, they do not allow readers, players, viewers, or listeners to have direct contact with one another. In contrast, players actively enact oppressive norms of behavior in online spaces, much as they do in the hallways, cafeterias, and classrooms that C.J. Pascoe (2011) describes in *Dude, You're a Fag*. Recent scholarship on virtual communities attributes these forms of online harassment to anonymity, contending that online harassment is enabled when people cannot be held personally accountable for their actions (Bernstein 2015; Citron and Franks 2014; Fox and Tang 2014). We maintain that the causes of online sexual and racial harassment are similar to the causes of those behaviors in real life and that while anonymity may amplify harassment, it does not cause it.

In an MMO, worlds are built in many senses, but perhaps most importantly, they are created through the persistent relationships and the social, symbolic, and economic capital created and maintained each time a player logs into the game. Players build relationships in MMOs that in turn build their abilities to level up, to complete quests and dungeons, and, for more advanced players, to participate in raids. This means that many players have a stake in their avatars' reputations: there may be consequences *within the world* when players are uncooperative, abusive, or aggressive.

Despite their myriad avenues for sexual harassment, those who experience harassment in online cultures enjoy forms of agency not available to people for whom embodied resistance can result in violent physical retaliation against their persons. As the following example demonstrates, anonymity—in this case, the disarticulation of body from avatar—and collective online organizing can serve as important tools for mitigating sexual harassment.

Queering Proudmoore

Proudmoore is one of *WoW*'s original player-versus-environment (PVE) realms, active since November 2004. It is a high-population Pacific Standard Time realm, with a player base in North America but substantial numbers of players in Australia, New Zealand, and Asia. In an MMO, the "massiveness" of the population requires that players be distributed to different physical servers (like memory banks) in order for the game to run smoothly. These "realms" are often divided based on location/time zone (e.g. on *WoW* there are Oceanic servers), but in some cases, they are also distinguished by the type of play. Some servers are player-versus-player (PVP), where players actively compete and battle with other players in direct combat. PVE servers are more common, since these allow players of all skill sets and levels to explore the world without the risk of being killed by other players. Role-playing servers ask players to engage more in the performances of identity and skill characteristic of role-playing games like *Dungeons & Dragons*. Because player characters cannot be easily or cheaply transferred from one server to another, their relative permanence and the relationships that accrue to specific player characters tie players to one another and deepen bonds of community and persistent climate.[2]

Stabile first heard about Proudmoore early in her fieldwork in *WoW*, mainly from LGBTQ players she met in the game, who referred to it affectionately as the "gay" server, perhaps *WoW*'s premier site for what Jenny Sunden describes as "transgressive play," meaning play that actively resisted heteronormative or racial norms. Stabile did not start playing on it until 2010, when she transferred some player characters to Proudmoore. Differences in climate on Proudmoore were immediately apparent. In Azuremyst and Eitrigg., two of the servers Stabile had played on, homophobic comments in trade and guild chat were common, especially in high-traffic areas or hubs where factions interacted, like the Barrens and Orgrimmar. Not only were public channels of communication on Proudmoore largely free of homophobia and rape jokes, LGBTQ-friendly guilds publicly recruited new members on trade channels. From 2013 to 2015, the authors of this chapter played together on the server (or realm) Proudmoore (members of a tiny guild named "The Party," Stabile played an Undead priest named Leonhotsky; Strait played a Tauren hunter named Porkheimer).

To say that Proudmoore *became* queer is something of a misnomer, since the LGBTQ presence on the server predates the launch of *WoW* itself, dating back to the beginnings of the MMO *City of Heroes* in April 2004. *City of Heroes* players created the guild <Rough Trade> and then went on to form the guild <Spreading Taint>, expanding their presence through a number of subguilds. The names of these guilds hint at the fact that many of these early "gaymers" were men, but, as demonstrated below, they were joined by lesbians, transgender players, and allies.[3] Some sources report that the *WoW*-based gay guilds formed while *WoW* was in beta ("Taint Proudmoore US." *WoWWiki*). When *WoW* launched in November 2004, these already-organized LGBTQ players migrated as a group to the new MMO. The server began functioning as a hub for LGBTQ players when members of <Rough Trade> formed the guild <Spreading Taint>.

The organized presence of <Rough Trade> was crucial to the climate that developed on Proudmoore. It encouraged the early proliferation of LGBTQ guilds, which were havens for players who felt bullied and alienated by the homophobic culture on other servers. In these guilds, players could communicate within guild chat without fear of reprisal. They could spend their leisure time with players who shared political views and dispositions. The LGBTQ guilds, in essence, allowed for the formation of queer communities who could help protect individual players and encourage them to learn the game and level up in a less hostile climate. Queer guilds <Stonewall Champions> (some of whose members went on to found <The Stonewall Family> in 2008) and <Spreading Taint> were established in 2005, just a few months after the game launched in November 2004. The first Gay Pride Parade in *WoW* took place on Proudmoore in June 2005, organized by members of these two guilds.

Although these LGBTQ guilds were already active from the game's launch and were actively contributing to improving the climate on the realm, some accounts trace Proudmoore's queer-friendly reputation to "a case where Blizzard had banned a gay-only guild, but then subsequently was forced to allow it after a court-case ruled in the favor of the claimants" (Ward 2006). In 2006, Sara Andrews, a lesbian player from the UK who played a mage on a different realm (Shadowmoon) was told by a game master (or GM—a Blizzard employee who oversees servers, moderates disputes, and sometimes punishes players for violations of the game's terms of service) that by using trade channels to publicize her guild as being LGBTQ-friendly, she had violated the game's terms of service. According to this GM, Andrews specifically had violated the policy prohibiting language that "insultingly refers to any aspect of sexual orientation pertaining to themselves or others." Andrews challenged this claim, arguing that she could hardly have been insultingly referring to herself. Moreover, she pointed out, homophobic language that clearly violated this policy routinely went unchallenged elsewhere in the game.

US-based LGBTQ guilds allied to Andrews' defense, mobilizing to demand that Blizzard institutionalize the right to openly recruit players to LGBTQ-friendly guilds. Members of <Spreading Taint> and <Stonewall Champions> wrote an open letter to Blizzard, criticizing the game developer's hypocritical stance. Lambda Legal—a US-based LGBTQ-rights legal group—also wrote an open letter to Blizzard, offering to assist them in crafting a nondiscriminatory clarification of the terms of service for Blizzard. In the wake of this publicity, Blizzard quickly backed down. Thor Biafore, senior manager of Blizzard's customer service, apologized to Andrews, telling her, "Please accept our apologies for the way our staff characterized your conduct, and rest assured that your account will not be penalized in any way for this occurrence." Blizzard also agreed to introduce training for the 1000 or so in-game administrators it uses to police Azeroth to help them deal more sensitively with LGBTQ issues, although it is not clear that this training ever took place ("World of Warcraft" Copes 2006).

In these ways, the organized presence of queer players on Proudmoore allowed activists to come to the support of Andrews and help to end the ban on LGBTQ recruiting throughout the game. At the same time, the publicity generated renewed interest in LGBTQ guilds like <Spreading Taint> and <Stonewall Champions>, enhancing the profile of an identifiably queer-friendly server. Through the overarching organizational structure provided by <Rough Trade>, queer guilds provided spaces for LGBTQ players to meet one another, play the game with each other, and band together in fighting homophobia on their server.

This support, plus the fact that defying homophobia in an online game differs in crucial ways from defying homophobia in real life, allowed queer players to challenge homophobic speech in the game in routine and everyday ways. Instead of a culture where queer-identified players felt marginalized and unsupported when they spoke out against homophobic behaviors, members of queer communities held players using homophobic language or imagery accountable to very different sets of gender norms. Players quickly discovered that homophobic language would result in reporting and censure. These private guild strongholds also held Pride Parades organized around queer political issues (like gay marriage) and engaged in queer naming practices that allowed players to quickly identify them as allies.

Playing queerly also educated and socialized other players, helping to create cultural change by creating new norms of interaction. Being queer became everyday on Proudmoore. One longtime member of <Spreading Taint> observed, "I've seen people from other non-GLBT guilds warn and scold others in Trade chat for making demeaning remarks or for using insensitive or homophobic remarks, explaining that Proudmoore is the wrong server to be behaving that way" (15 Minutes of Fame 2008). Game-related forums also indicate the degree to which queerness became normal on Proudmoore. One forum poster recommended Proudmoore to a new player, cautioning that "You should also familiarize yourself with LGBT if you haven't already, and if it is a problem for you then there maybe better options elsewhere. By familiarize yourself I mean be aware of its meaning and that we do have a lot of LGBT players and guilds on the server" (Help Me Choose a Realm! 2014).

Lessons

As game studies scholars have observed, harassers and victims alike must operate within the structural, algorithmic biases and restrictions of online games like MMOs (Chee et al. 2012; Galloway 2006; Nakamura 2008; Taylor 2009, 2012). The intransigence of built environments by means of programming, however, does not mean that cultural change is impossible within the game. For instance, until Andrews' challenge on Shadowmoon, the game regulated words related to sexualities in the same way it regulated profanities: by not allowing players to use them. According to Blizzard, the reasoning behind this stemmed from the attempt to rid the game of any real-world referents for which players could be targeted or harassed. Members of the Blizzard forum community (not only those affiliated with the guilds listed above) began to point out the hypocrisy of banning profanities and references to anatomy while allowing offensive words like "fag" to flow freely through the filter. When the issue hit the forums, Blizzard quickly amended the chat filter to exclude the words *homosexual* and *transsexual* when filtering for profanities (Profanity Filters 2012). The queering of Proudmoore occurred within those constraints, in spaces where members and allies of the LGBTQ community succeeded in cultivating tolerant and receptive persistent cultures across multiple games and platforms.

We can learn several lessons from the case of Proudmoore in regard to online sociality and cultivating positive and inclusive climates. First, organization was central to this successful intervention. Having already organized on *City of Heroes*, <Rough Trade> was well positioned to stake a claim to queer space in *WoW*. The formation of the original LGBTQ guilds crucially enabled subsequent transformations. Not only did these provide safe havens for gaymers and allies, they demonstrated the demographic power of queer players and formed an institutional base of support that helped to persuade Blizzard to publicly allow queer guilds. Without the existence and support of these guilds, the context for Proudmoore's myriad and multiplying acts of resistance would not have been possible.

The name of the Horde faction guild—<Spreading Taint> (a double entendre drawn from the lore of the game itself)—proved prophetic: by challenging homophobia and heteronormativity, these guilds spread a different model of interaction. Since its formation, the Rough Trade Gaming Community (RTGC) has amassed a thriving collective of LGBTQ gamers across a number of popular MMOs including *Star Wars – Knights of the Old Republic (TOR)*, *Elder Scrolls Online*, *Final Fantasy XIV*, and *Guild Wars 2*. In each game, the

RTGC has applied the same successful formula when creating LGBTQ game havens: players congregate generally on one realm and are centralized around one or two guilds, depending on the structure of the game.

Additionally, and especially in the contemporary moment, these groups are using external connections to build communities. As T.L. Taylor (2009) pointed out in regard to *Everquest*, established guilds have been organizing IRL (in real life) meet-ups for quite some time, strengthening social bonds that originated online. Today, most prominent guilds have active and functional websites on which to organize everyday guild functions. Additionally, many groups now utilize the affordances of social media to connect with one another, further closing the gap between real life and in-game life. In addition to IRL and social media connectivity, LGBTQ guilds host a number of recruitment sites (owing in part to Sara Andrews' challenge to the ban on LGBTQ guild recruitment), such as GayGuilds.com, where both Horde and Alliance guilds can congregate to recruit for various guilds across a number of *WoW* realms. The proliferation of social media has intensified the IRL social connections among players. Strait recalls her days as a guild master, when only one other player had her IRL contact information in the form of an AOL email address. Her current guild hosts regular gatherings and events, often facilitated by a website as well as an active Facebook group page.

The brief history of LGBTQ guilds on Proudmoore also hints at the role that policies and terms of service agreements can play in transforming play cultures (Chee et al. 2012). In particular, it highlights the utility of these policies for addressing hostile play climates. Although games are programmed with structural biases (e.g. the continued imposition of binary gender choices), and many admins and players are themselves biased, companies can be responsive to dissent when it comes to communities seeking redress particularly in the face of protests from organized LGBTQ guilds and communities like those on *WoW*. The broader LGBTQ MMO community and its large and prominent guilds also act as powerful resources for retention of long-term players and recruitment of new subscribers.

Some MMOs are developing machine learning methods to curb in-game harassment by incentivizing restraint when it comes to toxic behavior (Maher 2016). *LoL* has pioneered the efforts to impose behavioral regulation through system-end punitive processes, such as a more sophisticated "tribunal" system of reporting, which relies on vetted, well-behaved players, to essentially "blind review" reported players (Kou and Nardi 2013). The game's producer, Riot Games, has become notorious for employing their massive data reserves for social and behavioral science research to further efforts to control gaming culture from the infrastructural side. This approach may be effective in limiting negative experiences players face for a time, but does not account for the unseen and uncounted forms of bias that an online climate can foster. *LoL* has made strides in improving their game's social atmosphere through judiciary measures and provides ongoing research to improving inclusivity in MMOs through infrastructural adjustments.

The nature of changing or sustaining an inclusive climate online requires both the persistent discursive attention by well-organized groups in combination with responsive game developers, or game developers who can be persuaded to be responsive. There are allies in these spaces and industries who also care about improving the sociality and climate of their games instead of reproducing heteronormative, misogynist, and racist exclusions of marginalized demographics. From a user standpoint, good old-fashioned collective action, engagement, and the understanding that gaming parameters can be changed or creatively worked around are paramount to making online climates fully inclusive.

Notes

1. See http://gambit.mit.edu/projects/hatespeech.php/need for vivid examples of these forms of harassment.
2. The analysis that follows is based on nearly two decades' combined experiences as participant observers in *WoW* and other online games. Stabile began playing *WoW* in 2006, about 18 months after the game was launched, specifically for research purposes. She subsequently played *Guild Wars*, *The Lord of the Rings Online*, and *Knights of the Old Republic*. Strait began playing *WoW* shortly after its launch in 2005, while still in high school, and later played *Guild Wars*, *Dungeons & Dragons Online*, and *Runescape*.
3. In 2006, *gaymer.org* creator Chris Vizzini filed to trademark the term but with help of the Electronic Frontier Foundation was denied ownership by gay gamers who had for years been using the language (Kohler 2013).

Bibliography

15 Minutes of Fame: Proudmoore Guild Plays out GLBT Pride. 2008. *Engadget.* Accessed July 13, 2016. https://www.engadget.com/2008/10/21/15-minutes-of-fame-proudmoore-guild-plays-out-glbt-pride/.

Bernstein, Anita. 2015. Abuse and Harassment Diminish Free Speech. *Pace Law Review* 35 (1): 1.

Chee, Florence M., Nicholas T. Taylor, and Suzanne de Castell. 2012. Re-Mediating Research Ethics: End-User License Agreements in Online Games. *Bulletin of*

Science, Technology & Society 32 (6). https://doi.org/10.1177/0270467612469074. *bst.sagepub.com*. Web.

Citron, Danielle Keats, and Mary Anne Franks. 2014. *Criminalizing Revenge Porn.* Rochester, NY: Social Science Research Network. *papers.ssrn.com*.

Consalvo. 2012. Confronting Toxic Gamer Culture: A Challenge for Feminist Game Studies Scholars. *Ada: A Journal of Gender, New Media, and Technology*: n.p.

Cross, Katherine Angel. 2014. Ethics for Cyborgs: On Real Harassment in an 'Unreal' Place. *Loading…* 8 (13): n.p. *journals.sfu.ca*.

Daniels, Jessie. 2009. Rethinking Cyberfeminism(s): Race, Gender, and Embodiment. *WSQ: Women's Studies Quarterly* 37 (1–2): 101–124.

Dibbell, Julian. 1998. *My Tiny Life: Crime and Passion in a Virtual World.* New York: Holt.

Fox, Jesse, and Wai Yen Tang. 2014. Sexism in Online Video Games: The Role of Conformity to Masculine Norms and Social Dominance Orientation. *Computers in Human Behavior* 33: 314–320. *ScienceDirect*.

Galloway, Alexander R. 2006. *Gaming: Essays On Algorithmic Culture.* Minneapolis: University of Minnesota Press.

GAMBIT: Hate Speech Project. Accessed July 12, 2016. http://gambit.mit.edu/projects/hatespeech.php.

Help Me Choose a Realm! 2014. *Wowhead.* Accessed July 13, 2016. http://www.wowhead.com/forums&topic=204888/help-me-choose-a-realm.

Higgin, Tanner. 2009. Blackless Fantasy: The Disappearance of Race in Massively Multiplayer Online Role-Playing Games. *Games and Culture* 4 (1): 3–26.

Imarisha, Walidah, and adrienne maree brown. 2015. *Octavia's Brood: Science Fiction Stories from Social Justice Movements.* Oakland, CA: AK Press.

Kohler, Will. 2013. Its Okay To Be Gay-Mer! – Battle Over the Word 'Gaymer' WON! *Back2Stonewall*. n.p., 24 August. Web. 27 October 2016.

Kolko, Beth, Lisa Nakamura, and Gilbert Rodman. 2013. *Race in Cyberspace.* Abingdon: Routledge.

Kou, Yubo, and Bonnie Nardi. 2013. *Regulating Anti-Social Behavior on the Internet: The Example of League of Legends.* iConference 2013 Proceedings.

Maher, Brendan. 2016. Can a Video Game Company Tame Toxic Behaviour? *Nature News* 531 (7596): 568. https://doi.org/10.1038/531568a.

Marwick, Alice E., and Danah Boyd. 2014. Networked Privacy: How Teenagers Negotiate Context in Social Media. *New Media & Society* 16 (7). https://doi.org/10.1177/1461444814543995. *nms.sagepub.com*.

Nakamura, Lisa. 2002 Cybertypes: Race, Ethnicity, and Identity on the Internet (Hardback) – Routledge. Text. *Routledge.com*. n.p. Web. 12 July 2016.

———. 2008. *Digitizing Race: Visual Cultures of the Internet.* Minneapolis, MN: University of Minnesota Press.

———. 2009. Don't Hate the Player, Hate the Game: The Racialization of Labor in World of Warcraft. *Critical Studies in Media Communication* 26 (2): 128–144.

Nelson, Alondra. 2011. *Race After the Internet.* Edited by Lisa Nakamura and Peter Chow-White. New York: Routledge.

Nelson, Alondra, Thuy Linh N. Tu, and Alicia Headlam Hines. 2001. *Technicolor: Race, Technology, and Everyday Life*. New York: NYU Press.

Pascoe, C.J. 2011. *Dude, You're a Fag! Masculinity and Sexuality in High School*. Berkeley: University of California Press.

Phillips, Amanda. 2012. Laundry Day: Online Aggression. *Fembot Collective*, April 10. http://fembotcollective.org/blog/2012/04/10/laundry-day-online-agression/.

Profanity Filters, Homophobic Slurs, and Blizzard's Shaky Relationship with the LGBT Community. 2012. *Engadget.* Accessed July 15, 2016. https://www.engadget.com/2012/01/25/profanity-filters-homophobic-slurs-and-blizzards-shaky-relati/.

Stone, Alluquere Rosanne. 1995. *The War of Technology and Desire*. Cambridge, MA: MIT Press.

Taint (Proudmoore US). *WoWWiki.* Accessed July 15, 2016. http://wowwiki.wikia.com/wiki/Guild:Taint_(Proudmoore_US).

Taylor, T.L. 2009. *Play Between Worlds: Exploring Online Game Culture*. Cambridge, MA: MIT Press.

———. 2012. *Raising the Stakes: E-Sports and the Professionalization of Computer Gaming*. Cambridge, MA: MIT Press. Print.

Ward, Mark. 2006. Gay Rights Win in Warcraft World. *BBC*, February 13, sec. Technology. http://news.bbc.co.uk/2/hi/technology/4700754.stm.

'World of Warcraft' Copes with Gay Rights Fallout. 2006. *Msnbc.com*, February 16. http://www.nbcnews.com/id/11374783/ns/technology_and_science-games/t/world-warcraft-copes-gay-rights-fallout/.

Index[1]

---

[1] Note: Page numbers followed by 'n' refer to notes.

© The Author(s) 2018
T. Harper et al. (eds.), *Queerness in Play*, Palgrave Games in Context,
https://doi.org/10.1007/978-3-319-90542-6

Printed by Printforce, United Kingdom